The Call to Serve

THE CALL TO SERVE

Biblical and Theological Perspectives on Ministry in Honour of Bishop Penny Jamieson

EDITED BY
Douglas A. Campbell

Sheffield
Academic Press

Copyright © 1996 Sheffield Academic Press

Published by Sheffield Academic Press Ltd
Mansion House
19 Kingfield Road
Sheffield S11 9AS
England

Printed on acid-free paper in Great Britain
by Bookcraft Ltd
Midsomer Norton, Bath

British Library Cataloguing in Publication Data

A catalogue record for this book is available
from the British Library

ISBN 1-85075-625-2

CONTENTS

Part I
BIBLICAL PERSPECTIVES ON MINISTRY

Part II
HISTORICAL AND THEOLOGICAL PERSPECTIVES ON MINISTRY

FOREWORD

Most Rev. Brian Davis
Primate and Archbishop/Te Pihopa Matamua
The Anglican Church in Aotearoa–New Zealand and Polynesia
and Bishop of Wellington

The way the church has understood the role of its clergy and their leadership has been subject both to scrutiny and to change in recent years. One of the key issues has, of course, been the place of women among the ordained. The Anglican communion began to face this question seriously in the 1970s. First, the Episcopal church of the United States of America, and then the provinces of Canada and New Zealand, decided to ordain women as priests. Other provinces have since followed this lead.

In 1986 the general synod of the church of the province of Aotearoa–New Zealand acted to remove doubt that women were eligible for election to the episcopate, and in 1990 the diocese of Dunedin elected Penelope Jamieson as its bishop, the ordination to the episcopate taking place on 29 June. She was the world's first diocesan bishop.

It took a special combination of gifts to be a pioneer woman bishop, to cope with its various new challenges, and also to communicate creatively with those for whom the concept of a woman bishop was difficult. Bishop Jamieson has proved more than equal to the task.

Women now serve at all levels of leadership within the ordained ministry of the Anglican communion in Aotearoa–New Zealand, and make available to the church a variety of new gifts and perceptions. The result has been a more inclusive church, and one that is more sensitive to the aspirations and the needs of women as well as men.

I welcome this publication commemorating the consecration of the bishop of Dunedin, Penelope Jamieson, and the tribute it not only affords her but also the clergy and people of the diocese of Dunedin. Furthermore, the studies themselves make a substantial contribution to our understanding of Christian ministry. The editors, and all who have contributed, are to be warmly commended.

Editor's Preface

The publication of this collection would not have been possible without the provision of a generous subvention by the University of Otago. In particular, Dr I. Smith, Deputy Vice-Chancellor (research and international), is to be thanked for his support. Gratitude is also due to Sandra Lindsay for her word-processing assistance, and to Dr John Stenhouse, a sagacious colleague and (more significantly) a trusted friend. Most importantly, however, the contributors themselves are to be thanked for their initial enthusiasm for the project; for their patience during the long journey to publication; and for their rapid preparation of the volume's final draft. It is to be hoped that, as a result of this, the volume will not merely celebrate an important event in the history of the church, but will also contribute constructively to the church's ongoing struggles with issues of ministry and leadership.

DAC

ABBREVIATIONS

ANQ	*Andover Newton Quarterly*
ATR	*Anglican Theological Review*
Bib	*Biblica*
BJRL	*Bulletin of the John Rylands University Library of Manchester*
BSac	*Bibliotheca Sacra*
BTB	*Biblical Theology Bulletin*
CBQ	*Catholic Biblical Quarterly*
CSEL	Corpus scriptorum ecclesiasticorum latinorum
EvQ	*Evangelical Quarterly*
EvT	*Evangelische Theologie*
ExpTim	*Expository Times*
GTJ	*Grace Theological Journal*
HeyJ	*Heythrop Journal*
HTR	*Harvard Theological Review*
Int	*Interpretation*
JAAR	*Journal of the American Academy of Religion*
JBL	*Journal of Biblical Literature*
JEH	*Journal of Ecclesiastical History*
JETS	*Journal of the Evangelical Theological Society*
JSNT	*Journal for the Study of the New Testament*
JSNTSup	*Journal for the Study of the New Testament*, Supplement Series
JSOT	*Journal for the Study of the Old Testament*
JTS	*Journal of Theological Studies*
NIDNTT	C. Brown (ed.), *The New International Dictionary of New Testament Theology*
NovT	*Novum Testamentum*
NTD	Das Neue Testament Deutsch
NTS	*New Testament Studies*
OTL	Old Testament Library
RSR	*Recherches de science religieuse*
SBLDS	SBL Dissertation Series
SBLSBS	SBL Sources for Biblical Study
SBLSP	*SBL Seminar Papers*
SJT	*Scottish Journal of Theology*
SNTSMS	Society for New Testament Studies Monograph Series
SR	*Studies in Religion/Sciences religieuses*
ST	*Studia theologica*
TDNT	G. Kittel and G. Friedrich (eds.), *Theological Dictionary of the New Testament*

TS	*Theological Studies*
TynBul	*Tyndale Bulletin*
UBSGNT	United Bible Societies' *Greek New Testament*
VC	*Vigiliae christianae*
WW	*Word and World*
ZAW	*Zeitschrift für die alttestamentliche Wissenschaft*
ZNW	*Zeitschrift für die neutestamentliche Wissenschaft*

LIST OF CONTRIBUTORS

Ray Anderson
Professor of Ministry, Fuller Theological Seminary, Pasadena, California

Maurice Andrew
Professor of Old Testament (Emeritus), Knox Theological Hall, Dunedin

Ian Breward
Professor of Church History, Uniting Church Theological Hall, Melbourne

Douglas Campbell,
Lecturer in Religious Studies and New Testament, Department of Theology and Religious Studies, King's College London

Brian Davis
Primate and Archbishop, The Anglican Church in Aotearoa–New Zealand and Polynesia

Elizabeth Duke
(formerly) Lecturer in Classics, University of Otago, Dunedin

Ruth Edwards
Tutor with particular responsibility for Women's Ministry, Ripon College, Cuddesdon, Oxford.

L. Ann Jervis
Associate Professor of New Testament, Wycliffe College, Toronto

Irmgard Kindt-Siegwalt
(formerly) Executive Secretary, Commission of Faith and Order, WCC, Geneva

Christopher Marshall
Lecturer in New Testament, Bible College of New Zealand, Auckland

Rosemary Radford Ruether
Professor of Church History, Garrett-Evangelical Theological Seminary, Evanston, Illinois

Elisabeth Schüssler Fiorenza
Stendahl Professor of Divinity, Harvard Divinity School, Cambridge, Massachusetts

Graham Stanton
Professor of New Testament, Department of Theology and Religious Studies, King's College London

Alan J. Torrance
Lecturer in Theology, Department of Theology and Religious Studies, King's College London

T.F. Torrance,
Emeritus Professor of Theology, New College, University of Edinburgh, Edinburgh

THE CALL TO SERVE DUNEDIN:
AN ACCOUNT OF THE APPOINTMENT OF BISHOP PENNY JAMIESON

Douglas A. Campbell

1. *The Event as an Ecclesiastical Landmark*

On 25 November 1989 the Rev. Dr Penelope Jamieson was chosen by
an electoral synod of the diocese of Dunedin, in the Anglican province
of New Zealand, to be its bishop-elect. On 28 June 1990 she was
ordained bishop and, on the following day, Saturday 29 June, she was
installed as bishop of the diocese in a service that received international
media coverage. The event was hailed as a world first—if rather
overdue —for women: Rev. Dr Jamieson, who wished to be known as
Bishop Penny, was the first woman to be elected by a diocese to this
high ecclesiastical office.[1]

It was to acknowledge the importance of this event that a number of
scholars agreed to contribute studies on the concept of 'ministry' to a
commemorative volume—it seemed appropriate that the Christian
academic community should celebrate this event, albeit in its own somewhat tardy fashion. It is also appropriate, however, that such a volume
begin with a short account of the story of Bishop Penny's election. Its

---

1. In September 1988 Barbara Harris was appointed as assistant or suffragan
bishop in the diocese of Eastern Massachusetts, USA, by the diocesan bishop, Paul
Johnson (she was consecrated in February 1989). Without wishing to detract from
the significance of this appointment, it is important to note that Rev. Dr Jamieson's
selection was by a process of diocesan election, and to the highest episcopal office.
Hence there are both significant similarities, and differences, between her appointment and Bishop Harris's (not that either bishop, when questioned, is overly
concerned about 'who was first').

telling may serve to remind that the abstract discussions of biblical and theological perspectives on ministry that follow arise from an accumulation of concrete, localized contexts. They are intended, in turn, to contribute to the further shaping of such contexts, hopefully to the point where the story underlying Bishop Penny's election—a story so unusual that it provoked international attention—will become utterly unremarkable.

2. *The Event in its Local Context*

The central issue can be stated a little more precisely. For almost two millennia women have generally not been appointed to the main institutional leadership of the various Christian traditions; a leadership often defined in terms of 'ordination' to the office of 'minister' (Gk *diakonos*, literally 'servant', hence sometimes rendered 'deacon') or 'priest' (Gk *presbuteros*, literally 'elder'), or some equivalent, while higher levels of leadership, like that of bishop (Gk *episkopos*, literally 'overseer') are drawn from within this group. The reasons for this are complex and various but for our present purposes we need note only that, whereas in previous centuries the question of ordaining women does not seem to have been an issue, in this century, with increasing pressure to admit women to the priesthood, ordination has been actively opposed on grounds of gender. That is, an ideological position that women should not be priests merely because they are women (or because of the inverse position, namely, that priests must be male) has recently blocked their movement into the upper levels of the church's hierarchy—and this in increasing disparity with the conventions of surrounding society.[2] As is well known, many church traditions (including by far the largest, Roman Catholicism) still do not admit women to the priesthood, largely on these grounds.

The theological dimension can be set aside for a moment (especially since much of the following volume is taken up with it), and a more descriptive view pursued. Clearly, in order for the Rev. Dr Jamieson to be elected Bishop of Dunedin, this ideological conviction had to be neutralized in some way. Either its proponents had to be outmanoeuvred, or they had to consider other ideological considerations (that may have favoured her selection) more important, while the majority of the synod had to vote for different reasons altogether: for them the

2.   See in particular section d below.

notion of a female bishop had to be largely normalized.

A number of factors contributed to the creation of a situation in which the idea of a female bishop was normal; the situation of the Dunedin electoral synod in 1989. There are at least four[3] pertinent factors that created the general context for this precedent-setting decision.[4] Within this context we must then consider the dynamics of the synod itself.

a. *The Admission of Women to Prominent Leadership Roles in Other Church Traditions*
An important step towards the normalization of female priests within Anglicanism was taken when other denominations preceded it in admitting women to official leadership, with few obviously detrimental results.[5]

---

3. In an earlier version of this paper I speculated that a fifth factor was also important, namely, the characteristic commitment of Scottish ethnicity (regionally significant) to the education and high occupational status of women. While remaining an important feature of local provincial history, however, the slowness of the diocese to embrace female ordination suggests that this tradition was not a significant factor within the local Anglican tradition which, by all accounts, is (and was) fundamentally quite 'conservative'. The best history of the region is Erik Olssen's *A History of Otago* (Dunedin: John McIndoe, 1984), with useful comments on the distinctive education of women in Dunedin on pp. 45 and 93.

4. I have been guided in what follows particularly by an excellent Honours dissertation by Angela Webber, supervised by the Dept of History at the University of Otago: 'An Easy Passage? The Evolution of an Anglican Female Priesthood in the Church of the Province of New Zealand' (Honours dissertation, University of Otago, Dunedin, 1994). Also helpful is R. Neave (ed.), *The Journey and the Vision: A Report on Ordained Anglican Women in the Church of the Province of New Zealand* (Auckland [Newmarket]: The Women's Resource Centre, 1990).

5. Women had been ordained within Congregationalism in the USA since 1853, although this practice was not immediately followed in New Zealand. The first female Congregational minister in New Zealand, Rev. Nancie Ward, was originally ordained in Scotland, and emigrated to New Zealand (specifically to Napier) in 1951, presenting the church with something of a *fait accompli*. Phyllis Guthardt was admitted to the Methodist ministry in November 1959; Margaret Martin was ordained within Presbyterianism in May 1965; and Patricia Preest, having been ordained a deaconess in 1957, was ordained within the Baptist tradition in 1974. The earliest church tradition to admit women to the ministry in New Zealand was the Salvation Army. In 1883 a contingent of officers sent to New Zealand included female officers, while in 1892, of 269 full-time officers in New Zealand, 146 were women. The Auckland Unitarian Church was also ministered to by a couple, Wilna and William Constable, in 1929. These last two traditions were less important with respect to progress within Anglicanism, however (see immediately following

This progression undoubtedly helped Anglicans to acclimatize to the idea of female ministers.

But another factor made these ordinations (especially in Congregationalism, Methodism and Presbyterianism) still more pointed for New Zealand Anglicans. In the late 60s and 70s a significant ecumenical drive towards formal church union took place,[6] resulting in an official constitution in 1971, *The Plan for Union*, that only failed narrowly at the point of its final ratification by the Anglican General Synod in 1974.[7] Indeed, many parishes had already merged in anticipation of the wider integration. The position of Congregationalism, Methodism and Presbyterianism on gender and ministry consequently directly confronted Anglicanism throughout consultation and the planned merger itself (where it was not negotiable). This exposure undoubtedly normalized the principle and practice of female ministers for many individual Anglicans.[8]

above). On this, and related, issues see A. Davidson, 'The Church and Women in the Twentieth Century', ch. 14 in *Christianity in Aotearoa: A History of Church and Society in New Zealand* (Wellington: The New Zealand Education for Ministry Board, 1991), pp. 141-53; also interesting is ch. 8, 'Women's Contribution to Missionary and Colonial Christianity', pp. 74-84; also Neave (ed.), *The Journey and the Vision*, p. iv.

6.   Methodist, Presbyterian, Anglican, Associated Churches of Christ, and Congregationalist traditions, were involved.

7.   Three dioceses also subsequently rejected *The Plan*. In 1980, a 'covenant of mutual recognition' was also rejected—by one vote—in the house of bishops (!).

8.   Anglican representative John Mullane, a crucial participant in the process by which women were ordained, stated afterwards: 'My own involvement with the Christchurch thing about the ordination of women had a bit of a personal conversion about it. I started off as conservative over the issues as anybody when I first got ordained and really got confronted with the inappropriateness of the issue as far as it affected men through the church union movement who were confronted with "you've got to do it, whether you like it or not" kind of thing. That was the initial stage. It wasn't a matter of commitment to any principle. But as we started to work on that I started to believe that it was not only important making statements about priesthood, but it was an issue of human rights and that kind of thing as well, but that we were lacking something in not having women ordained' (recorded in Neave [ed.], *The Journey and the Vision*, p. 3/3).

The broader, rather unsettling, effect of the plans for merger on the communion as a whole should also not be overlooked: this upheaval and controversy took place at just the time that the question of female ordination was being considered, perhaps delaying progress in the interests of stability.

b. *Increasingly Flexible Directives from the Central Policy-Making Bodies of International Anglicanism*
Although officially citizens of an independent province, New Zealand Anglicans still looked towards certain international gatherings of Anglican leaders (notably of bishops) for policy advice, especially to the Lambeth conferences and the directives of the ACC (the Anglican Consultative Council). In response to requests from certain provinces, and renewed interest in the office of deaconess, these bodies consulted and produced a succession of increasingly flexible pronouncements on the question of gender in relation to ministry.

In typically Anglican fashion, these pronouncements were sometimes rather ambiguous, but this in itself was significant. The Lambeth conferences of 1920 and 1930 conferred increasing legitimacy on the ordination of deaconesses (although the 1930 conference added the important disclaimer that this order was *sui generis*, that is, not part of, or directly analogous to, the traditional ordained ministries). More importantly, the conference of 1968, followed by the ACC, pronounced the question of gender and ministry inconclusive, and hence a matter of preference for individual provinces. This last decision of course effectively undermined firm opposition to female ministers, because any such opposition presupposed biblical and theological clarity on the matter. In encouraging independent decisions, it also effectively legitimized the role of local factors for each province in the decision. Encouraged (if not abandoned) by these decisions, the Anglican province of New Zealand had to find its own way to a decision on gender and ministry, which by this point had moved to a consideration of women's admission to the priesthood.

c. *The Admission of Women to the Ordained Offices of Deacon and Priest in New Zealand Anglicanism*
Of particular significance, and in close relation to the foregoing, was the progression within New Zealand Anglicanism of women to official inclusion within the lower levels of the ordained ministry, namely, the diaconate, followed by the priesthood.[9] Once this had taken place the

9. I am leaving aside temporarily the question of whether any tier of ordained leadership within the Anglican (or any other) tradition should be described in terms of 'priesthood'. Here, simply for the sake of clarity, I am using the term to describe the second level of the ordained leadership within Anglicanism that intervenes between the diaconate and the episcopate.

election of a female bishop was almost inevitable, since the main ideological and sociological battles had been largely fought and won. The critical progression was probably into the diaconate, because at this point the perimeter of ordination was breached.

The order of deaconesses underwent something of a revival in the nineteenth century. It was not a large movement, but it provided an important avenue for women called to some sort of church leadership. It was, as has just been noted, also never officially part of the communion's ordained leadership. Pressure within New Zealand to extend ordination to the order of deaconesses mounted during the 1960s, and was spearheaded by a small group of women from the diocese of Christchurch. From 1963–64 a deaconess originally ordained in the UK, Glenys Lewis, was specifically commissioned and funded to travel around New Zealand explaining and promoting the order. In 1964 the province's General Synod ratified a service for ordaining deaconesses to the diaconate.[10]

With this decision the province had basically admitted that women could be ordained, although with the gradation between the diaconate and the priesthood, many within the communion probably had not fully grasped this concession. Equally importantly, however, female deacons could now minister within the churches in a wide capacity. Many laity from this point on found it difficult to distinguish between a priest and a deacon: in practical terms, women were now ministers. Hence, in terms of sociological exposure to women leading worship within New Zealand Anglicanism, although the number of female deacons was not large, the process had begun by the mid-1960s.

The progression of women into the priesthood from this point, however, was not overly rapid. In 1970 the General Synod set up a commission to consider the question of ordaining women to the priesthood. It reported its findings—which were basically positive—back to the General Synod in 1972 (the General Synod is biennial), and the idea was approved, although only 'in principle'.[11] The process of amending the province's constitution began in 1974. In 1976 the bill was finally

10. For further details see Webber, 'An Easy Passage?', pp. 8-18; and G. Lewis, 'The Story of the Deaconess Order in NZ from 1962–1977', in Neave (ed.), *The Journey and the Vision*, pp. 2/1–2/3.

11. The direct approval of the motion failed to pass, by one vote, in the house of clergy. The amended version passed reasonably easily, with 12 votes switching sides when the phrase 'in principle' was added.

passed by the General Synod, to sit for a further year before being adopted into the constitution, at which point, as was constitutionally permitted, an appeal was launched. After a full hearing, this was dismissed in November 1977. The first women were ordained into the priesthood of the Anglican church in the province of New Zealand in December of that year.

It is interesting to note that, although the diocese of Dunedin supported the movement of women into the priesthood, and the diocesan bishop who immediately preceded Bishop Penny, Peter Mann, was in the forefront of the movement at the church's central levels, it was not itself overly progressive in comparison with other dioceses. (As has already been noted, the move for female ordination had come primarily from the diocese of Christchurch.) The diocese of Dunedin's first female minister, Claire Brown, was ordained deacon in July 1983, having applied for ordination in 1977. She was ordained to the priesthood in September 1984. This made Dunedin one of the last dioceses in New Zealand to ordain a women to the priesthood—and this caution was quite deliberate.[12]

The vicissitudes of the progression apart, Anglicanism in New Zealand had been admitting women increasingly into an official leadership role since the early 1960s. The progression was typically—and perhaps wisely—incremental. Hence the church had been exposed to female leaders, in increasing numbers and levels of authority, for almost three decades by the time the Dunedin synod met in 1989 to consider candidates for the office of its bishop.

d. *The Ongoing Pressure from Surrounding Culture and 'Second Wave' Feminism*

The broad parallelism between the admission of women into official leadership roles in many New Zealand denominations, described briefly above, and the general impact of 'second wave' feminism, is almost certainly no coincidence.[13] In the late 60s and throughout the 70s,

12. Compare Auckland and Waiapu in 1977, and Aotearoa, Christchurch, Waikato and Wellington in 1978. Only Polynesia (1985) and Nelson (1987) were slower (so Neave [ed.], *The Journey and the Vision*, p. 4/2).

13. For some details of 'second wave' feminism, especially in the Otago area, see Olssen, *A History*, pp. 226-27; a colourful sample of some of the New Zealand literature of the period is S. Coney, 'Starting to Fight Back: The *Broadsheet* Years', Part II in *Out of the Frying Pan: Inflammatory Writings 1972–89* (Auckland:

women (along with a number of other groups) agitated publically and effectively for an end to discrimination and for equality of opportunity. The connection with 'first wave' feminism should also not be over-looked. In many ways the first wave, building from the late nineteenth century, overlapped with, as well as prepared for, the second. Indeed, the very demand for female ordination was typical of the Christian proclivities of first wave feminism.

Clearly, as a movement on behalf of women largely by women, this was not an agitation internal to the church's leadership. The counter-vailing ideology of resistance to mere cultural agendas by the church should also not be discounted.[14] These factors suggest that the broader movement within society by women into leadership roles would not in itself have been enough to force change within the church. Indeed, the ongoing resistance to this change by traditions with a significant Western presence (such as Catholicism, various Orthodoxies, and most Pentecostal denominations) confirms that. But it would be equally insensitive to suggest that this social movement had no influence on the movement of women into official positions of leadership within certain church traditions, especially when such movements happened in a reasonably clear correlation with that broader social progression. The notion of female leaders *per se* was increasingly normalized by 'second wave' feminism, while many of the arguments of the proponents of liberation seemed equally valid within a Christian context.[15]

Penguin, 1990), pp. 63-130.

14. See Webber, 'An Easy Passage?', pp. 20-23.

15. One might say that the premises were similar enough to make a transfer rhetorically effective. For example, that liberation was a question of justice resonates with the strong biblical and theological emphases on that attribute of God, while to make liberation (itself resonant with the biblical theme of freedom) dependent on human dignity and worth was consonant with the biblical doctrine of the creation of humanity in the image of God (Gen. 1.26-27—and this was not the first time that this doctrine had been historically significant). One should also add to such approaches the impact of scientific assertions about gender (biological, psychological and otherwise), such as, that it is culturally varied and so should not be rigidly stereotyped. Finally, it should be noted that non-conservative Christians were likely to weigh such 'cultural' arguments more heavily, being less committed to the position that biblical injunctions were inviolable and 'worldly' judgments inherently problematic. There were undoubtedly many such Christians within the Anglican communion in New Zealand at this time, although it is difficult to be more precise than this. The inverse view may be the more revealing here in that many evangelicals strongly resisted female ordination within Anglicanism, but were clearly in a

These four, rather broad, sets of considerations probably explain why the Dunedin electoral synod of 1989 found the notion of a female candidate for the office of bishop so acceptable.[16] As one editorial put it: 'Twelve years ago ordained women were a curiosity, but now it feels as if Anglicans have accepted them as so natural that the arrival of a woman bishop is no more than the inevitable extension of the path Anglicans are following.'[17]

It is now time to consider the story of the synod proper.

3. *The Dunedin Electoral Synod of 1989*

Of course, not all the story of the synod can, or should, be told.[18] But certain features are both reasonably obvious and significant, namely, the peculiarly familiar ethos of the Dunedin diocese, the presentation of the candidates, and the effect of the transferable vote electoral system. These local considerations all played their part in a process that ultimately happened to select a female bishop. The most important could be described alternatively as (a) the absence of lobbying; (b) competing ideological considerations; and (c) electoral mechanics.

minority, being concentrated to a significant degree only in the diocese of Nelson. The Bishop of Nelson, Right Rev. P.E. Sutton, opposed the move, however, not for evangelical reasons but rather on practical grounds. The diocese of Waiapu also resisted the move primarily because it was opposed by its indigenous clergy and laity, of whom there were a particularly significant number in this diocese: here the ideology of opposition was explicitly 'cultural', not biblical and/or theological (as was the opposition of the ethnically defined diocese of Aotearoa, and the Pacific Island diocese of Polynesia).

16. See the survey reported in Neave (ed.), *The Journey and the Vision*, pp. 5/1-20, Appendix, pp. xxiv-xxv. The results of the questionnaire, sent out in 1989, are not reported exhaustively (and the sample size is not particularly large). However, of the collected comments, very few report division over the issue and, even then, it is usually only initial opposition. There is admittedly some evidence of ongoing dissent, but it is extremely scant.

17. *New Zealand Herald*, 28 November 1989. Note that the General Synod had just passed a motion explicitly stating that the ordination of female bishops was acceptable.

18. I have been greatly assisted here by personal interviews with almost a dozen of the synod's participants—the first two observations here rely particularly on their reports. Confidentiality, however, forbids acknowledging them as they deserve.

a. *The Absence of Lobbying*

The leadership of the Dunedin diocese, and consequently its synod, is quite small—in 1989 the house of clergy consisted of just over 30 clergy (of whom, significantly, less than half a dozen were women). Coupled to the natural intimacy associated with a relatively small group is a tradition of friendliness: emotive and divisive speeches and debates are frowned upon (in contradistinction to other dioceses and church traditions). Coupled with this is a general absence of aggressive lobbying. Indeed, given the approach of the synod, any such activity would risk being counter-productive.[19]

Moreover, Rev. Dr Jamieson was a relatively late candidate and largely unknown as a person to the electoral synod (this was not unusual for candidates for bishop of the diocese: probably because of its small size, they tended to be drawn from outside). Certainly her nominators had researched her biography, but she was not well known,[20] being a minister in another diocese, and then not for an overly long time.[21] This reinforces the point that little organized lobbying seems to have taken place: there simply was not enough time or information available for it, even discounting traditional Dunedin synodal practice. She was, in fact, the proverbial 'dark horse' in the selection race.

All of this counts strongly against any suggestion that Rev. Dr Jamieson was selected as part of some feminist drive for high office. While the desire to elect a woman may have influenced a handful of participants (see section c below), this does not seem to have been a decisive factor. Other considerations plainly governed Rev. Dr Jamieson's selection over against the issue of gender; an issue that seems to have been normalized by this time for reasons already discussed.

19. A participant commented, most intriguingly, that the one more aggressive speech of the proceedings had just this effect, counting (insofar as this could be assessed) against the candidate that the rhetoric was intended to support.

20. She was known by sight only to one of her two nominators, who had met her and heard her speak at an Ordained Anglican Women's Conference held earlier that year (1989)—Neave notes the unexpected strategic importance of the conference here (*The Journey and the Vision*, p. ii).

21. Rev. Dr Jamieson applied for ordination in 1979, was accepted as a candidate in 1980, was ordained to the diaconate in 1982, and to the priesthood in 1983, being installed in a parish in the diocese of Wellington.

b. *Competing Ideological Considerations*
The obvious considerations were her excellent qualifications, not merely in general, but given the specific needs of the diocese as perceived by the electoral synod. In addition to an impressive academic record,[22] Rev. Dr Jamieson was known to be articulate, and committed spiritually. There was, in fact (as more than one participant told me), a strong correlation between her profile and the formal profile for candidates drawn up by the diocese's search committee. This aspect of the decision was therefore plainly meritocratic. When she was presented to the synod alongside the alternatives, Rev. Dr Jamieson was clearly an impressive candidate in terms of abilities and qualifications.

An additional dimension may also be significant here, however. The Anglican communion in New Zealand, as elsewhere, embraces a considerable spectrum of Christian belief and practice. The candidates for Bishop of Dunedin in 1989 reflected this spectrum, ranging, on theological matters, from the conservative or evangelical end of the spectrum through to a pronounced liberalism. One strong candidate, for example, was widely thought not to believe in the bodily resurrection of Christ.

Setting aside the theological implications of this for the moment, the impact on the electoral synod of this position was probably quite important. Those most likely to oppose the selection of a female bishop for the ideological reasons already discussed were also those most likely to occupy the conservative or evangelical end of the spectrum, taking biblical and theological orthodoxy most seriously. It seems that fundamental considerations of Christian orthodoxy overwhelmed any decisions on the basis of an ideology of gender for this group—the resurrection of Christ was clearly a more important matter than the gender of the bishop. Hence, precisely the group that one might have expected to object to the selection of a female candidate on grounds of gender was effectively redeployed, possibly in favour of Rev. Dr Jamieson, who was perceived (correctly) to be warmly orthodox. In other words, for one voting group, Christian ideological considerations in relation to Christ

22. Rev. Dr Jamieson had an MA (Hons.) in Linguistics from the University of Edinburgh. From 1970–75 she was a junior lecturer in Linguistics at the University of Victoria (Wellington). She was awarded a PhD in 1976 for work primarily on Tokelau Island children and their families for whom English was a second language. Clearly, these qualifications were weighed against her relative inexperience as a parish minister (no doubt with different members of the synod weighing these considerations in different measure).

were considered to be more central than ideological considerations based on gender.[23]

c. *Electoral Mechanics*

Because of the large number of candidates that can be initially forwarded for the office of bishop, and a desire to achieve the democratic benchmark of a majority, the synod (like many other church bodies) uses a transferable vote system. Under this system successive ballots are taken until one candidate achieves an absolute majority. The majority is effectively produced by removing the lowest polling candidates from the list. The supporters of these candidates are then free to vote for another candidate, hence their vote 'transfers'. Hopefully, enough will eventually transfer to one candidate for an outright majority of over 50 per cent of the relevant voting body to be attained without an embarrassingly large number of ballots (mathematically this must happen at some point).

Clearly, in order for any candidate to achieve an absolute majority, a considerable number of these transferring votes must be attracted. Hence it is important within this system to be perceived as 'the next best', especially to supporters of a minority candidate who is removed at an early stage in the balloting.[24] It is also important to achieve that state much-prized in American Presidential nomination races, namely, momentum. It would seem that votes often tend to be cast for perceived front-runners or winners. Probably, when voting within a transferable system, those voters who have already had their first preference disqualified tend to be more susceptible to any 'bandwagon' effect.[25] Conversely, some voters in this position go on to cast their ballots 'negatively',

23. A similar logic probably also applied along axes other than the theological, for example, in terms of perceived managerial style, interpersonal skill, or evangelistic ability. Again, however, such things are extremely difficult to evaluate precisely, although they undoubtedly played their part (and of course perceptions of these types of issues would not have affected specifically evangelical or conservative voting behaviour).

24. Evangelicals therefore had to reorientate relatively early in the balloting process, with the removal of their candidate from the list.

25. Most literature on voting behaviour using the single transferable vote focuses on political systems and multi-member electorates with written ballots (where the dynamics are slightly different), but the peculiar electoral tendencies of the system are still clear in, for example, V. Bogdanor, 'Proportional Legislation: The Single Transferable Vote', ch. 5 in *What is Proportional Representation?* (Oxford: Martin Robertson, 1984), pp. 75-110, esp. pp. 78-94.

seeking to block a candidate perceived as counter-productive by helping another less perceptibly negative candidate to victory.[26]

While this effect should not be exaggerated within a small voting constituency like the Dunedin synod, and one that took its responsibility so seriously, it may have had a minor role to play in Rev. Dr Jamieson's selection. It is significant that she was ahead after the first ballot. This is certainly the ideal position from which to accumulate transferring votes. Perhaps even more importantly, such a strong position after the first ballot may also have allayed any fears that supporting her candidacy would have been to waste votes: from this point on her candidacy clearly had every chance of success and, indeed, only a few subsequent ballots were necessary for her selection. Moreover, although several participants stated that ballots were not governed by the desire to elect the world's first diocesan bishop, the realization does seem to have dawned on many rather late in the process that this direction, if followed, would 'make history'. One can suggest, therefore, that the late transfer of votes may have been assisted by a desire to make history (although the sources actually disagree at this point: some participants recollect this as a distinct factor in the balloting, while others claim that there was no such agenda—even if there was such a realization). The election of Rev. Dr Jamieson may also have been aided by the desire merely to elect one candidate decisively (an important speech of support was couched in these terms by a minister who had travelled from a country district—was it a long road home?).

These rather mechanical electoral factors should not be exaggerated, but neither should they be completely ignored. Perhaps they should be balanced against another observation made by several participants, namely, that the decision was a very prayerful one.

With the selection made, it was time for the ordination, installation, and appropriate celebration, which leads us on to some further brief remarks about the nature of this volume.

4. *Perspectives on Ministry*

Scholars both local and abroad, and from many different church traditions, were enthusiastic about contributing to a volume celebrating

---

26. Here the transferable vote therefore functions to eliminate the least preferred option rather than to elect the most preferred: for a possible instance of this see section b above—and 'anonymity' will clearly assist this type of transfer.

Rev. Dr Jamieson's appointment. An obvious theme for such a volume was a consideration of the issue at the heart of her selection, namely, ministry, particularly in the specific sense of the nature, role and function of those called to lead the church.[27] Our approach to this theme naturally falls into two halves. First, many of the critical scriptural texts and authors are revisited for their insights into ministry.

We begin with a study of the critical Old Testament paradigm of the prophet by Maurice Andrew. His suggestions lead in slightly unexpected literary and hermeneutical directions, which nevertheless open up inclusively for the question of 'prophetic' ministry today. We are involved in a textual process of prophecy, he argues, recapitulating its powerful, oscillating themes of judgment and restoration, rather than actually copying ancient examples. The analysis of the New Testament is dominated, as one might expect, by studies of Pauline texts. In my own article, by discussing the famous Reformational slogan 'the priesthood of all believers' in relation to Romans, I seek to redirect Paul's well-known faith language in a more constructive direction for ministry by emphasizing the vicarious function of Christ. Ann Jervis offers a convincing resolution of one of Paul's famous 'texts of terror', namely, the injunction in 1 Corinthians 14 that women should be silent in church, utilizing sociological and textual arguments to suggest that the constituency of this injunction was (and is) not women in general. Christopher Marshall then discusses the broader theme of Paul's 'spirituality' as the driving force for his own extraordinary ministry.

Having addressed this earliest stratum of the New Testament, discussion then turns to the Gospels. Two complementary studies here by Graham Stanton and Ruth Edwards present us with careful summaries of how Matthew and John depicted the leadership and ministry of the early church. And each Gospel author, as we might expect, has unique insights to contribute to the unfolding theme.

After this broad scriptural engagement, the question of ministry can be approached from integrated theological and historical angles. These more theoretical studies all consider the question of gender although, significantly, none makes it determinative for the notion of ministry. Moreover, none of these studies pretends to be exhaustive, while many

27. Perhaps a doubly suitable theme since Bishop Penny herself led a series of bible studies and theological reflections on the theme of 'priesthood' at the 1989 Conference of Ordained [Anglican] Women in New Zealand: see 'Appendix 1: Our Priesthood', in Neave (ed.), *The Journey and the Vision*, Appendix pp. i-iv.

reflect quite specific contexts (although, as we have just seen, local contexts are often critical in the outworking of decisions concerning the nature of ministry, and who should minister).

Ray Anderson, in a powerful argument, describes the Pentecostal, Spirit-driven impetus of mission and ministry. Ian Breward describes the delicate progression, particularly within Australian churches, towards a recovery of the incarnational nature of the diaconate, evidenced in its historical concern for the marginalized. Elizabeth Duke introduces many of the refreshing insights of the radical Reformation into our discussion by describing Quaker views of ministry. Irmgard Kindt-Siegwalt, drawing upon the discussions of the WCC, gives a panoramic depiction of the movement of the world-wide church towards the ordination of women—an often halting, dislocated process heavily informed by local contexts. Rosemary Radford Ruether criticizes ecumenical arguments tabled in the Roman Catholic debate on female ordination. She suggests that these considerations, designed to slow or even to halt progress towards the ordination of women, are incoherent and even counter-productive. Elisabeth Schüssler Fiorenza gives a programmatic description of a radical democratic future for the church and its leadership. Alan J. Torrance attacks false notions of inclusivism in ministry, arguing that only a proper attention to the distinctive, exclusive truth of the Christian gospel can actually promote a radically inclusive approach to the other in ministry. Finally, Thomas F. Torrance, drawing extensively on biblical and patristic material, makes a powerful case directly for female ordination.

In this way, through the entire volume, a scriptural, then historico-theological, set of perspectives is assembled concerning a critical issue for the church of our time, namely, who should lead it and, perhaps more importantly, how. It remains only to commend the resulting studies to the one in whose honour they have been written, namely, Bishop Penny herself.

Part I

BIBLICAL PERSPECTIVES ON MINISTRY

THE PROPHETIC EXAMPLE:
REFERENTIALITY OR TEXTUALITY?

Maurice E. Andrew

Most discussions of ministry today make reference to the archetype of the prophet, who is usually assumed to be central to, and definitively described by, the Old Testament. This necessitates a prelude to any analysis of ministry consisting of a careful scrutiny of the prophetic phenomenon. However, as with so many such analyses, what we find is that the prophet as a discrete historical entity rather dissolves on closer analysis, to be replaced instead by the socio-literary process of 'prophecy'. This in turn suggests that our understanding of ministry should be illuminated, not so much perhaps by 'the prophet', as by involvement in the process of prophecy and its crafted literary statements of judgment and restoration.

1. *The Social Context of Prophecy*

The nature and role of the prophets has been much discussed recently. Some believe that sociological methods are illuminating.[1] Others think

1. For example, R.R. Wilson, *Prophecy and Society in Ancient Israel* (Philadelphia: Fortress Press, 1980); T.W. Overholt, *Prophecy in Cross-Cultural Perspective* (SBLSBS, 17; Atlanta: Scholars Press, 1986); *idem*, 'Prophecy: The Problem of Cross-Cultural Comparison', in B. Lang (ed.), *Anthropological Approaches to the Old Testament* (London: SPCK, 1985), pp. 60-82; *idem*, 'Prophecy in History: The Social Reality of Intermediation', *JSOT* 48 (1990), pp. 3-29; D.L. Petersen, *The Roles of Israel's Prophets* (JSOTSup, 17; Sheffield: JSOT Press, 1981); F.E. Deist, 'The Prophets: Are We Heading for a Paradigm Switch?', in V. Fritz (ed.), *Prophet und Prophetenbuch: FS für O. Kaiser* (Berlin: de Gruyter, 1989), pp. 1-18. For a survey of these and other studies, see J.S. Kselman, 'The Social World of the Israelite Prophets: Review Article', *RSR* 11 (1985), pp. 120-29;

these methods convey little that is certain about the Old Testament prophets, and believe it is more appropriate to treat them from a literary point of view in their present written form.[2] Those of the first view strongly emphasize the necessity of recognizing the social context. An often quoted sentence from Wilson is: 'There can be no socially isolated intermediaries'.[3] This is from a chapter on prophecy in modern societies, but in another article directly referring to Old Testament prophets, Wilson writes: '[t]he OT prophets did not carry out their activities in isolation but were an integral part of their society'.[4] Those of this view are usually also confident that they can define the historical circumstances of prophets: 'Prophets...such as Jeremiah and Ezekiel, were priestswho were occasionally transformed into prophets...The prophets ...were not harassed unless their messages became too strident and threatening to the society (Jer. 26.1-24; 38.1-13)'.[5] Here, material in the book of Jeremiah is assumed to be historical; however, scholars taking the literary approach may be sceptical. Carroll writes:

> What status does the presentation of Jeremiah have in the book traditionally associated with his name? Is it historical, biographical, theological, imaginative, fictional or what? How may the genre(s) of the material be determined? The problem generates many questions, but few answers are forthcoming because the interpretation of the data is undetermined by corroborative evidence.[6]

Those taking the sociological view nevertheless confidently use the term 'intermediary' to describe the role of the prophets. Kselman writes that,

---

for a critical discussion, C.S. Rodd, 'On Applying a Sociological Theory to Biblical Studies', *JSOT* 19 (1981), pp. 95-106.

2.   R.P. Carroll, 'Prophecy and Society', in R.E. Clements (ed.), *The World of Ancient Israel* (Cambridge: Cambridge University Press, 1989), pp. 205-25; A.G. Auld, 'Prophets through the Looking Glass: Between Writings and Moses', *JSOT* 27 (1983), pp. 3-23; R.P. Carroll, 'Poets not Prophets', *JSOT* 27 (1983), pp. 25-31; *idem*, 'Whose Prophet? Whose History? Whose Social Reality? Troubling the Interpretative Community Again: Notes towards a Response to T.W. Overholt's Critique', *JSOT* 48 (1990), pp. 33-49.

3.   Wilson, *Prophecy and Society*, p. 30.

4.   R.R. Wilson, 'Prophet', in P.J. Achtemeier (ed.), *Harper's Bible Dictionary* (San Francisco: Harper & Row, 1985), p. 829.

5.   Wilson, 'Prophet', p. 829.

6.   R.P. Carroll, *Jeremiah: A Commentary* (OTL; London: SCM Press, 1986), pp. 33-34.

> After showing the inadequacies of such traditional terminology as
> shaman, witch, sorcerer, medium, diviner, mystic, or priest for the
> biblical prophet, Wilson settles on the neutral 'intermediary' as the most
> useful and comprehensive category into which such figures as the biblical
> prophets may be placed.[7]

This indicates that sociological approaches may also proceed from
comparisons of different cultures. In fact, Overholt writes,

> [T]he specific *content* of their [i.e. Jeremiah's and the American Indian
> Handsome Lake's] respective messages is culturally conditioned and,
> therefore, quite dissimilar, [but] the prophetic *activity* of the two conforms
> to the same general pattern…The basic components of this model are
> two: a set of three actors and a pattern of interrelationships among them
> involving revelation (r), proclamation (p), feedback (f), and expectations
> of confirmation (e).[8]

Overholt writes elsewhere that 'religious intermediation is a very widely
distributed phenomenon, and it conforms rather strictly to a particular
pattern'.[9] He gives the example of Amos, where 'a prophet is someone
to whom Yahweh has spoken and who freely communicates the
contents of this revelation to an audience…'. But there are problems in
deriving from this a widely accepted social function that might apply to
all prophets. With reference to Overholt's statement that a prophet is
someone to whom Yahweh has spoken, and who communicates the
content of the revelation to an audience, Carroll makes the point: '*Quite
so*, but many of the prophets represented in the Bible might be better
defined as "someone to whom Yahweh has *not* spoken but who freely
communicates their own thoughts to an audience"'.[10] He is referring to
Mic. 3.5-8 where, concerning the prophets who cry 'peace' when they
have something to eat, Yahweh says that it will be night to them,
without vision. Presumably no revelation has been given to these
prophets. Certainly there is a revelation expressed in the passage itself—
'thus says Yahweh'—and this is assumed to be to Micah, who is an
intermediary to an audience, in this case, to the prophets. The extraordinary thing, however, is that Micah himself is not said to be a prophet
(neither here nor in any part of the book). Carroll comments that

7. Kselman, 'The Social World of the Israelite Prophets', p. 121.
8. Overholt, 'Prophecy: The Problem of Cross-Cultural Comparison', pp.
63-64.
9. Overholt, 'Prophecy in History', pp. 9-10.
10. Carroll, 'Whose Prophet?', p. 38.

defining that speaker as a prophet is simply not part of the text, but part of its history of reception. As far as Mic. 3.8 is concerned—'I am filled with power, with the Spirit of the Lord'—it might be added that both the reference to the Spirit, and the almost overbearing self-confidence, are not typical of the pre-exilic prophets. Possibly, at least part of the passage is a later interpretation rather than a historical description of a social role that functioned at a particular time. Possibly the understanding of intermediation changed, and later interpreters thought it had been performed by people in whom it had not at first been recognized. This is perhaps borne out by the term *nabi'* (the Hebrew word most commonly translated 'prophet') being applied to the figures now known as prophets only gradually and later on.[11]

To return to Amos 7 (vv. 10-17): here it is startling that Amos says that he is *not* a prophet. Since Amos 7.14 also gives Amos's ordinary occupation, it seems likely that the term *nabi'* is being used in another, professional sense—possibly that of an intermediary accepted at the time in society. But just this role is repudiated for Amos. Certainly it is claimed, to use Overholt's words again, that Amos 'is someone to whom Yahweh has spoken and who freely communicates the contents of this revelation to an audience...'.[12] The question is, however, who is making this claim? It is, furthermore, striking that Amos 7.10-17 is the only story about Amos cast in the third person. The rest of the book, apart from the title in 1.1, purports to quote his words. Was this story, then—possibly quoting some of Amos's own words—told by editors in order to present the nature of Amos's authority, and with it that of the whole book: he was just doing his job, but none other than Yahweh took him from it and commissioned him to speak to the people? Was it, therefore, later editors who drew explicit conclusions about Amos being an authentic intermediary?

This possibility is made the stronger by recognizing that the passage interrupts the ordered account of Amos's visions. The first three visions are recounted in 7.1-9, and are taken up again in chs. 8–9, immediately after the story about Amos. Where the visions are interrupted is also significant: in the first two, Amos is able to intercede for Israel, and Yahweh relents. In the third, however, immediately before the story,

---

11. For more details see Auld, 'Prophets through the Looking Glass', pp. 3-23; *idem*, 'Prophets and Prophecy in Jeremiah and Kings', *ZAW* 96 (1984), pp. 66-82; Carroll, 'Prophecy and Society', p. 213.

12. Overholt, 'Prophecy in History', p. 10.

there is no more intercession: Yahweh has said, 'I will never again pass [Israel] by' (7.8). This statement is repeated after the story, but preceded by an even more radical proclamation: '[t]he end has come on my people Israel'. This was an incredible claim to make, especially as it did not turn out to be literally true. In this regard, the ending of Amos 7.7-17, between the two statements about Yahweh's complete destruction of Israel, is significant: 'Israel will surely go into exile away from its land'. Israel may not have been completely destroyed, but they did suffer the most dire catastrophe and, what is more, it was not just 'some upstart from down south' who said this, but through Amos it was Yahweh's proclamation.

If this interpretation is along the right lines, then the passage is not primarily a reflection of a social function that applied to all prophets at all times. The editorial interpretation still implies that there was feedback from people, but it is not necessarily feedback from people of the prophet's time—it may even be reticent about the role of prophets in earlier times. Given these factors, it may be more appropriate to speak of *prophecy* rather than of *individual prophets*; prophecy in the sense that something comprehensive is being created. Prophecy connects different periods of time; it interprets the present or near future through the past; and it is still hoping for an assenting response from the people of the present, who may themselves be future to the figure who later came to be regarded as a prophet. There may therefore be people playing a role within the prophetic process who are anonymous, but who were confronting the situation they were in. Moreover, in their kind of response, they demonstrate that people embedded in prophecy are performing something similar to what present-day readers must also undertake.

In drawing a distinction between 'a prophet' and the original hearers, and the response of later people also found within the process of prophecy, we can see that, when it is said that 'the biblical prophets...were singularly dependent upon acceptance by others for any measure of authority...',[13] this acceptance by others may actually have been *later* than any accorded 'the biblical prophets' themselves in their own time. Thus, what is found in prophetic books is not necessarily a straightforward description of a social function at one time, but more a

---

13. B.O. Long, 'Prophetic Authority as Social Reality', in G.W. Coats and B.O. Long (eds.), *Canon and Authority: Essays in Old Testament Religion and Theology* (Philadelphia: Fortress Press, 1977), p. 4.

history of the reception of prophecy over a long period. Actually, we know more of the nature of prophetic books *in extenso* than of a certain social function, however illuminating the latter may be in some instances. Long may well be right in claiming that prophetic authority has a social, and not merely a theological, dimension.[14] But when, for example, Joseph Blenkinsopp writes, '[a]fter receiving a message that he was to transmit to those concerned, ...[Samuel's] prophetic role was publicly acknowledged (1 Sam. 3.20)',[15] it must be questioned how historical this acknowledgment was with regard to Samuel and the people of his time. Questions arise about the historical role of Samuel, because as well as being called *nabiʾ*, he is also said to be a 'man of God'. This draws attention to the fact that *nabiʾ* is by no means the only term used for those later designated 'prophets'. As well as 'sons of the prophets', there are also two words for 'seer'. 'Man of God' is itself someone who can be consulted for a fee about some particular problem (1 Sam. 9.6-8). Furthermore, Samuel is also described as acting like a (minor) judge (1 Sam. 7.15-17). It seems likely, therefore, that 1 Sam. 3.2, in speaking of Samuel as *nabiʾ*, is a later interpretive legitimation of his activity. The term *nabiʾ* is therefore being used for a figure considered to have had broad significance at a crucial stage in Israel's history. It was a time when, as might be said today, the structures of society were undergoing comprehensive change.[16]

To summarize thus far: the use of terms for 'prophet' is more complicated than at first appears—certainly, there is more than the one common designation, *nabiʾ*. *nabiʾ* itself was only gradually and later used for the great figures now thought of as prophets. Furthermore, when it is so used, it does not designate all the prophets as uniform figures, but can take different meanings. Sociological descriptions may be partially helpful, though they apply mainly to figures other than those we usually think of as prophets. Moreover, the claims represented by the descriptions were sometimes repudiated by later interpreters of prophecy

14. Long, 'Prophetic Authority', p. 3.

15. J. Blenkinsopp, 'Introduction to the Prophetic Books', in J.L. Mays (ed.), *Harper's Bible Commentary* (San Francisco: Harper & Row, 1988), p. 537.

16. Moreover, at a time in New Zealand which is at least comparable, and when most people think of a prophet as someone saying something challenging about one particular political or social issue, it may be salutary to realize that at least one biblical perspective on prophecy suggests a figure who has comprehensive significance for many aspects of society.

and applied to the figures we now think of as prophets. Hence, prophecy (like all theology) is never totally comprehended by one group of people, or one period. Our main conclusion must be that the process of prophecy includes those people who were already responding to the utterances of the figures they regarded as prophets; these responders, and their responses, are already embedded in the prophetic books. It is a direct implication of this that prophecy today legitimately calls for the response of present readers as well.

2. *Prophecy as Literature*

No one should assume that the confidence with which some scholars propose new approaches to the prophets means that they can be followed as confidently. Deist uses the term 'paradigm switch', and sees this happening through the application of sociological and anthropological models. But Carroll, in an article which many people think does represent a paradigm switch, maintains that '[a]t best the theoretical component [of sociological theories] tends to produce ideal-typical reconstructions which lack that sharp particularity of the real and also mask from the reader the high degree of reconstruction of the texts entailed by such arguments'.[17] Possibly such disagreement arises because of the desire to derive a global method and description which fits all the prophets. But, as Wilson writes, 'no single picture can incorporate all of the biblical data'.[18]

One reason for this is the editing process which reflects the response mentioned above, and through which we now have prophecy in its present written form: it is the only source for our present knowledge of the prophets. As Barton comments: 'The great figures of any nation's history may be important for either of two reasons: for what they do, and for what they are afterwards thought to have done'.[19] The editors of the prophets were vehicles for the second kind of estimation, and an awareness of their work leads us to recognize prophecy as literature. Once again Carroll puts it sharply: 'We know prophecy now as literature rather than as spoken word. Such a shift from orality to literacy has removed prophecy from its original social setting to a decontexualised,

17. Deist, 'The Prophets', p. 16; Carroll, 'Prophecy and Society', pp. 208-209.
18. Wilson, 'Prophet', p. 826.
19. J. Barton, *Oracles of God: Perceptions of Ancient Prophecy in Israel after the Exile* (London: Darton, Longman & Todd, 1986), p. 1.

timeless setting and any search for the *Sitz im Leben* of specific prophecies is irrelevant'.[20]

This statement also raises the question whether any 'single picture' can encompass all the biblical data. I concur that we do know prophecy primarily as literature, rather than as spoken word. Even when prophetic words are quoted directly, we do not know how literally this is to be taken and, in any case, their purport is influenced both by the way they are arranged and by editorial comments. Nevertheless, this literary presentation can be so skilful that it makes readers 'hear' the prophetic words by being engaged with them. Hence, Carroll's statement does not make the necessary distinction between what exists literarily, and what effect that literature has—it may be, to remain with our previous example, that Amos 7.10-17 was *written* later and inserted subsequently into the presentation of Amos's visions. But it is written so effectively that the present reader 'hears' and is caught up in the dramatic encounter between Amaziah and Amos conveyed in the spoken words, 'Do not prophesy at Bethel', answered by 'I am not a prophet, but Yahweh took me from behind the flock, and Yahweh said to me...' (vv. 13-15). The literature embodies itself as spoken word. Perhaps it comes from a time later than Amos, but it is convincingly set in his time. Thus, Carroll's 'decontextualised, timeless setting' does not do justice to the skill of the writer. Readers believe that Amos is prophesying 'in the days of King Jeroboam' (Amos 1.1; 7.10), whether this can be demonstrated by modern historical scholarship or not. The editor goes to a great deal of trouble to make the time of the prophet relevant. This editor—and perhaps a circle around him—may have wanted to give Amos authority for their time, but they do it so persistently through an 'Amos' that later readers are more likely to be led back to an Amos in his own time. Thus, in relation to the question of accepting prophetic authority, it is not only that later people (such as editors) respond to it for their own time, but they do so *through* earlier times, and in the whole process, lead even later readers (like us) backwards *and* forwards in time. Hence, prophecy owes a response both to originating individuals and to later interpreting groups. The phenomenon of the prophetic is therefore constituted by a preparedness to be challenged both by great individuals and by anonymous groups at different times and in various situations.

Thus, in the matter of a 'decontextualised, timeless setting', I think Carroll is only partially right—to the extent that there are passages in

20. Carroll, 'Prophecy and Society', pp. 207-208.

the prophets where a different context than that of the prophet is of concern, and it may be difficult to say exactly what either context is. This does not entail, however, that there was *no* context, and sometimes it is possible to bring significant arguments for one rather than another. If Old Testament editors wish to be 'timeless', I can only say that they are not successful. The details of particular contexts keep on slipping through. Even if Amos 7.10-17 wants to talk about the exile, it does so through the accusation that 'Amos is conspiring against Jeroboam' (v. 10). Whether or not Amos ever did say 'Jeroboam will die by the sword' (v. 11) is not the main point: the passage is not 'timeless'. Here the sixth century BCE exile is presented through a situation in the eighth century BCE. Hence, even if a prophetic book has evolved to its present form over a number of centuries (certainly the case with Isaiah), though that is a long time, it is still a finite period, and a quite different context from the time in which we live. Thus, prophets, even if in varying degrees, are presented so effectively within literature that they are, in a sense, released from that literature.

This release does not confine them to one time or to one social function—that is also part of the truth of Carroll's statement. Recognizing the editorial process shows that the prophetic challenge often lies in the integration of different periods and their situations. An example of this is the editorial arrangement of prophetic books, where a pattern of restoration is laid alongside judgment. The prophetic dynamic lies in the continued address to people who not only do not recognize judgment, but who also, after judgment, find it hard to recognize that judgment can lead to restoration. Even the book of Amos, which is composed almost entirely of judgment, ends with a section on restoration that, from a literal point of view, hangs briefly and awkwardly at the end (9.11-15).[21] While one prophet may say different things at different times, it is questionable whether the one who said 'the end has come over my people Israel' (8.2) would also say 'I shall raise up the booth of David that is fallen' (9.11)—especially since the expression 'the booth of David' comes from the Jerusalem royal tradition, whereas the rest of the book makes no reference to it. Moreover, if the booth of David is to be raised up, and breaches and ruins repaired, the implication is that there has already been a fall. The 'booth of David' fell in 587 BCE, when the Babylonians destroyed Jerusalem and terminated the Davidic kingship. It

21. For a different view, see S.M. Paul, *A Commentary on the Book of Amos* (*Hermeneia*; Philadelphia: Fortress Press, 1991).

seems likely that the last part of the book is based some time after the destruction and exile (v. 15), some 200 years after Amos in the time of Jeroboam (c. 786–746 BCE).

How is a book which speaks primarily of judgment and then abruptly introduces restoration to be understood? For it certainly is abrupt: 9.10 states that 'All the sinners of my people will die by the sword', then v. 11 reads 'On that day I shall raise up the booth of David that is fallen...', where 'that day' refers not to the past, but to an indeterminate future. Indeed, in one place just before this, there is even a literal contradiction: Amos 9.8 says that Yahweh will destroy the sinful kingdom from the face of the earth—only to break off and say that Yahweh will not utterly destroy the house of Jacob. Literally, of course, it is impossible to destroy from the face of the earth and then not destroy utterly. Moreover, having said that the house of Jacob will not be utterly destroyed, 9.9 goes on to say that the house of Israel (without any clear distinction between this and the house of Jacob) will be shaken, but after this again (as we have seen) the booth of David will be raised up (v. 11).

There are thus a series of statements juxtaposing judgment and retractions of judgment. If one speaks of the prophets having a pattern of revelation (from God), proclamation (by the prophet) and feedback (from the people), such an overall formula takes no account of such contradictions. If a book speaks of judgment throughout, and then abruptly introduces restoration, this must be deliberate: it is part of the editorial makeup of the work, and this itself is part of prophecy in the written form in which we have it. Clearly, the prophecy of Amos in its written form seems to want to preserve the tradition of what Amos said, claiming that what he said was the word of God. The proclamation of judgment, and of an unprecedented close encounter with God, was an essential part of the process. In fact, however, though Israel was defeated and taken into exile, this prophecy also records realistically that it was not completely destroyed, as Amos probably expected. Indeed, not only was Israel not completely destroyed, but it was possible through the very judgment that Amos proclaimed to express the hope that Israel would again be restored, and that the Israel whose destruction *from off the earth* (9.8) had been predicted would never again be uprooted *from off the earth* (v. 15: note that the expression *me^{c}al $^{\jmath a}$dama* is used in slightly different ways in the two cases). Thus, a deliberate linguistic link may well have been created between judgment and restoration:

restoration placed alongside judgment expresses the insight subsequent to Amos that judgment can lead to restoration, but also that restoration has to remain aware of its roots in judgment. The past cannot be left out of account.

The pattern of judgment and restoration is prophecy's most pervasive expression of the integration of different periods of time. Prophecy has heard that which is most uncompromising, and in this hearing it sifts over time what has been said and what happens, accepts the catastrophes, and finds an interpretation in all this which expresses hope for the future. In terms of times, places and people, therefore, it embraces more dimensions than merely the social function of an intermediary exercised at a given time by one prophet with one group of people. It expresses its interpretation through literature.

The editorial make up may also claim the prophet as an intermediary between God and people. When words like '[t]he time is surely coming, says Yahweh...' are attached to the book of Amos (9.13), the claim is being made that they are a legitimate extension of Amos's words and, at the same time, that they are a revelation from God. Further, when it is said, 'I shall restore the fortunes of my people Israel, and they will rebuild the ruined cities and inhabit them...I shall plant them upon their land, and they will never again be plucked up...', it is fairly certain that the prophet is seen as an intermediary for the people who had been through the defeat and devastation of Judah, and uprooted from their land in the sixth century BCE. Even if the people were still using sixth century events as a paradigm for later circumstances, it would remain true that the defeat and exile of that time was the basis for their existence; the foundation both for their chastening and their hope. This does not give us exact information about their identity and circumstances, but it does supply us with essential particulars—the ones that *they* regarded as essential.

Some today would want to make the point that these editors are 'only' *claiming* that these words are a revelation from God. Over against this, it is often thought, is the fact of Amos's revelation from God. But as Barton writes,

> The Old Testament itself provides little information about the mechanism
> by which the prophets acquired their supernatural knowledge...A number
> of types of inspiration occur in the Old Testament—dreams, auditions,
> waking visions, communications through angels—but it is difficult to find

any case where there is any great significance in the mode in which the revelation comes.[22]

We have no direct access to what happened to Amos: we only have the intermediary of the written book of Amos. Thus, references to revelation also come to us through editors. Moreover, *we* are now the people who must make our own response and decision, just as the editors did. We may decide that it makes no sense for them to have written in terms of 'says the Lord'. At the same time, we may make the response of repeating in our own way their looking back and being seared; their realization of their own people having been inadequate; their acknowledgment of having gone through harrowing times; and their confidence that they can begin a new life. Prophecy as literature written later than the time of the prophets, therefore, entails an interpretation for present and future times, but does this so persistently through the past of the prophets that they release themselves from that literature and continue to challenge people in far later contexts than even that of the literary editors.

3. *Judgment and Restoration*

The continuing challenge of prophecy, as I have noted, comes through a pattern of judgment and restoration, which is perhaps prophecy's most pervasive expression of the integration of different periods of time. It is not only a characteristic of Amos, but is one of the main features of prophecy—in fact, the book of Isaiah goes further than Amos. Here the pattern is not found merely in a section added to the end of the book, but is woven into the text, both (so to speak) in the individual stitches and into the very warp and woof of the book. The first chapter (which may be taken as a programmatic beginning for the whole composition[23]) is mainly concerned with judgment. But after speaking of smelting dross and removing alloy, it goes on to the restoration of judges as at the first (vv. 25-26)—only to return again to judgment for the rest of the chapter. So, judgment alternates with restoration in the course of a few verses. But when ch. 2 begins with a new title in v. 1, indicating an originally independent collection, it opens with a unit on restoration (the

22. Barton, *Oracles of God*, pp. 116-17.
23. See G. Fohrer, 'Jesaja 1 als Zusammenfassung der Verkündigung Jesajas', *ZAW* 74 (1962), pp. 251-68; S. Niditch, 'The Composition of Isaiah 1', *Bib* 61 (1980), pp. 509-29.

famous passage on beating swords into ploughshares: see 2.2-5). After more on judgment, it is striking that there is a comparable passage on the restoration of Zion in 4.2-6. This unit is more prosaic, and shares hardly any of the history of effectiveness of 2.2-5, but, from the point of view of overall composition, this is irrelevant. There is a deliberate editorial principle discernable here of alternating judgment with a series of passages on restoration. This is confirmed by the two best-known 'messianic' passages, which occur in the first main section of the book (chs. 1–12): '[t]he people who walked in darkness have seen a great light' (9.1-7), and '[a] shoot will come out of the stump of Jesse' (11.1-9). This latter passage concludes the series (confirmed by the doxology of ch. 12, and the start of an entirely new section with oracles against the nations in ch. 13).

It is almost overwhelming that in a section where the judge is one of the officials who represent the break-up of society (ch. 3), the final hope is for one who 'will not judge by what his eyes see, or decide by what his ears hear, but will judge the poor with righteousness...' (11.3-4). This is a theology of greater and more integrated scope than that of Amos. Furthermore, it has not been spoken in a day, or even written in a few years: it seems expressed with a poetic power forged over many generations. This prophecy seems to draw what the people have been through into a broad, painful and triumphant scope.

Scope is indeed the right word for the prophecy of Isaiah. For the alternation of judgment and resoration is not only found in succeeding verses and in a series of units punctuating a complete section, but also fashions the book as a whole. Chapters 1–39 keep returning to passages which are credible in the latter part of the eighth century BCE, and in fact end with a prediction to Hezekiah, who reigned at that time, that all his house would be taken to Babylon (39.6). Chapters 40–45, however, are concerned with the restoration of the people, the details making clear that Jerusalem has already been destroyed (44.28—over 100 years after Isaiah), and that it will now be restored. The prophet's very opening is that Jerusalem has paid her penalty (40.2), and it is all expressed with surging confidence. Seen from literary, historical and theological points of view, there is no prophecy more unified than Isaiah 40–55.

It might be thought from this that restoration brings everything to a satisfactory conclusion. Chapters 56–66, however, are a collection of diverse material indicating considerable conflict between groups in the post-exilic community (65.13; 66.5).[24] The restoration of Jerusalem c. 520 BCE was not the unimpeded process which might be expected from Isaiah 40–55 (although these words have continued to inspire people ever since), but had to be worked out in the depressed conditions of Jerusalem itself, and in conflict with the region's inhabitants.

Broadly speaking, therefore, the three main parts of the book of Isaiah (chs. 1–39, 40–55 and 56–66 express, first, the particulars of judgment in a society faced with unprecedented crisis; secondly, the surge of hope at a turning point after the crisis; but also, thirdly, a sober accommodation to the realities of a situation not easily redeemed—and possibly in the end God's word was heard above all in the exhortations to capitalize on the limitations of restoration.

The series of responses over a period of no less than centuries is not comprehended either by the categories of social function, or by a timeless literature. It is true that it is difficult to identify exactly the people, or whole series of peoples, who are addressed by this prophecy. But they were people who had to struggle with accepting judgment. For some, at least, living in depressing circumstances, it may have been just as difficult to accept restoration, and they could only be set on the first stages to that acceptance by an eloquent prophecy, and even after that still had to effect the restoration together with people who had quite different conceptions of how it should be achieved. The pattern of judgment and restoration, therefore, reveals the issues, the crises and the opportunities in which the editors were involved, and which they continued to present to new readers. Thus, the main challenge for people—and, especially, Christian leaders—today is to realize that they also must live through, in order to be a part of, prophecy.

4. *Prophecy and People Today*

In her essay 'Journey of a Metaphor', Phyllis Trible presents a female organ, the womb, as a metaphor for the compassion of God.[25] Theology, she suggests, is communicated through certain ways of speaking and

---

24. See, for example, P.D. Hanson, *The Dawn of Apocalyptic: The Historical and Sociological Roots of Jewish Apocalyptic Eschatology* (Philadelphia: Fortress Press, rev. edn, 1979).

25. P. Trible, *God and the Rhetoric of Sexuality* (Philadelphia: Fortress Press, 1978), pp. 31-59.

writing about God. She describes Jer. 31.15-22 as 'a drama of voices'.[26] Writing that '[t]hese voices organize structure, fill content, and mold vision to create a new thing in the land (cf. v. 22b)...', she says, in fact, that 'this new thing is the poem itself'. Thus, far from accepting the conventional wisdom that 'God speaks through the prophets', Trible suggests that receiving the content will come through discerning a literary form. She does not see the first strophe of this text (Jer. 31.15) as a direct address of God to people, but rather as an announcement of the weeping of the ancestral mother Rachel (it is the well-known text, 'a voice is heard in Ramah...Rachel is weeping for her children'). Trible describes this as a mother embracing children with many tears and fading speech, which is directed *to all who may hear through the ages* (my emphasis). In effect, then, readers are drawn into an emotional experience of hearing a weeping mother.

Indeed Yahweh responds to *Rachel* in the second strophe (vv. 16-17). The promise to her that children will return from the land is reinforced by the statement 'says the Lord', but Trible points out that 'Yahweh never draws attention to the divine self'. And while there are no first-person pronouns, possessive pronouns address Rachel: 'your voice, your eyes, your work, your future'. Trible thinks that, on the whole, the woman dominates in this strophe. It is not a bald promise that people will return. Instead, to appreciate it, the reader must see through the focus on Rachel.

The third strophe does change emphasis (vv. 18-19). Now the sons are named in Ephraim. Yahweh too is present in the 'I' as subject and with Ephraim as object: 'I have heard Ephraim rocking in grief'. But despite this, Yahweh is not addressing the people, as some assume that prophecy usually suggests. Here, a brief introduction with Yahweh's 'I' leads to a long quotation in which Ephraim speaks: 'For after I turned away, I repented'. Trible defines it thus: 'Ephraim implores God with a voice of repentance and confession'. So, in these three strophes, 'Rachel cries; Yahweh consoles; Ephraim confesses'. Though Trible does not make the point here, it is interesting that up to this stage, there is nothing about the prophet. Thus, the assumption that all prophecy is expressed under the rubric of God, prophet and people is not confirmed comprehensively here. Nor is it a matter of 'direct' address from God to people. 'The drama of voices' expresses itself in different ways: 'Rachel cries; Yahweh consoles; Ephraim confesses'. Hence, the 'new thing' of

---

26. See *God and the Rhetoric of Sexuality*, pp. 40-50.

the poem is being conveyed through a relation of varied spokespeople and emotions.

Though the 'I' of Yahweh has been mentioned in v. 18, it is not until the fourth strophe (v. 20) that Yahweh is quoted extensively, and it is also in emotional terms: 'Is Ephraim my darling child?' Trible thinks that this 'suggests that God identifies with Rachel's caring for her children'. She translates the rest of the strophe, 'For the more I speak of him, the more I do remember him. Therefore, my womb trembles for him; I will truly show motherly-compassion upon him. Oracle of Yahweh.' She justifies her translation of 'womb' for the Hebrew word usually rendered 'inner parts' by observing that the latter is paralleled by 'womb' in various passages (Gen. 25.23; Ps. 71.6; Isa. 49.1). 'Truly show motherly compassion' comes from her consideration that two verbal forms of the same root from which 'womb' (*rḥm*) comes are used. She concludes: 'an exclusively female image extends its meaning to a divine mode of being'. Trible summarizes by saying that 'strophe four is the voice of Yahweh the mother'. Rachel mourns the loss of the fruit of her womb; Yahweh mourns the same child. 'Yet there is a difference. The human mother refuses consolation; the divine mother changes grief into grace.' So it is not only that Yahweh speaks in generally emotional terms, as I noted earlier. Yahweh's mercy is expressed through a particularly female emotion that outbids, however, the human female. Thus, there are deeper dimensions here than the point that 'the prophets predict the mercy of God for people'.

Up to this point, the presentation has been through Rachel, Ephraim and Yahweh, and the prophet is only putatively present in formulas like 'Thus says Yahweh' and 'oracle of Yahweh'. But in the fifth strophe, as Trible puts it, the prophet appears with the role of delivering the message of God's maternal compassion. She adds in a note (pp. 58-59 n. 36), however, that she cannot prove that the voice belongs to Jeremiah, since the speaker is not identified, and she adds that this focuses attention solely on the speech, which is replete with female semantics. She does, however. go on to speak of 'Jeremiah' commanding, speaking and questioning. The final strophe is both summary and innovation. The first strophe begins with a mother crying for lost children, but in the last the prophet commands them to make guideposts for their return home (31.21-22). Now too the children change sex: 'Ephraim the son becomes Israel the daughter'. This means that the promise is expressed by a prophet speaking through a woman. 'This change of imagery converges upon the center of the poem to surround male with female.'

Trible points out that in the fifth strophe Jeremiah twice commands that Israel return (to the land), and that this was what was promised and requested earlier. The final climactic line in the poem is 'For Yahweh has created a new thing in the land: female surrounds man'. Earlier Yahweh spoke and was addressed; now Yahweh is spoken about, using a new verb, 'create' (*bara'*), a word used only for the creative work of God. Trible concudes that 'female surrounding man' receives its meaning from the whole work of art.

Carroll, however, thinks that the connection between vv. 15-17 and vv. 18-20 is redactional, because the latter passage deals with children who in the former are dead. He also treats vv. 21-22 as a separate unit, seeing speaker, addressee and deity as distinctive in these verses.[27] He gives a survey of the difficulties of the meaning of the phrase 'female surrounds man'.[28] At the end of his exegesis, he says that he does not know what v. 22b means. Trible, however, finds enough thematic and literary unity to give a plausible sense to the present form of the passage. She sees 'female surrounding man' as

> Rachel the mother embracing her sons with tears and with speech; it is Yahweh consoling Rachel about Ephraim; it is Yahweh declaring motherly compassion for Ephraim; it is the daughter Israel superseding [*sic.*] the son Ephraim. And it is more than these images. Female surrounding man has power to dry up the tears of Rachel; to fulfill the compassion of Yahweh; and to overturn the apostasy of Israel. And it is other than all these images, for it is Yahweh's creation of a new thing in the land. In short, it is the poem itself…the very form and content of the poem embodies a womb: woman encloses man. The female organ nourishes, sustains, and redeems the male child Ephraim. Thus, our metaphor is surrounded by a cloud of witnesses.[29]

It is a moot point whether the metaphor has taken over from what it conveys, despite their necessary connection. On the other hand, after writing 'the very form and content of the poem embodies a womb…', Trible adds, '[t]he female organ nourishes, sustains and redeems the male child Ephraim'. This is confirmed at the beginning where she writes of the metaphor (of the womb) being the mode of comparison,

27. Carroll, *Jeremiah*, p. 569.
28. Carroll, *Jeremiah*, pp. 601-603.
29. Trible, *God and the Rhetoric of Sexuality*, pp. 49-50.

and she uses similar expressions later, seeing the womb as a vehicle for God's compassion (for the whole people).

As we have seen, the question of the redaction of this passage can be raised, and possibly that of its social function as well. Trible's interpretation, however, does not address these questions. It resembles other interpretations in this even if they do not have the same particular emphases. Their approach is to demonstrate dimensions within the present form of a passage through the relation of its parts. Often they lend it a personal address by assuming that the prophet named in other parts of the book is the speaker.

The effect of such interpretation is to bring a certain kind of people to light, both those heard in the passage and those reading it now. Literally, the prophet may not have been Jeremiah. I agree with Carroll that, since Jeremiah proclaimed the destruction of the land and people without any reservation, it is difficult to imagine him performing the *volte-face* which is entailed if the book of the restoration (in chs. 30–31) is attributed to him.[30] Carroll thinks the cycle shows some influence of Hosea and Second Isaiah, and shares some common elements with the Ezekiel tradition. He attributes it to 'anonymous circles during and after the exile which cherished expectations of restoration'. He thinks this attribution is vague, but it does give a sociological context in broad terms, and such a context does not have to be exact to be helpful. Though Trible makes little direct reference to sociological context or editorial activity, the kind of work she does adds (at least for 31.15-22) an illuminating dimension, bringing a certain kind of people to light; those who think that a feminine way of describing God's compassion is the one which will bring the promise of return to birth. Moreover, to understand it as Jeremiah speaking gives it a radically transformed personal focus.

People today are drawn into this kind of interpretation by the interpreter's use of appealing language like '[t]he human mother refuses consolation; the divine mother changes grief into grace'. Trible is plainly hoping that readers will enter into this neglected dimension. Interpretations like 'Ephraim the son becomes Israel the daughter' challenge readers to be the kind of people who identify themselves as female recipients even if they are male. This is prophecy as a revolution of roles. Trible confirms that she is interested in bringing people today to recognize a dimension of prophecy missed before, when she writes of

30. Carroll, *Jeremiah*, p. 569.

the womb as a metaphor for God's compassion: 'Though readers of the Old Testament have often been slow to perceive this speech, they have long been recipients of its manifold blessings.'[31] It is also clear that while this way of interpreting prophecy is not primarily interested in sociological or editorial aspects, it is not an easy option. In the way people today select some snippet of prophecy, they usually assume that they know what it is about. Trible's interpretation, which is not just easy reading, makes it clear that it is necessary to make a considerable effort in order to understand and connect the details of the text. Thus, with this kind of interpretation too, people must be prepared, both intellectually and existentially, to become part of the prophecy themselves.

In the three approaches to prophecy considered—sociological, literary, and an interpretation of a particular passage—we have seen that prophecy is not simply a neutral description of what individual prophets said or did in one time. Those unexciting people, editors, are part of the prophecy we have. They bound together past, present and future; saw the significance of the combination for themselves; and offered a goal for people in the future. As far as we know them, they form an anonymous group; they do not emerge as great individuals. No Amos, Isaiah or Jeremiah will arise now to be prophets for us—if they did, probably we would not recognize them. It may be, however, that prophetic communities will evolve. Realizing that prophecy is not one-dimensional, these communities will learn that prophecy is not totally clear at one place or time, but involves the integration of different situations and times. They will struggle to speak at the right time, but will also be more prophetic the more they listen to various voices. 'God creating a new thing' means that people can change their means of receptivity. The God who usually spoke in masculine terms, but who can show motherly compassion, indicates that prophecy does not have to come to expression in a masculine—or any other—customary way. It entails, for example, that all forms of ministry, including episcopal, can be feminine or, indeed, take forms we cannot yet conceive of.

31. Trible, *God and the Rhetoric of Sexuality*, p. 56.

A REFORMATIONAL SLOGAN ON MINISTRY AND PAUL'S GOSPEL OF GRACE

Douglas A. Campbell

Introduction

The slogan 'the priesthood of all believers' is a Reformational clarion-call in relation to clericalism. However, this famous saying, which has supposedly had such revolutionary implications for the nature of church leadership, has some unexpected ramifications. A careful scrutiny suggests that its original Reformational context sharply reduces its relevance today. Moreover, its original scriptural function is also severely limited in its contemporary application. A different, rather more Pauline, construal of the saying, however, may suggest the precise opposite of irrelevance: understood in a radically Pauline way the saying may encapsulate the heart of the gospel, and also comprise a critical insight into Christian ministry—hence it is a trumpet well worth sounding today.

1. *The Historical Context of the Slogan*

As is well known, Luther coined the phrase 'the priesthood of all believers'. It was an important strut in the argument of one of his three powerful 1520 pamphlets, 'On the Babylonian Captivity of the Church',[1]

---

1. Available in numerous translations: the version used here is from H.T. Lehmann and A.R. Wentz (eds.), *Luther's Works*. XXXVI. *Word and Sacrament II* (Philadelphia: Muhlenberg, 1959), pp. 11-126. Also significant is one of his four defences against Jerome Emser written in 1521, 'Answer to the Hyperchristian, Hyperspiritual, and Hyperlearned Book by Goat Emser in Leipzig—Including Some Thoughts regarding his Companion, the Fool Murner', in E.W. Gritsch and H.T. Lehmann (eds.), *Luther's Works* (Philadelphia: Fortress Press, 1970), XXXIX, pp. 137-224.

which was a sustained attack on three clusters of privilege claimed by the clerical and papal leadership of sixteenth-century Catholicism. 'The priesthood of all believers' was a theological volley aimed at levelling one of these 'walls' (as Luther called them), specifically, that of general clerical privilege, and this was doubtless a constructive thing to say in the sixteenth century. Certainly Luther in doing so merely stood in a long line of anti-clerical protest that stretched back to at least the middle of the twelfth century.[2] The Gregorian papacy and church supported an astonishing class of religious professionals, hedged around with benefits and pleasures. Admittedly, one should not exaggerate the fallen state of the clergy at this time: no doubt there were many pious people living within the sprawling bureaucratic culture that was the church's leadership in Western Europe in the fourteenth and fifteenth centuries. Moreover, the hostile rhetoric of the Reformation was given to overdrawn caricature. Nonetheless, some truth also undoubtedly lies within the polemic. The clergy tended to define itself as 'the priesthood' and, helped partly by the analogy of the Levitical priesthood, it had arrogated to itself a number of religious privileges that separated it significantly from the average Christian layperson. Catholicism at this time had the distinct aroma of class.[3]

2.   Both here and for the following points 'a reliable if hard-edged' account may be found in P. Johnson, *A History of Christianity* (New York: Athenaeum, 1985), esp. pp. 191-328 (quote from a review by Martin E. Marty, printed on the back cover).

3.   This is perfectly exemplified in the two extensive linguistic paradigms, forming an overarching binary opposition, that completely organized this society. On the one hand there was the clerus/clerici (hence, 'clergy'); *hiereus/hiereteuma*; litterati; and, on the other, the *laos/lakios*/laici (hence, 'laity'), *idiotai*/idiotae/illiterati, *biotikoi*, saeculares, populi/populares (see H. Küng's discussion 'The Priesthood of All Believers', in *The Church* [trans. R. and R. Ockenden; repr; London: Search Press, 1971 (1967)], pp. 385-86). Christopher N.L. Brooke observes (fascinatingly) that this distinction was often most apparent in hairstyle, the clergy having the tonsure (in the West, 'of St Peter'). Brooke also observes, however, that while various factors were converging, particularly from the reign of Urban II late in the eleventh century, to reinforce this basic social divide, it was still both blurred and opposed at times. The most notable instance of opposition was the Franciscan (although it was not alone), and the most notable—and recurrent—case of 'blurring' was in the area of lay brothers/monks, who constituted a borderline category, neither fully clerical and hence entitled to offer the sacraments, nor fully lay (and signified in their ambiguous hairstyle: no tonsure, or a reduced one, but uniformly bearded). This binary division represented a modification of the earlier threefold division of society into 'those that

Luther's famous dictum was, as I have said, simply part of a gener-alized offensive against this situation. The critical point to note, however, is that as a result of this its content *is essentially negative*.[4] That is, it criticizes a situation characterized by clericalism, specifically where the clergy are terming themselves 'priests'.[5] In this context 1 Pet. 2.4-10 is an effective brief rejoinder, suggesting that this title and its associated privileges belong to all Christians and not merely to a few: 'you [all] are a chosen race, a royal priesthood, a holy nation, God's own people...' (v. 9, NRSV). Moreover, the claim that 'you all' have access to this status probably generated an exhilarating sense of freedom and dignity among the traditionally dispossessed.

But clearly the slogan is limited by this context. Only where the church is characterized by a leadership monopoly, and one somehow analogous to priesthood, can the statement be deployed effectively. Here it will still function adequately and, as Luther intended, as a critique. Equally clearly, however, it cannot function apart from such a context as an enduring statement of some positive dimension in the church, unless it is redefined.[6] If the church many Christians belong to today is only

---

fight; those that pray; and those that work' ('Priest, Deacon and Layman, from St Peter Damian to St Francis', in W.J. Sheils and D. Wood [eds.], *The Ministry: Clerical and Lay* [Oxford: Basil Blackwell, 1989], pp. 65-85).

4.   Paul Althaus anticipates much of my discussion here in his description of 'the Evangelical Priesthood' in Luther's thought, and its positive development in terms of the two specific ministries of preaching/witnessing and forgiveness (*The Theology of Martin Luther* [trans. R.C. Schultz; Philadelphia: Fortress Press, 2nd edn, 1966], pp. 313-18, esp. nn. 86 and 87, p. 314). It is interesting, however, that (as has to be done surprisingly often) he distinguishes Luther's understanding from that of later Protestantism: 'The church is founded on Christ's priesthood. Its inner structure is the priesthood of Christians for each other. The priesthood of Christians flows from the priesthood of Christ...[Hence] Luther never understands the priest-hood of all believers merely in the "Protestant" sense of the Christian's freedom to stand in a direct relationship to God without a human mediator' (pp. 313-14). George Yule also distinguishes Calvin's thought from later Calvinist Scholasticism: 'Calvin's View of the Ministry of the Church', in Sheils and Wood (eds.), *The Ministry: Clerical and Lay*, pp. 167-76.

5.   T.W. Manson gives a good, brief summary of the main positions of the Reformers in *Ministry and Priesthood: Christ's and Ours—Two Lectures* (London: Epworth Press, 1958), pp. 36-39, esp. n. 5 p. 37.

6.   Küng notes this clearly, and also makes such an attempt: 'Priesthood', pp. 372-80.

vestigially clerical, then it is a pointless observation—something quite forgettable (a point we will return to shortly).

One might object that this dismissal on grounds of literal context is too hasty—that the history of the church in recent centuries suggests that the slogan is constantly being reapplied, often in a revivalist context.[7] But it is important to scrutinize this periodic reaffirmation carefully.[8] In part the slogan's revival seems traceable to the Protestant and Nonconformist matrix of these periodic awakenings (via Pietism),[9] where it probably functions as much as an affirmation of continuity with the Reformation as a critique of clericalism (such revivals were—and regrettably are—often characterized by anti-Catholic rhetoric).[10] When it is stripped of these emotive Reformational resonances, little seems left of the principle's original point. Certainly, the more specific criticisms of priestly privilege that should accompany its proper use seem absent.[11]

Something substantive is possibly still salvageable. The periodic reuse of the statement does seem to suggest that (with unfortunate frequency)

---

7.   Another, rather Protestant, basic introduction to Christian history illustrates this well: the saying is a repeated element in the description of the various post-Reformation revivals in T. Dowley *et al.* (eds.), *A History of Christianity—A Lion Handbook* (Berkhamstead: Lion, 1977).

8.   We could add that the New Testament tends to be misappropriated at this point. It can be claimed that the New Testament reflects a small-group setting (usually in houses) and a fairly informal leadership structure, hence this supposedly remains normative for later Christianity. But the problems that gave rise to institutionalization ('early Catholicism') simply had not arisen in much of the New Testament period—the church was not large, significant, or old enough. So it is hardly surprising that second-century problems do not find their solutions in the pages of the New Testament. Is it wise to dismiss institutional structures on the grounds that the New Testament precedes them?

9.   See W.R. Ward, 'Pastoral Office and the General Priesthood in the Great Awakening', in Sheils and Wood (eds.), *The Ministry: Clerical and Lay*, pp. 303-27. He comments: 'The majority parties among the Churches insist on maintaining a corporative attitude towards their professional ministries, apparently oblivious of the fact that the rest of the world manages its affairs much better by contracts of service, and making up its mind what it wants from its employees...the Pastoral Office has clearly swallowed up the General Priesthood. They ['the clergy'] are the true Levites, not the eternally nonconformist priesthood after the order of Melchizedek' (pp. 326-27). See also Küng, 'Priesthood', pp. 363, 368-69, 377-78.

10.   Since Vatican II much less convincing (see Küng, 'Priesthood', pp. 380-82).

11.   Moreover, do these revivals spring from an Orthodox or Catholic context, within which a critique of clericalism might be relevant?

ordinary Christians find it liberating to be reminded that they are individually significant in furthering God's designs: 'everyone has their part to play'. This suggestion is important, especially when revivals are enthusing large numbers of Christians outside traditional church structures, but it is hardly programmatic. It amounts to little more than a principle of good business management. In large institutions the leadership may monopolize initiative, but a vigorous institution requires the active participation of all its members, however anonymous they may feel. Nevertheless, one hears as much on most regimental parades. While granting that this is something worth saying, is this all that is left of Luther's fearsome anti-clerical volley?

2. *The Scriptural Function of the Slogan*

One possible solution to this problem is to explore the saying's original scriptural attestation—surely in the New Testament we will find a positive and enduring understanding? Here, however, we find that the Evangelical connection we might expect to hold between the principle's scriptural and later historical contexts is severely dislocated.

The most often quoted text is 1 Pet. 2.4-10 (especially vv. 5 and 9), while the ideas stated clearly here are echoed in the book of Revelation (1.6, 5.10 and 20.6), and perhaps also in Titus (2.14). The magisterial letter to the Hebrews is, at least at this point, not apparently relevant, since it discusses the supersession of the Levitical priesthood in Christ. The Petrine text and its associates, following Exod. 19.6, discuss the entire people of Israel, collectively referred to as priests, and apply this designation contemporaneously to the entire Christian community. Exod. 19.6 is itself a covenantal request directed through Moses to all Israel before Sinai.[12]

This original context makes the drawing of any inferences for Christian leadership, where this is understood on analogy to Levitical priestly leaders, problematic. Moreover, Luther's use of the text to attack a priestly clericalism may have been superficially plausible, but fundamentally invalid. One can imagine Catholic clerics (such as 'the Leipzig goat' Emser) rejecting Luther's attack in the following terms: 'We admit the importance of your text, and the conclusion that all Christians are

---

12. Strictly speaking, the event recounted in Exodus takes place before the Levitical priesthood has been established. Therefore, a reading which follows the story's own narrative structure cannot detect Levitical implications at this point.

priests in this sense. But the priesthood we occupy as clerics corresponds to the *Levitical* priesthood which God ordains and describes later on in the Pentateuch. This is a different and quite distinctive ordinance, so your text and your criticism are improper. In a sense, there are two "priest-hoods" in the church (and it is a great error to confuse them): the first is the general Israelite priesthood, suggested by the Sinai narrative, to which all belong, and the second is the select, Levitical priesthood, to which only the few belong. If one merges the two, one confuses the Scriptures. Most importantly, all belong to the former, but only we belong to the latter.' Of course, this rebuttal may not have greatly troubled Luther, caught up as he was in the ecclesiastical convulsions of the early 1500s, but it makes our task today rather more difficult. Up to this point, however, our examination of the New Testament data has perhaps been too superficial.

When we begin to explore motifs related to priesthood in the New Testament, an awkward sense of metaphorical plasticity becomes apparent. In the central 1 Peter text, as well as in some of Paul's writings (not forgetting the Gospel of John), the Christian community repeatedly receives metaphorical qualifications in terms of various features of the Old Testament temple and its cultus. The precise nature and application of these metaphors varies quite widely.[13] In Romans, for example, Christ himself functions as an annual sacrifice of atonement, as a sin-offering (or at least as 'an atoning act'), as a priestly intercessor, as the stone laid fundamentally under the temple, and as a priestly servant (see 3.25; 8.3b, 34; 9.32-33; 15.8). Paul also functions as a priestly servant making acceptable offerings (of the Gentiles) to God, within a reiterated reference to his life as one of sacred religious service (see 1.1, 5, 9; 15.15b-16). The Christian community is described within this metaphorical ambit as a sacrifice, is exhorted to undertake an appropriate religious service to God, gains access or entrance into God's presence, and is purified in the manner of sacred temple objects (see 12.1; 5.1-2; 15.16b).[14]

The 1 Peter text also reflects this metaphorical layering. In v. 5 Christians are 'living stones...built into a spiritual house [i.e. temple]', as well as 'a holy priesthood...offer[ing] spiritual sacrifices acceptable to

---

13. A point also made by Manson: see *Ministry and Priesthood*, pp. 47-51, 64.

14. The letter to the Ephesians is similarly rich in this imagery, while the letter to the Hebrews is simply a *tour de force* (but the distinctive perspective of Hebrews should not be allowed to dominate discussions of cultic imagery in the New Testament).

God'. The main emphasis of the section then follows, namely, a description of Christ as a 'stone' that fulfills the prophecies of Isa. 8.14, 28.16, and Ps. 118.22[15]—and in the context of 1 Pet. 2.5 it is reasonable to assume that this stone is also part of a temple, although the point is not developed as, for example, the letter to the Ephesians elaborates it (see esp. 2.14-22).

By now the general tenor of the New Testament discussion of priesthood in relation to Christians should be apparent. Priesthood is but one element in a quite generalized application of cultic imagery to various aspects of the Christian community. It is drawn, like the rest of the images, from the context of the Jewish cultus, that is, the Jerusalem temple and all its accoutrements. Moreover, it is not itself applied uniformly to a specific referent (again, like its accompanying images), but to different referents—at times to Christ, to Paul, or to the Christian community as a whole. In view of this generalized transfer of temple imagery, rather than speaking of the priesthood of all believers, we should speak of the cultic characterization of various aspects of the Christian community.

The import of Luther's slogan may now be stated more precisely. The slogan presupposes that a given image or set of images (usually priesthood, so P), rooted in a broader cultic reservoir of imagery (C), is being applied to a certain, rather narrow, constituency (I: in Luther's case, the Catholic clergy; in the New Testament, the referent of the reservoir of imagery, i.e. the cultus itself, with a more generalized reference to Israel possible on the basis of Exod. 19.6). The slogan's contention, however, is that the Christian community (II), which differs significantly from this prior constituency, has legitimate title to the metaphor(s) (which are deemed to be important enough to fight over). In essence, P, and any other metaphors in C, should be transferred from I to II.

Hence, for the slogan to function meaningfully, P and C must be valued significantly, and I must differ significantly from II. In fact, it gives special force to the slogan if I is behaving oppressively towards II: then the transfer 'turns the tables', if only metaphorically. The slogan

---

15. On this motif see R.N. Longenecker, *The Christology of Early Jewish Christianity* (London: SCM Press, 1970), pp. 50-53. On the theme of priestly fulfilment in the New Testament in particular relation to Christ see O. Cullmann, *Christology of the New Testament* (trans. S.C. Guthrie and C.A.M. Hall; repr.; Philadelphia: Westminster Press, 1959 [1957]), pp. 83-107, esp. pp. 104-107; and Longenecker, *Christology*, pp. 113-19.

also clearly functions significantly where new identities are being created. It urges a transfer of images, along with their associated sanctity and loyalties, to another body, whether the early Christian community or Protestantism. Consequently it is a slogan that facilitates movement, or, put more negatively, it may legitimize division, as meaning is transferred from an old constituency to a new one.[16]

Four interpretive consequences implicit here are important for our broader discussion:

1. It is dangerous to speak solely of one image and one referent (in other words, of a single transfer), namely, of priesthood being transferred to believers or Christians in general. Any scrutiny of the New Testament data will undermine the centrality of this specific application essentially by complicating it: priesthood goes to other referents (like Christ or Paul), while other images come to Christians. The reification of one particular transfer then seems both biblically insensitive and arbitrary.

2. More importantly, as I have already suggested briefly when discussing Luther, the claim of transfer is only rhetorically significant when the reservoir of images is still meaningful. In the early church this claim was not merely meaningful; it was incendiary—a revolutionary act. The massive functions of the temple were devolving onto the small Christian community! Christ was displacing one of the centre-pieces of Judaism![17] But

16. For a possible reconstruction of the sociological dynamic here in the early church (although largely disowned by its author) see F. Watson, *Paul, Judaism, and the Gentiles: A Sociological Approach* (SNTSMS, 56; Cambridge: Cambridge University Press, 1986).

17. A good case may be made for the particular notion of temple-fulfilment causing (at least in part) the first, very vicious, outbreak of persecution against the nascent Christian movement. Certainly Stephen's rather puzzling speech in Acts 7 is comprehensible in these terms, namely, the Christian movement's displacement of the cultus—it is an 'anti-temple' speech. As the author of Acts describes it, this claim caused various Jews present to stop up their ears, grind their teeth, and howl with rage, before lynching the claimant (7.54, 57-58). We often fail to grasp the staggering audacity of this point because we forget the importance of the temple in Jerusalem. No metaphor or analogy is really available from our own culture that carries the same weight of sanctity and importance. It was this massive cultural value that certain early Christians—'the radical wing' of the early church—transferred to themselves and their meetings. Unfortunately, the precise theological rationale for this transfer is crucial, although seldom articulated (see point 4 below). One can

for the vast majority of Christians today, this is a non-issue— and even for orthodox Jews, the temple along with its offici- ating priesthood has not stood for the most part of two thousand years.[18] What does it have to say to the modern, profoundly Gentile, Christian, whose only exposure to the Jerusalem temple and the metaphor of priesthood is the occa- sional homily drawn from the Pentateuch? How does it benefit such a person, other than perhaps hermeneutically, to be told that the status of a general Israelite priesthood has been trans- ferred to them? One might as well claim Roman citizenship in addition.

3. As we have seen, the slogan's content is essentially defined by a prior constituency, to which it reacts negatively. Privileges claimed by constituency I are asserted now to belong to II, that is, to a more general group. Thus the *positive* force of the saying is the application of P (or another image from C) to II, *but this can only ever be of rhetorical benefit*. The original cultic reservoir for these images (C) means that any transfer of meaning must be highly figurative—it is virtually impossible to draw direct equations between aspects of a temple cultus and a human community. So Christians are not *literally* stones in a new temple, and Jesus' death was not literally a mercy-seat (see 1 Cor. 3.10-17 and Rom. 3.25). These transfers are metaphor- ical—although Christian interpreters are so used to them that this tends to go unnoticed. Hence, in terms of practical, con- crete guidance for the structure of the new community, the

speculate that the presence of the Spirit was critical, the 'fact' of Jesus' resurrection, and some perceived connection between these and the function of the temple (so Stephen's speech). But such questions are the subject of a voluminous scholarly literature, within which little agreement is apparent. On the above view of Stephen's speech see R.N. Longenecker, 'Acts' in F.E. Gaebelein (ed.), *The Expositor's Bible Commentary* (Grand Rapids: Zondervan, 1981), IX, pp. 326-54, esp. pp. 337-44. H. Räisänen surveys approaches to this speech well, but to my mind supplies no alternatives superior to Longenecker's: 'The "Hellenists": A Bridge between Jesus and Paul?', in *Jesus, Paul and Torah* (trans. D.E. Orton; JSNTSup, 43; Sheffield: JSOT Press, 1992), pp. 149-202.

18. Much of the original temple loyalty was transferred rabbinically to the relevant Mosaic texts, although it still rests in part on the geographical node of the temple mount. Note that in a post-Auschwitz age any deployment of a slogan so offensive to Jews is further complicated.

slogan is largely useless. It can only score rhetorical points for II as it emerges from its historical parent, I (and, as the foregoing point notes, for this to happen the prior reservoir C needs to be current).

4.   Finally, the slogan does not give the rationale for the transfer it lays claim to: it merely asserts that the transfer ought to take place. For the early Christians, as for Luther, something about Christ (presumably!) effected this transfer, even though type I constituencies deny it. But the slogan presupposes this: it is not stated explicitly. This doubles the conundrum of the saying's lack of positive content. Not only is its positive force largely figurative, but the critical rationale that lies behind its basic assertions is not supplied.

When these four limitations are taken into consideration, our saying looks increasingly useless—like a cannon that has been discharged in an ancient battle and never reloaded. Only a new understanding of the saying offers a way forward.[19]

3. *A New Perspective on 'Believing'*

As we have seen, the slogan draws together three basic semantic components:

1.   the motif of 'priesthood', P (in 1 Pet. 2.5 *hierateuma*; this may be replaced by alternative cultic motifs from C);
2.   the significant qualification of 'all' (in the New Testament *pantes* or its equivalent;[20] present by implication in the inclusive second person plural verbs used in 1 Pet. 2.5-11, and supplying the sense of transfer to type II constituencies); and

19. Küng attempts this—but also illustrates my basic contention concerning its difficulties well, as he constantly oscillates between affirmations of the negative force of the slogan, grounded in church history, and the elucidation of a more positive content, which is increasingly distanced from the actual saying and its metaphors (and the saying's history), and seems more akin to the notion of simply 'being a Christian'—why use this saying to speak of what it means to be a Christian? (see 'Priesthood', pp. 372-87).

20. This is a particularly important word and theme in Romans: *pas* (everyone/all), or its equivalent, occurs some 71 times (once additionally in 16.26; and once in a variant in 3.22).

3. 'believing'; the participial form of the verb 'to believe', derived from the Greek stem *pist-*.

The critical point in the slogan is usually assumed to be the qualification of (1) by (2), that is, the suggestion that 'the priesthood' now extends to 'all'; all, that is, who belong to the new community. Motif (3), 'believers', has usually been understood as a synonym for 'Christians', so we may paraphrase the traditional reading as 'the priesthood of all Christians'.[21] But, far from occupying an innocuous position, the motif of 'belief' or 'faith' may reorientate the statement in a significant new direction. This reorientation will be attempted through a brief exploration of the chief New Testament witness to 'faith', namely, Paul and his letter to the Romans.[22]

pist- words in Paul are generally understood in terms of human acts, specifically, the moment of belief in the good news and the ongoing trust that together grasp the gospel's offer of salvation. Such a reading is widely followed by scholars, preachers and laypeople today. It is easily comprehensible—if not completely self-evident—to a Christian generation with a long legacy of theological contractualism, an intellectual heritage of anthropocentric rationalism and individualism, and a political and legal tradition based on consent.[23] Hence the standard synonym for Christians used in our slogan, 'believers'.

An alternative interpretation, however, gaining ground of late (especially in North America), reads *pistis* in many of its Pauline occurrences with reference to Christ himself, and not to the Christian.[24] Such a

---

21. Much of the secondary literature reflects this, alternating without distinction between 'believers' and 'Christians'.

22. The key Pauline words are *pistis* (the noun 'faith') and *pisteuō* (the verb 'to believe' or 'to trust'). 'Believers' comes from the latter, but Paul's discussions are actually dominated by the former (108 uses in a ten-letter canon; the verb occurs 48 times). Paul's use of *pist-* words is also heavily concentrated in Romans and Galatians (notably Rom. 1–4 and 9.30–10.11, and Gal. 2.15–3.29).

23. See J.B. Torrance, 'Covenant and Contract: A Study of the Theological Background of Worship in Seventeenth-Century Scotland', *SJT* 23 (1970), pp. 51-76; *idem*, 'The Contribution of McLeod Campbell to Scottish Theology', *SJT* 26 (1973), pp. 295-311.

24. An excellent summary of the position may be found in R.B. Hays, 'ΠΙΣΤΙΣ and Pauline Christology: What is at Stake?', in E.H. Lovering (ed.), *SBLSP* (Atlanta, GA: Scholars Press, 1991), pp. 714-29; with more detailed arguments concerning Galatians in his *The Faith of Jesus Christ: An Investigation of the Narrative Substructure of Galatians 3.1–4.11* (SBLDS, 56; Chico, CA: Scholars Press, 1983).

reading draws not so much on the notion of decision, which may be a peculiarly modern, Western concern, but on older notions of relational obedience and religious witness. These are perhaps more to be expected in ancient, heavily stratified societies that often punished religious dissenters with persecution and even execution. In such a social context, the word *pistis* would not suggest 'belief' so much as 'trust' or the stronger notion of 'faithfulness'; that of an unwavering fidelity to God's will and call, to the point of death if need be.

If this approach is correct, then Paul speaks quite frequently of the steadfast fidelity of Christ in his letters to the Galatians and to the Romans.[25] But this rather complicates Paul's general use of *pist*-language: we now have to interpret two separate sets of *pist*- statements (see esp. Gal. 2.16 and Rom. 3.22—and 1.17?). Paul speaks of the trust and belief of Christians in God and in the gospel (usually using verbal forms), but also of the trust and fidelity of Christ himself (usually using the noun). How do these two notions relate to one another?

Formally, there are probably only three options: the relation is (1) fortuitous; (2) imitative; or (3) participatory.

1. It seems immediately unlikely that the relationship is merely fortuitous (that is, there is no real relationship between the two notions, and the apparent linguistic similarity is accidental). One of the reasons that an allusion to Christ's own faithfulness has been overlooked for so long is that Paul's references to it occur in the context of numerous other references to the believing of Christians in general. Sometimes these references even seem to jostle within the same sentences, for example, Gal. 2.16: 'seeing that a person is not justified through works of law but through the fidelity of Jesus Christ, we too have believed in Christ Jesus so that we might be justified through the fidelity of Christ and not through works of law...' (my own translation). Paul also seems to use closely related prooftexts for each aspect of this. Gen. 15.6 speaks

For Romans see my *The Rhetoric of Righteousness in Romans 3.21-26* (Sheffield: JSOT Press, 1992), pp. 58-69, 204-18; 'The Meaning of ΠΙΣΤΙΣ and ΝΟΜΟΣ in Paul: A Linguistic and Structural Investigation', *JBL* 111 (1992), pp. 85-97, and 'Romans 1.17—A *Crux Interpretum* for the ΠΙΣΤΙΣ ΧΡΙΣΤΟΥ Debate', *JBL* 113 (1994), pp. 265-85. See also I.G. Wallis, *The Faith of Jesus Christ in Early Christian Traditions* (SNTSMS, 84; Cambridge: Cambridge University Press, 1995), esp. pp. 65-134. A typical more traditional response is J.D.G. Dunn, 'Once more, ΠΙΣΤΙΣ ΧΡΙΣΤΟΥ', in Lovering (ed.), *SBLSP* (1991), pp. 730-44.

25. See esp. Gal. 2.16, 20; 3.22, 26; Rom. 3.22, 25, 26; also Phil. 3.9 (2×?); and perhaps Eph. 3.12; 4.13.

of 'believing' and receiving righteousness (using the verb *pisteuō*); probably something to be read with primary reference to Christians, while Hab. 2.4 (given the correctness of a christological approach to *pistis*) speaks of the 'faithfulness' of 'the righteous one', that is, of the Messiah, Christ himself (using the noun *pistis*).[26] These texts both revolve around words drawn from the *pist-* and *dik-* word groups, and it is simply implausible to deny a deliberate connection, especially when Paul uses them, and phrases drawn from them, in close proximity.[27] But what is its precise nature?

2.   One possible reply is that Christ's faithfulness is exemplary. Like most contemporary martyrological literature, Christ's example of faithfulness to the point of death should inspire a similar spirit of self-sacrifice and devotion in its audience, in this case, the Christian community.[28]

---

26. See my 'Romans 1.17'; also R.B. Hays's '"The Righteous One" as Eschatological Deliverer: A Case Study in Paul's Apocalyptic Hermeneutics', in J. Marcus and M.L. Soards (ed.), *Apocalyptic and the New Testament: Essays in Honour of J. Louis Martyn* (JSNTSup, 24; Sheffield: JSOT Press, 1989), pp. 191-215.

27. The defender of the traditional reading is almost necessarily committed at this point to such a position, however. If it is granted that many of Paul's uses of the noun *pistis* refer to Christ, then the traditional reading of the verb, namely, that of Christian belief in the gospel, cannot really be imputed to Christ as well. Is Paul stating that Christ's belief in good news (about himself?) from God was central? This is redundant, if not slightly silly. Hence the two phrases must be interpreted separately—it must be argued that Paul is stating something rather different when he switches from the noun to the verb. But this is (to attempt) to separate what the traditional interpreter has invariably interpreted together (one of the position's strengths), and also to reduce the traditional claims largely to the much less numerous verb. In short, by this stage the battle has been largely lost. Hence the perhaps surprising fact that the traditional reading is not really considered from this point on in my argument.

Also significant is the impact that this observation has on the suggestions of commentators who *accept* the christological reading, but nevertheless interpret the critical phrases at some distance from the participial phrases that speak of Christian belief in general. Such suggestions also run afoul of the symmetry between the two propositions concerning 'faith'. For example, R. Hays interprets Christ's faithfulness as an expression of God's covenant faithfulness ('ΠΙΣΤΙΣ and Pauline Christology', *passim*). How does this attractive reading integrate with Christian belief, however? Is Paul speaking of a covenantal type of activity when he uses the verb *pisteuō* to denote an act by Christians in general? (Hays may well say 'yes' here).

28. See esp. the Maccabean cycle of literature (notably 2 Macc. 6 and 7; *3 Maccabees* and *4 Maccabees*); see also J.S. Pobee, *Persecution and Martyrdom in*

Hence, his faith is copied by ours. Such a suggestion can also draw on various exhortations in terms of example scattered through Paul's letters.[29] However, several considerations almost immediately undermine this approach.

First, the broader contexts of Paul's discussions involving *pist-* clusters are not exemplary, inspirational or exhortative. There are no appropriate verbs to this effect, nor are there accompanying statements making such applications. These discussions seem basically soteriological (hence verbs like 'to live', 'to be justified', and so on), where the *pist-* clusters oppose some sort of salvation premised on 'works of law'. Moreover, it is difficult to conceive of how an exemplary, martyrological soteriology would achieve Paul's aim here. A martyrological fidelity *to* the law was well known in the Judaism of Paul's time, but in what sense could such fidelity *displace* the law? Yet this is what Paul seems to be vigorously asserting.[30]

Secondly, advocates of the centrality of Christian belief to Paul's discussions usually understand this act as eminently feasible: it is a simple act within the grasp of every person—in fact, it is sometimes defined as a non-act.[31] This simplicity contrasts with the ostensible difficulty of achieving salvation by accumulating virtuous deeds. God has made a generous offer of salvation conditional on these easy terms, and we would be foolish (if not immoral) to refuse it. This belief is also usually defined cognitively, as a mental assent to the gospel about Christ (which

the Theology of Paul (JSNTSup, 6; Sheffield: JSOT Press, 1985), and D. Seeley, *The Noble Death: Graeco–Roman Martyrology and Paul's Concept of Salvation* (JSNTSup, 28; Sheffield: JSOT Press, 1990).

29. Notably 1 Cor. 4.16; 11.1; Phil. 3.17; 1 Thess. 1.6; 2.14; 2 Thess. 3.7, 9; and see also Eph. 5.1. The preponderance of the theme in the Thessalonian context is no doubt significant; on this see A.J. Malherbe, *Paul and the Thessalonians: The Philosophic Tradition of Pastoral Care* (Philadelphia: Fortress Press, 1987), esp. pp. 52-54.

30. Also, does Christ's own faithfulness have any effect in Paul's thinking beyond the merely exemplary? If not, would any other suitable example of faithfulness suffice at this point, for example, Moses, or Elijah, or Akiva? In this model, Christ's role seems strangely adumbrated for the strongly christocentric apostle.

31. See, for example, J.A.T. Ziesler (discussing Rom. 4.5): 'this makes it crystal clear that for Paul, faith is not anything one does, and is not equivalent to faithfulness. *It is almost a non-thing*, the simple willingness to receive...' (*Paul's Letter to the Romans* [London: SCM Press; Philadelphia: Trinity Press International, 1989], p. 125, emphasis added).

can be reduced to certain propositions); it is basically a positive response to preaching.

The martyrological nature of Christ's own faith, however, introduces some difficulties here. The Christian's faith, if it is to imitate Christ's, is no longer what most commentators have assumed it to be, namely, a positive, mental assent to certain ideas. It is both different from, and far more difficult than, this definition. Christ's *pistis* was a 'faithfulness unto death', hence, if Christians are to follow this example, so must their faith be (see esp. Rom. 4.17-22). Essentially, a martyrological reading of Christ's faith (which is really unavoidable), and an exemplary understanding of the relationship between Christ's and our faith, necessitates a symmetrical reading of our faith as the same. But it seems unlikely that Paul was asking this much of the average Christian (and, if he was, not many of us are now qualifying...).

Thirdly, while Paul will exhort Christians to imitate Christ on occasion, it is not a sustained theme in his writings, so the imitative construal can gather little wider support from Paul.[32] He seems to have a rather different understanding of Christ's function from the imitative, but this observation really leads us on to the third formal alternative, which I will discuss at greater length.

3.   At this point we still wish to understand the relationship between Christ's faith and that of the Christian, while we suspect strongly that it is not merely exemplary. Although *pist-* words are most heavily concentrated in the first four chapters of Romans, the question of the Christian's relation to Christ is analysed most carefully in the following four chapters, namely, chs. 5–8. Paul's discussion here may give us a formal model for relating Christ's faith to our own, even if the specific issue of 'faith' is not raised (although our analysis at this point must be regrettably superficial). So here I am endorsing the 'participatory' reading of Paul,[33] and then attempting to understand Paul's use of faith

32.   Malherbe states 'Paul usually calls his readers to imitation' (*Paul*, p. 52), but I am not sure that the foregoing eight references sustain this confidence (he himself supplies five; two from the disputed 2 Thessalonians; p. 52 n. 74).

33.   A disputed but nevertheless (I would argue) entirely accurate reading of the 'centre' of Paul's theology: see, for a cautious summary account, J.A.T. Ziesler, *Pauline Christianity* (Oxford and New York: Oxford University Press, rev. edn, 1990 [1983]), pp. 46-65; a stronger reading in C.F.D. Moule, 'The Corporate Christ', ch. 2 in *The Origin of Christology* (Cambridge: Cambridge University Press, 1977), pp. 47-96; the original, quite vibrant, interpretation by G.A. Deissmann, *St Paul: A Study in Social and Religious History* (trans. L.R.M. Strachan; London:

language in its light (rather than the other way around, as is usually done).[34]

In ch. 5 of Romans Paul speaks of the critical 'submission' or 'obedience' of Christ that counterbalances the fateful disobedience of Adam (see esp. 5.19). It is by means of that 'single act of righteousness' that life comes to everyone (*dikaiōma* in 5.18). Thus Christ functions, Paul suggests, as a universal figure, like Adam: what happens to him happens to all—we could hardly wish for a clearer exposition of his vicarious function. The subsequent three chapters of discussion tend to work within this basic perspective. Chapter 6 describes an immersion of the Christian within the death of Christ, and a rising through him to new life (especially in vv. 1-11). Key summarizing phrases for this may be found in vv. 11 and 23: we are alive to God '*in* Christ Jesus'. Chapter 7 drops back to a (controversial!) description of the previous stage of life 'in' the flesh and in relation to the law—a somewhat tortured recollection for Paul—but also conceived of essentially vicariously (especially if Adam is being alluded to).[35] Then ch. 8 speaks once again of the risen life through the Spirit *within which* the Christian experiences Jesus's intimacy with his *Abba*-God.[36]

This whole, powerful section of argument is characterized by participation in Christ. It is this identification with—and indeed 'immersion' in—Christ that generates the changed existence of the Christian (significantly, *pist-* words only occur twice in this argument: in the first

Hodder & Stoughton, 2nd edn, 1910); and its English popularization in J. Stewart, *A Man in Christ: The Vital Elements of St Paul's Religion* (London: Hodder & Stoughton, 1935). Basically the same notion is discussed extensively by Morna Hooker under the rubric 'interchange': see her *'PISTIS CHRISTOU'*, *NTS* 35 (1989), pp. 321-42; *idem*, 'Interchange in Christ', *JTS* 22 (1971), pp. 349-61; *idem*, 'Interchange and Atonement', *BJRL* 60 (1978), pp. 462-81; *idem*, *Pauline Pieces* (London: Epworth Press, 1979); and *idem*, 'Interchange and Suffering', in W. Horbury and B. McNeill (ed.), *Suffering and Martyrdom in the New Testament* (Cambridge: Cambridge University Press, 1981), pp. 70-83.

34. This is probably because of the order of the argument in Romans. However, Paul's order here is not informed by systematic concerns.

35. A cogent presentation of this perspective on ch. 7 is found in R.N. Longenecker, *Paul, Apostle of Liberty* (repr.; Grand Rapids: Baker, 1976 [1964]), pp. 86-97, 109-16.

36. The importance of the Spirit here has recently been underscored by G.D. Fee, in *God's Empowering Presence: The Holy Spirit in the Letters of Paul* (Peabody, MA: Hendrickson, 1994), pp. 515-91.

verse of the section's somewhat transitional preface, and in 6.8).[37] If I understand it correctly, this central argumentative discussion in Romans suggests, first, that Jesus for Paul functions *vicariously*, that is, on our behalf; and, secondly, that *by participating in him* through the Spirit his life and righteousness become ours.[38] Critically—and wondrously—the entire process is a gift. The entry of Jesus into our enslaved condition is unsolicited and born of the mercy of God,[39] and our new being, available in him, is given to us through the Spirit. 'Grace' is therefore an entirely appropriate description for the gospel as Paul explicates it in these chapters, since an unconditional element quite clearly underpins any sense of exchange or transfer as it is described here. But what has this to do with faith/*pistis*?

A priori one would expect *pistis* to function like any other benefit available in Christ. Just as life, righteousness and obedience are given to us in him, so we would expect faithfulness to be given to us in and through him. That is, the answer to our over-riding question concerning the relationship between Christ's faith and our own is essentially partici-patory: Christ is the primary 'possessor' of faithfulness, but by entering into him and assuming his character we too can receive this quality of fidelity (and here the stronger reading of these words as 'faithfulness unto death' can be accommodated). Viewed from Christ's perspective, this is a vicarious function in that his faith becomes ours. Viewed from the Christian's perspective, faith is a gift, so the system is unconditional, while the gift is received through participation in Christ himself.

If the argument in Romans 5–8 suggests this model of relationship in formal terms, are there any textual clues that confirm this inference specifically for the *pist-* word group? Here three further observations may be significant.

1. In 1.5 Paul links faith and obedience tightly together: 'through whom we received grace and apostleship *with the goal of the*

37. Furthermore, in 5.1 the reference seems to function retrospectively rather than prospectively, recalling the argument of ch. 4.

38. Peerless accounts of the vicarious function of Christ, with particular reference to Calvin's theology, are J.B. Torrance, 'The Vicarious Humanity and Priesthood of Christ in the Theology of John Calvin', in W.H. Neuser (ed.), *Calvinus Ecclesiae Doctor* (Kampen: Kok, Uitgeversmaatschappij, n.d.), pp. 69-84; *idem*, 'The Vicarious Humanity of Christ', in T.F. Torrance (ed.), *The Incarnation* (Edinburgh: Handsel, 1981), pp. 127-47; see also Yule, 'Calvin's View' (n. 4).

39. See esp. 5.5, 6-8; 8.3, 28-39.

obedience of faithfulness in all the Gentiles on behalf of his name...' This is almost certainly an epexegetical genitive, that is, the one substantive reiterating and amplifying the meaning of the other, to which it is attached in a genitive construction.[40] The equation is then repeated in 16.26.[41] This observation must now be linked to ch. 5 where, as has already been noted, it is Christ's *obedience* that is central to the entire cosmic drama of salvation (the same word as in 1.5: *hupakoē*). At this point and following, our obedience is obtained *in* Christ, and nowhere else. If faith, however, is basically coterminous with obedience for Paul in Romans, as 1.5 suggests, then *by direct implication* our faith too is obtained in the faithfulness of Christ, just as ch. 5 suggests. The vicarious achievement and offer of obedience to us in Christ, recounted in 5.15-21, really amounts to exactly the same thing as an offer of faithfulness, if we take Paul's earlier (and later) semantic equation seriously.

2.   Faith is explicated at certain other points in Romans in terms of *the death* of Christ. The two motifs are tightly linked in 3.25, are probably implicitly paralleled in 4.24-25, and correspond to each other precisely in 5.1 and 9. Certainly the idea of death on the cross encompasses the notion of obedience (so it is also probably not far from the discussion of 5.19). But for Paul we die as we participate in the death of Christ, and he makes just this point at length in 6.1-11. Our death is in the vicarious death of Christ—'he dies for us'.[42] Hence, if faith is coterminous with the idea of 'the death of Christ', then a wealth of discussion in Romans (and elsewhere in Paul) also confirms that we receive this vicariously in Christ. To die through Christ also amounts to the same thing as receiving faithfulness through him—a 'faithfulness [if need be] *unto death*'.

3.   In 12.3 Paul states explicitly that 'each one of you...should

---

40.   See the excellent discussion in C.E.B. Cranfield, *A Critical and Exegetical Commentary on the Epistle to the Romans* (2 vols.; Edinburgh: T. & T. Clark, 1975, 1979), I, pp. 66-67.

41.   16.26 is often dismissed with vv. 25 and 27 as a non-Pauline gloss, produced in some relation to Marcion, but the evidence for this is not overly weighty. For a countervailing interpretation see P. Stuhlmacher, *Der Brief an die Römer* (NTD; Göttingen and Zürich: Vandenhoeck & Ruprecht, 1989), pp. 225-27.

42.   See esp. Gal. 2.19-20.

think of themselves considerately [or, soberly], *as God has given to each the measure of pistis*.[43]

Thus, while Paul seldom explicitly speaks (in Romans[44]) of the gift of faithfulness to us in Christ, I would argue that the idea is still a necessary inference from his discussion, while certain small textual hints more directly reinforce that. The reason that such an equation is not made clear by Paul probably lies in the function of *pistis* within his discussion as an intertextual allusion to Hab. 2.4, and less directly to Gen. 15.6. In Romans 1–4 and Galatians 2–3 Paul seems concerned to ground his understanding of salvation through Christ and the cross in the Old Testament, and especially in the story of Abraham (Gen. 12–22). Hence, it may not actually be the word he would have chosen had he been completely free to do so—in less constrained contexts, as we have just seen, Paul chooses 'obedience' and 'submission', or 'death'. These equations would probably have been quite clear to the early Christians, however, accustomed to reading Hab. 2.4, like many of their other Old Testament texts, messianically, with reference to Christ, and also used to equating (in good Jewish fashion) the ideas of obedience, faithfulness and submission. I would argue that it is only the intrusion of a neo-Protestant agenda, with its emphasis on the absolute centrality of faith for Paul, allied with its understanding of this in terms of human decision, that obscures this equation for contemporary readers.

Enough has probably been said by this point to suggest the basis for my alternative reading of the saying 'the priesthood of all believers'. I suggest that the motif 'believers' should be understood here, not contractually and anthropocentrically as is usually the case, but vicariously and christocentrically. 'Believing' is really something we obtain as a gift from God, by participating in the prior faithfulness of Christ. Such a reading speaks of the very heart of the gospel of grace—the gift of a new being to us in the vicarious work of Christ, brought to us individually through the Spirit, in accordance with the loving purposes of

43. The ardent advocate of the christological perspective may well detect a reference to Christ here (which may make more sense in context). This would not alter the basic point that God gives through Christ, although the statement would not then witness directly to the gift of faith to the Christian via Christ (the gifts are 'grace' and, hopefully, 'sober thinking', from the verb *sōphronein*)—there is little discussion of this view in the commentaries.

44. Ephesians makes this quite explicit but Paul's authorship is questioned here: see Eph. 2.8-10; 3.12, 16-19; 4.4-6, 13 (esp. the first and last citations).

God the Father. With this interpretive position in place, however, we can derive still more insight from Paul as we address quickly the two remaining motifs in Luther's slogan, namely, priesthood and universality.

4. *A New Perspective on the Saying*

Paul does not make much use of the idea of priesthood *per se*— although he does use it to describe himself in Rom. 15.16.[45] But, as we have seen, he does use cultic and temple imagery from time to time. The metaphors are supplied less frequently and far more aphoristically than the theme of *pistis*, hence it is even more incumbent on the later interpreter to supply the underlying rationale for these characterizations. Once again, Paul's central discussion of Christ's vicarious function in Romans 5–8 is attractive. Moreover, the close relationship between the death of Christ, already linked with *pistis*, and the scattered use of cultic metaphors to describe this in Romans, reinforces this. Hence, I would suggest reading the motif of 'priesthood' also in a vicarious fashion: Christ fulfils the Jewish cultus so through and in him all the associations of that phenomenon may legitimately be transferred to the new Christian community.

Thus, if we understand them in what I take to be a Pauline fashion, the two motifs of 'priesthood' and 'believing' in Luther's dictum function symmetrically, as motifs pointing in parallel towards the vicarious function of Christ. Christ is the one true priest *and* the one true faithful one, and both these sets of benefits are made available to Christians through and in him. This last observation about availability leads us in turn to the third and final component in our saying, namely, the notion of universality implicit in the word 'all'.

It is important to emphasize that these vicarious benefits are available to 'all'. One ostensible reading of Calvin has led in the past to repugnant distortions of the gospel of grace in just this sense, with God's salvific purposes being limited to the elect.[46] This limiting of the value of the atonement is deeply destructive to Christian well-being, and to our

45. On this critical but often overlooked text see D.W.B. Robinson, 'The Priesthood of Paul in the Gospel of Hope', in R.J. Banks (ed.), *Reconciliation and Hope* (Exeter: Paternoster Press, 1974), pp. 231-45; and L.A. Jervis, *The Purpose of Romans* (JSNTSup, 55; Sheffield: JSOT Press, 1991).

46. See J.B. Torrance, 'Covenant and Contract', pp. 63, 67-69; and *idem*, 'The Contribution of McLeod Campbell', *passim*.

understanding of the character of God. It is also fundamentally false, as the God who offers up the only Son becomes inexplicably narrow and wrathful in applying the benefits.

Paul once again correctly emphasizes the real dimensions of the gospel when he repeatedly speaks of 'all' those who receive it in Romans. In fact, such is his enthusiasm for this often innocuous word that its occurrence in his argument seems to present him with an almost irresistible temptation to digress—at times rather to the detriment of his style![47] Of course, it is debatable whether he has 'all' the Jews or 'all' the Gentiles in mind at any given occurrence, but his basic point is obvious and unquestionable: Christ's vicarious function is on behalf of everyone. Luther's saying therefore also preserves this crucial dimension of the Pauline gospel: the vicarious faithfulness and priesthood of Christ are intended for all, without exception.[48]

To draw our discussion of 'the priesthood of all believers' to a close: I have argued that the traditional understanding of the saying, whether in its Reformational or its original scriptural context, tends towards irrelevance—although it was doubtless dynamic enough within these original settings. The saying functions essentially negatively, as a critique, rather than as a positive statement of some deep Christian truth, hence its limitations when it is removed from a suitably desperate setting. However, I have also suggested that the saying can be reinterpreted in a more Pauline fashion. In particular, the slogan's use of the famous Pauline principle of faith—as long as we understand it aright—leads us directly to the vicarious and christocentric reality that stands at the heart of the gospel. In view of these arguments, I would paraphrase Luther's slogan as follows:

> All are priests and faithful believers
> in the one true priest and faithful one.

Reinterpreted in this fashion, the saying speaks quintessentially of the God of grace acting through the gospel of Christ by means of the Spirit. As such, it is indeed an enduring statement of Christian truth—and of Christian ministry, since it emphasizes that at the heart of Christian life

47. See esp. 3.22-24 and 10.11-13 (-16?).

48. So Manson (briefly and rather unsystematically), *Ministry and Priesthood*, pp. 64 and 70; and (much more coherently) Küng, 'Priesthood', esp. pp. 363, 66-67, 70, 72-73 (and, according to Althaus and Yule, Luther and Calvin: see n. 4 above).

and leadership is the prior, vicarious life and leadership of Christ, in which 'we live and move and have our being'. It follows that Christ's life *and leadership* must be available to and through all who so live, participating in the one true priest and believer. Furthermore, to exclude any from these possibilities would be to misunderstand—and to misrepresent radically and destructively—the very heart of the gospel of grace, as it is witnessed to by Paul.

THE GREATEST OF THESE IS LOVE
(1 CORINTHIANS 14.34-35)[*]

L. Ann Jervis

For two reasons the words of 1 Cor. 14.34-35 impress many modern readers as offensive: they deny freedom of speech and they appear to do so on the basis of gender. Several recent interpreters have sought to lessen this passage's offense by interpreting it as an interpolation by a post-Pauline editor.[1]

This paper argues that, attractive as the interpolation theory may be, it remains too problematic to be historically probable. Instead these words should be regarded as Paul's. Paul wrote them next to his words about prophecy (1 Cor. 14.29-40)[2] because the behaviour he found reprehensible took place during the exercise of that charism. The passage is less restrictive than has been thought previously: it limits 'the women'[3] from

---

*   This article first appeared as '1 Corinthians 14.34-35: A Reconsideration of Paul's Limitation of the Free Speech of Some Corinthian Women', *JSNT* 58 (1995), pp. 51-74.

1.   See J. Bassler, '1 Corinthians', in C.A. Newsom and S.H. Ringe (eds.), *The Women's Bible Commentary* (London: SPCK, 1992), pp. 327-28; also G.D. Fee, *The First Epistle to the Corinthians* (repr.; Grand Rapids: Eerdmans, 1991 [1987]), who argues for this position, providing also a concise bibliography, p. 699 n. 4. Fee's attempt to lessen the passage's offense by stating that if the text is not authentic 'it is certainly not binding for Christians' (p. 708) appears to be based on the assumption that authorial authenticity and biblical authority are synonymous.

2.   There is only one reference to glossolalia in this section, i.e., v. 39 ('spiritual' in v. 37 is not limited to speakers of tongues, and may in fact refer to those who discern prophecies; see 1 Cor. 2.13).

3.   I agree with A. Wire (*The Corinthian Women Prophets: A Reconstruction through Paul's Rhetoric* [Minneapolis: Fortress Press, 1990], p. 156) who considers that this injunction is to all women, not simply wives. The reference to 'their men' at

asking questions of the prophets which disrupt prophetic utterance, therefore it does not censure other types of speech such as prophecy, the interpretation of prophecy, tongues, teaching and so on. A brief comparison of the passage with some of Philo's words regarding the function of silence and speech in the spiritual life serves to nuance our understanding of Paul's words. It will be argued that a distinction should be made between Paul's prescription and his diagnosis. While his remedy for the situation was undeniably patriarchal, Paul diagnosed the problem as the type of speaking the women engaged in rather than that women were the speakers. In all probability Paul's chief concern was the peaceful exercise of prophecy rather than the subordination of women. 1 Corinthians 12–14 demonstrates that Paul's overall aim was to persuade the Corinthians that their spirit-filled worship should manifest the greatest spiritual gift of all, love. His censuring of 'the women's' speaking in 14.34-35 should be interpreted in the context of that aim. Before presenting this reading of the passage, however, it is important first to outline why I find the interpolation theory unsatisfactory.

1. *Problems with the Interpolation Theory*

Many consider that 1 Cor. 14.34-35 is best understood as the work of a post-Pauline editor. In this view the content of the passage reflects the church's developing 'subjectionist' tendencies.[4] The interpolation theory marshalls support from the fact that the verses appear at two locations in the manuscript tradition.

The passage's occurrence at two locations in the textual tradition indeed calls for comment. The textual displacement of vv. 34-35 (in some manuscripts the verses appear after v. 40) strongly suggests that the words were originally a gloss. In fact, the evidence for two different textual traditions, both equally early,[5] suggests that the words appeared initially in the margin of the letter (rather than being originally interpolated into the text) and were inserted at two different places during

---

home (v. 35b) refers to any number of household relationships between women and men. See also Fee, *Corinthians*, p. 706 n. 29.

4. So W. Munro, *Authority in Paul and Peter: The Identification of a Pastoral Stratum in the Pauline Corpus and 1 Peter* (Cambridge: Cambridge University Press, 1983), p. 15.

5. See G.D. Fee, *God's Empowering Presence: The Holy Spirit in the Letters of Paul* (Peabody, MA: Hendrickson, 1994), p. 274.

subsequent scribal copying.[6] Such a gloss is not best explained, however, as the product of an editor with a viewpoint different from Paul's for (1) there is no precedent in the Pauline letters that I know of for a gloss intended to contradict directly Paul's own view;[7] (2) there is precedent for Paul adding words late in the process of composing a letter and for this resulting in a variety of textual traditions;[8] and (3) the passage appears in every extant manuscript, which should caution us against too readily adopting an interpolation hypothesis. The best interpretation of the textual evidence is that of Antoinette Clark Wire who concludes that the words were originally a gloss either by Paul, an amanuensis or the first person to copy the letter.[9]

The most popular presentation of the interpolation theory proposes that the words were written by a person who shared the views on women evinced by the Pastoral epistles. An editor with sentiments similar to those expressed in 1 and 2 Timothy and Titus added what would become 1 Cor. 14.34-35 so as to emphasize the unacceptability of

6. So Fee, *God's Empowering Presence*, p. 275.

7. As we shall see, the argument that this is a post-Pauline gloss involves proposing that the gloss's writer wanted to counteract Pauline egalitarianism; see for example W. Munro, 'Women, Text and the Canon: The Strange Case of I Corinthians 14.33-35', *BTB* 18 (1988), pp. 26-31.

8. See particularly the manuscript discrepancies over the second grace benediction of Rom. 16 (v. 24). As H. Gamble has demonstrated, this is best explained by supposing that initially Paul closed his letter at v. 20, then he added the greetings at vv. 21-23 as an afterthought and so proceeded to append another grace benediction (v. 24) (*The Textual History of the Letter to the Romans* [Grand Rapids: Eerdmans, 1977], p. 94).

9. *The Corinthian Women Prophets*, p. 149; see E. Schüssler Fiorenza, *In Memory of Her: A Feminist Theological Reconstruction of Christian Origins* (New York: Crossroad, 1990), and E.E. Ellis, who writes, 'no MS lacks the verses and, in the absence of some such evidence, the modern commentator has no sufficient reason to regard them as a post-Pauline gloss' ('The Silenced Wives of Corinth [I Cor. 14.34-35]', in E.J. Epp and G.D. Fee [eds.], *New Testament Textual Criticism: Its Significance for Exegesis. Essays in Honour of Bruce M. Metzger* [Oxford: Clarendon Press, 1981], pp. 213-20, p. 220).

The proposition that these verses are 'anti-Montanist' (D.R. MacDonald, *The Legend and the Apostle: The Battle for Paul in Story and Canon* [Philadelphia: Westminster Press, 1983], p. 88) also founders on the textual issue. It is almost certain that if the verses originated as late as the end of the second or early third century (the time of the Montanists) there would be some manuscripts without them in the textual tradition.

women speaking in public.[10] It is not adequately recognized, however, that there are several tensions between pertinent aspects of those letters and our passage. For instance, 1 Cor. 14.34-35 prohibits women from learning in public (if the women want to learn something they are to learn at home), whereas 1 Tim. 2.11 commands women to learn (*manthanō* is in the imperative) with the clear implication that this is to take place in the assembly.

Moreover, the 'interpolation-by-a-Pastoral-type-editor' theory must make sense of the supposed editor's choice of location for his gloss. The most straightforward explanation of the editor's rationale for positioning these words is a compulsion to qualify Paul's directions concerning prophecy to conform to his own views and communicate with his contemporaries. That is, the supposed editor would have added these words either to persuade or to placate readers in his own milieu. As J.A. Sanders says, textual variants are evidence of how 'the biblical authors and thinkers themselves contemporized and adapted and reshaped the traditions they received'.[11] What is not typically recognized about this hypothesis is its corollary—that the editor's locating of the gloss means that his concern was not a general one about the role of women, but rather a very specific one about women speaking in relation to the exercise of prophecy. That is, unless we posit a totally arbitrary editor (and we would not then be able to argue for his intentionality in any respect) we must presume that he purposely positioned his gloss in connection with Paul's words on prophecy. This corollary is difficult to sustain in light of the ecclesiastical milieu reflected in the Pastoral letters.[12]

---

10. See n. 1 above. Also J.P. Sampley, *Walking between the Times: Paul's Moral Reasoning* (Minneapolis: Fortress Press, 1991), p. 79; and S. Heine, *Women and Early Christianity: A Reappraisal* (trans. J. Bowden; Minneapolis: Augsburg Press, 1987), pp. 135-37. See also MacDonald, *The Legend and the Apostle*, pp. 86-89; V.P. Furnish, *The Moral Teaching of Paul: Selected Issues* (Nashville: Abingdon Press, 1986), pp. 90-92; G. Dautzenberg, *Urchristliche Prophetie, ihre Erforschung, ihre Voraussetzungen im Judentum und ihre Strucktur im ersten Korintherbrief* (Stuttgart: Kohlhammer, 1975), pp. 257-74, 290-300; and R.W. Jewett, 'The Redaction of 1 Corinthians and the Trajectory of the Pauline School', *JAAR* 44 (1978), Supp. B, pp. 389-444.

11. 'Text and Canon: Concepts and Method', *JBL* 98 (1979), pp. 5-29, 28-29.

12. That is, unless we adopt what in my view is a facile solution—an editor who was completely unattached to a milieu similar to that reflected in the Pastorals but who nonetheless felt compelled to add words so that Paul's letter might agree with 1 Tim. 2.11-15—we need to account for information from 1 Timothy concerning the

The Pastoral letters give little evidence that the churches to which they were written experienced prophecy in a manner comparable to the Corinthian church. When prophecy is mentioned in the Pastorals its function is that of furthering and guarding the faith (1 Tim. 1.18-19). Reference to prophetic utterance (1 Tim. 4.14) bears greater similarity to Old Testament prophets designating a religious leader on behalf of God (e.g. 1 Kgs 19.16) than to the communal experience of the Spirit reflected in the Pauline literature. There is nothing in the Pastoral literature comparable to Paul's words about earnestly desiring 'the spiritual gifts, especially that you may prophesy' (1 Cor. 14.1). It is noteworthy that the gift of tongues, which is such a prominent topic in verses proximate to our passage, is not even mentioned in the Pastoral letters. Furthermore, in the Pastorals the Spirit is referred to as the agent of God (1 Tim. 3.16), who participates in the salvation of humanity (Tit. 3.5-7). The Spirit instructs and warns (1 Tim. 4.1) and is the agent who indwells the believer to whom it gave the truth of the gospel (2 Tim. 1.14). The spiritual gifts are the indwelling of power and love and self-control (2 Tim. 1.67). The Pastorals do not refer to believers as spiritual *pneumatikoi*; this word does not even occur in the Pastorals. Whatever else the word 'spiritual' signifies (such as recognition of the truth of the gospel—1 Cor. 2.13; Gal. 6.1), it certainly includes reference to the ecstatic experience of spiritual gifts, for the letters in which this word describes believers are also letters to communities in which the Spirit is an experiential, ecstatic reality (1 Corinthians and Galatians [3.3-5]). The lack of the word *pneumatikos* in the Pastoral letters is, then, a further indication that the churches to which these letters are addressed have an experience and understanding of spiritual gifts that is distinct from that of Paul and the Corinthians. Overall, the impression gained from the Pastoral epistles is of much less 'enthusiastic' assemblies than those of Paul. And consequently it is difficult to understand why an editor influenced by an ecclesiastical environment such as that reflected in the Pastorals would add his words to Paul's letter where he did.

There remains this conundrum: the editor presumably added his words to Paul's discussion of prophecy because he was concerned about women speaking in such circumstances, but why then did he leave untouched Paul's words in 1 Cor. 11.2-16?[13]

general ecclesiastical environment (not necessarily the actual venue) out of which the editor came and how this relates to his intentions in adding his gloss.

13. The best possible resolution of such a contradiction is a theory about the

Moreover, there are problems with the interpolation theory's typical presentation of the passage's warrants. The theory argues that the passage uses the warrants of 'law', 'shame' and 'what is permitted'/ 'custom' in an 'unPauline' way and that the reference to 'all the churches' indicates a general rule which fits uncomfortably in Paul's very particular letter.

The warrant of *law* (v. 34) is seen as unusual, for no text is specified.[14] 'Law' in this passage appears to be used in an absolute sense uncharacteristic of Paul.[15] The exceptional nature of this warrant is further emphasized if the conventional attribution of the law as Gen. 3.16 is accepted.[16] With Gen. 3.16 as the subtext the passage comes to mean that, since according to the creation order women belong on a lower rung of the divinely created ladder, they cannot speak publicly. Such an attitude is demonstrably foreign to Paul who disdains distinctions and hierarchies 'in Christ' and who affirms the earliest Christian understanding that divisions either of ethnicity, social status or gender do not belong in Christian community (Gal. 3.28; also 1 Cor. 12.13). For Paul believers are reflections of and partakers in the new creation—a new creation in which God's original intention for harmony and peace has been inaugurated in this time (Rom. 5.17-21; 2 Cor. 5.17). Furthermore, Paul considers that the framework of life for believers no longer includes the curses of Genesis 3.[17]

composite nature of 1 Corinthians. Yet, as I have argued elsewhere, the various partition theories for 1 Corinthians are unsatisfactory. The peculiarities of the form of 1 Corinthians are, in my view, most readily explained by regarding it as a single letter written to correspond with several different concerned groups within Corinth (L.A. Jervis, *The Purpose of Romans: A Comparative Letter Structure Investigation* [JSNTSup, 55; Sheffield: JSOT Press, 1991], pp. 57-59).

14. See G. Dautzenberg, 'Auf Stellung der Frauen in den paulinischen Gemeinden', in *Die Frau im Urchristentum* (Freiburg: Herder, 1983), pp. 182-224, p. 199; and MacDonald, *The Legend and the Apostle*, p. 87. Also R.W. Allison, 'Let Women Be Silent in the Churches (I Cor. 14.33b-36): What Did Paul Really Say, and What Did it Mean?', *JSNT* 32 (1988), pp. 26-59, p. 29; and Fee, *Corinthians*, p. 707.

15. So Fee, *Corinthians*, p. 707.

16. *UBSGNT* 3rd edn refers the reader to Gen. 3.16.

17. As Robin Scroggs writes: Paul envisages that 'the new creation, while it reveals a *con*junction with the pre-Fall creation, shows a complete *dis*junction from the old world. It is a community of people freed from the curse of history begun in Gen. 3' ('Paul and the Eschatological Woman', *JAAR* 40 [1972], pp. 283-303, p. 287). See L. Scanzoni and N. Hardesty, *All We're Meant To Be: A Biblical*

The appeal to *shame* (v. 35) is also regarded as awkward and peculiar in the context of Paul's writing. For shame functions as a means of social control, conveying and depending on cultural values, whereas supposedly Paul does not appeal to such values. Gordon Fee states that the appeal to shame as a 'general cultural matter' is atypical of Paul.[18] Robert Allison argues that the appeal to shame in 1 Cor. 14.35 is an absolute appeal which would have been inappropriate for a specific circumstance.[19]

The interpolation theory considers that the word *epitrepetai* (v. 34) sounds an uncharacteristically authoritative tone. Victor P. Furnish, among others, contends that this is 'not Paul's way of phrasing his ethical teaching' and is close to the Pastoral style.[20] Finally, the reference to *all the churches* (although not part of the supposed interpolation) nevertheless functions in most manuscripts in conjunction with it, indicating to some that this was a convenient spot for an editor to import a general rule into Paul's letter to Corinth.

In fact, however, Paul regularly uses the aforementioned warrants in support of his directives, especially in 1 Corinthians.[21] Moreover, the prevalence of comparable warrants in Hellenistic rhetoric[22] should make us cautious about using them as evidence for establishing authorship.

It further needs to be noted that there are several weaknesses in the

---

Approach to Women's Liberation (Waco, TX: Word Books, 1974), pp. 23-27; see also the helpful article by P. Trible, 'Eve and Adam: Genesis 2–3 Reread', *ANQ* 13 (1973), pp. 251-58; and J. Beker who writes: for Paul 'the death of Christ functions as the negation of the old world's values and as the transference of believers into a resurrection mode of existence' (*The Triumph of God: The Essence of Paul's Thought* [trans. L.T. Stuckenbruck; Minneapolis: Fortress Press, 1990], p. 52).

18. *God's Empowering Presence*, p. 279.

19. 'Let the Women Be Silent in the Churches', p. 38.

20. *The Moral Teaching of Paul*, p. 92.

21. J.C. Hurd points out that Paul typically appeals, especially in 1 Cor. 7–16, to five warrants for his directives: Jesus, Scripture, common sense, custom and his own authority (*The Origin of I Corinthians* [Macon, GA: Mercer University Press, 1983], p. 74). See P.J. Tomson, *Paul and the Jewish Law: Halakha in the Letters of the Apostle to the Gentiles* (Assen: Van Gorcum; Minneapolis: Fortress Press, 1990), pp. 81-86. The appeals of 1 Cor. 14.34-35 can be seen to correspond to two of these typically Pauline appeals, i.e. law = Scripture; shame = custom; what is permitted = custom; and all the churches = custom.

22. B. Mack points out that Hellenistic persuasion relied on appeals to traditional views and values, such as what is right, lawful, advantageous and honorable (*Rhetoric and the New Testament* [Minneapolis: Fortress Press, 1990], p. 37).

interpolation theory's presentation of the individual warrants in 1 Cor. 14.34-35. With regard to the *law*, while it is true that no law is specified in v. 34, on its own this is not enough to indicate that a reference to law works differently here than elsewhere in Paul. In 1 Cor. 7.19 Paul appeals to 'the commandments of God' in a similarly abstract way and for the purpose of persuasion. Furthermore, it is far from self-evident that the reference to law in v. 34 is at odds with Paul's other appeals to law, that is, that the appeal to law in this passage indicates that the author had a view of the role of law in Christian ethics different from Paul's. P.J. Tomson has demonstrated that an appeal to law for the purpose of directing behaviour is typical of Paul, who claimed the authority of law without at the same time being obligated to it.[23] And S. Westerholm notes that while some instances, such as 1 Cor. 9.8-10 (and 1 Cor. 14.34), may appear to prescribe behaviour on the basis of a precept from the law, in fact not even in these cases 'is Torah treated as the direct source of Christian duty'.[24] We may also observe that at other points Paul refers, as in 1 Cor. 14.34, to the law 'saying' (*legō*) something (e.g. 1 Cor. 9.8; Rom. 3.19; 7.7). Moreover, the Pastoral letters do not provide this directive with a more comfortable home, for they do not contain a single occurrence of a persuasive appeal to law for the purpose of directing behaviour.

As mentioned above, the law in v. 34 is often identified with Gen. 3.16—an identification that serves to strengthen the case of those holding the interpolation theory. Here it is necessary to state the obvious: 1 Cor. 14.34 does not give a specific reference for the 'law', and any candidates for the reference will make sense only in the context of a particular reading of the passage. As women's speaking or silence does not figure in Gen. 3.16, this 'law' is a sensible choice only with an *a priori* understanding that the agenda of 1 Cor. 14.34-35 concerns the promotion of gender hierarchy. The circular nature of the argument is clear.

The appeal to *shame* in 1 Cor. 14.35 is not unusual. Paul appeals to shame for specific reasons in 1 Cor. 11.6.[25] It is further important to

---

23. *Paul and the Jewish Law*, p. 268.

24. *Israel's Law and the Church's Faith: Paul and his Recent Interpreters* (Grand Rapids: Eerdmans, 1988), p. 201.

25. *Contra* Allison, 'Let the Women Be Silent in the Churches', p. 38. It is difficult to see the distinction Fee makes between the use of 'shame' in the two passages 1 Cor. 11.6 and 1 Cor. 14.35, only the latter of which he describes as using

notice that *aischron* does not fit more readily in the Pastoral letters than in those of Paul. In fact, it only occurs once in the Pastorals (Tit. 1.11) and there it is not used as a warrant.

The appeal to *what is permitted* is no less fitting in Paul than in the context of the Pastorals, where the only example of *epitrepō* is the first person singular at 1 Tim. 2.12. There this verb should be read as expressing a personal opinion advising a temporary restriction.[26] In 1 Cor. 14.34, on the other hand, *epitrepō* is in the third person singular and communicates not personal opinion but common custom.[27]

The reference to *all the churches* cannot usefully be adduced as evidence of interpolation. First, it was not originally part of the gloss, as the textual evidence shows.[28] Secondly, the fact that Paul typically appeals to the custom of Christian churches[29] should give us pause before we read this as the importation of a general (and therefore foreign) rule into Paul's situation-specific letter. In 1 Corinthians Paul regularly seeks to persuade by appealing to the Corinthians' concern to conform to the general practice of the churches.[30]

Enough difficulties persist with the interpolation theory to invite a reconsideration of 1 Cor. 14.34-35 as Paul's own words. The rest of this paper is based on the assumption that 1 Cor. 14.34-35 is authentic and

shame as a 'general cultural matter' (*God's Empowering Presence*, p. 279). Surely in 1 Cor. 11.6 Paul is also appealing to a cultural connection between women and shame in order to persuade his readers. See n. 64 below.

26. So G.N. Redekop, 'Let the Women Learn: 1 Timothy 2.8-15 Reconsidered', *SR* 19 (1990), pp. 235-45, p. 242.

27. It is worth considering that the author of 1 Timothy might have used the word *epitrepō* for his directive because of his familiarity with 1 Cor. 14.34-35.

28. Only vv. 34-35 are displaced in the manuscript tradition. It is also important to note that the text flows smoothly without vv. 34-35. Verse 33b refers, as Calvin noticed, 'not merely to the first part of this verse, but to all he has outlined above' (*The First Epistle of the Apostle Paul to the Corinthians* [trans. J.W. Fraser; Grand Rapids: Eerdmans, 1980 (1960)], p. 305). Verse 36 would have followed v. 33 as a challenge (similar to other challenges in 1 Cor. 5–16, for example, 1 Cor. 5.2, 12; 6.2-3, 15; 9.4; 12.29-30) in which Paul emphasizes the correctness of his advice, highlights the appropriateness of his readers' present behaviour and acknowledges that he is aware his readers feel justified in their current actions and beliefs.

29. B.J. Malina points out that the custom of Christian churches is a typically Pauline standard (*The New Testament World: Insights from Cultural Anthropology* [Louisville: John Knox, 1981], p. 115).

30. Fee points out that in 1 Corinthians Paul regularly appeals to the standards of his other churches (1 Cor. 4.17; 7.17; 11.16) (*Corinthians*, p. 698).

will proceed to offer an alternative reading of the passage.[31]

2. A Re-Examination of 1 Corinthians 14.34-35 as Paul's Words

'The Women's' Speaking

How do we understand the speaking that Paul censures in the present passage? One thing can quite firmly be advanced: when 'the women' spoke they were asking questions and seeking to learn.[32] For the verses state that while it is not permitted for 'the women' to speak in church, if they want to learn anything they should ask questions of their men at home (v. 35). The context argues against understanding the speaking as glossolalia,[33] or teaching,[34] for whether the passage was originally written in the margin next to v. 33 or v. 40 it occurs in the context of a discussion of prophecy. This fact has led several interpreters to conclude that the behaviour Paul is censuring is that of the discerning of prophecy.[35]

---

31. The proposition that these verses (and perhaps also v. 36) are Paul's quotation of his opponents' opinion (see for instance N.M. Flanagan and E.H. Snyder, 'Did Paul Put Down Women in 1 Cor. 14.34-36?', *BTB* 11 [1981], pp. 10-12; and P.F. Ellis, *Seven Pauline Letters* [Collegeville, MN: Liturgical Press, 1982], pp. 102-103) founders when it is noticed that, in passages where Paul quotes his opponents' slogan, both the slogan and the retort relate to issues in the surrounding verses (see for instance 1 Cor. 6.12-13; 7.1). The verses surrounding our passage, on the other hand, are not about gender-specific actions in worship. Another difficulty with this proposition is the lack of supporting evidence that the Corinthians held the view of the supposed slogan. In fact, the opposite evidence presents itself—at the Corinthian worship men and women prophesy together (1 Cor. 11.2-16) (see Fee, *Corinthians*, p. 705). Fee points out further that 'there is no precedent for such a long quotation that is also full of argumentation' (*Corinthians*, p. 705).

32. See Schüssler Fiorenza: 'The community rule of 14.33-36...has a specific situation in mind, namely, the speaking and questioning of wives in the public worship assembly' (*In Memory of Her*, p. 233).

33. *Contra* A. Verhey, *The Great Reversal: Ethics and the New Testament* (Grand Rapids: Eerdmans, 1989), pp. 116-17.

34. *Contra* Calvin, *Corinthians*, p. 306.

35. For example R.P. Martin: 'It may well be that 1 Corinthians xiv, 34-36, 40 (the command for women to keep silence in the worship) has to do with the same situation as is envisaged in 1 Thessalonians v. 21, namely, the need to test the prophecies, especially if the women members of the Church at Corinth...possessed the prophetic gift. It may be, then, that (in view of 1 Corinthians xiv, 32, 33) some women had abused the gift' (*Worship in the Early Church* [Westwood, NH: Fleming H. Revell, 1964], p. 136). See Ellis, 'The Silenced Wives of Corinth'; *idem*, 'Paul and the Eschatological Woman', in *Pauline Theology: Ministry and Society*

Yet Paul uses the word *eperotaō* here, rather than *diakrinō*, the word he uses when discussing the weighing of prophecy. Furthermore, if Paul is here referring to the 'weighing of prophecy' he would be advising 'the women' to carry out that function at home. Such private judging of prophecy would be in contravention both of the method Paul has just prescribed (the other prophets are publicly to discern prophecies) and the function of true prophecy as a community edifier (14.4) and public witness (14.24). It is also important to note Paul's unqualified use of *laleō* in vv. 34-35. In ch. 14, in all but one instance other than vv. 34-35 (i.e., v. 11), the word *laleō* is qualified so as to make it refer to spiritual speaking: tongues (14.2, 4, 5, 6, 9, 18, 23, 27, 29), prophecy (14.3, 29), speaking in connection with revelation, knowledge, prophecy and teaching (14.6), and speaking, presumably in connection with interpreting tongues (14.19).[36] The unqualified use of *laleō* is distinctive.[37] It is best to understand Paul as censuring a type of speaking which he regards as unspiritual and uninspired. The women's speaking appears to be a type that Paul wishes clearly to distinguish from the spiritual speaking to which he has referred throughout ch. 14.

Information from Philo

Our understanding of the nature of Paul's response may be enhanced by a sideways glance at Philo Judaeus. Philo represents a Hellenistic Jewish mindset which was perhaps comparable to that of the Corinthian spirituals.[38] Something like his opinions about matters of spiritual speech[39] may have been shared by the Corinthian believers. I am not

(Grand Rapids: Eerdmans, 1989), pp. 53-86, esp. 67-71; W.L. Leifeld, 'Women, Submission and Ministry in 1 Corinthians', in A. Mickelsen (ed.), *Women, Authority and the Bible* (Downers Grove, IL: IVP, 1986), pp. 143-54, esp. pp. 150-51; and Wire, *The Corinthian Women Prophets*, p. 156.

36. See Fee, *Corinthians*, p. 676.

37. *Contra* C.K. Barrett (*A Commentary on the First Epistle to the Corinthians* [New York: Harper & Row, 1968], p. 332) who argues that because the verb is used throughout ch. 14 in the sense of inspired speech it should be read that way also in vv. 34-35. My point is that the word's use in 1 Cor. 14.34-35 is singular, as indicated by the fact that it is not directly linked to references to spiritual speech.

38. So R.A. Horsley: 'the principles and ideas of the Corinthians are extensively paralleled in Philo's writings and in Wisdom' ('Spiritual Marriage with Sophia', *VC* 33 [1979], p. 48).

39. Though Philo does not use *pneuma* language he is concerned with how to speak appropriately of and to God. My argument rests not on there being a direct

suggesting that the Corinthians knew Philo's writings but rather that they may have had an approach to spirituality similar to Philo's. Information from Philo is then helpful in understanding the perspective of the Corinthian spirituals and so Paul's response to them. As A.J.M. Wedderburn suggests, Philo 'provides *indirect* evidence of the view against which Paul was contending in 1 Corinthians'.[40]

Both Philo and Paul stress that spiritual speech should be 'intelligible'. For Philo intelligible spiritual speech is the property of the wise who are able to express the true things of God with a mind to which God is revealing himself.[41] Paul's point, on the other hand, is that spiritual speech should be intelligible to others in the community (1 Cor. 14.14, 15, 19).[42] It is conceivable that Paul appeals to the importance of the mind in the process of directing the Corinthians' behaviour during spiritual worship in order to get his recipients' attention. His purpose is to change their preconceptions and stress that spiritual speech is not the privilege of the wise for the purpose of attaining the revelation of God.[43]

similarity or dependence between Philo and Paul but rather on the assumption that the Corinthian spirituals may have misunderstood Paul's teaching in accordance with a Jewish Hellenistic religious understanding such as we can find in Philo.

40. 'Philo's Heavenly Man', *NovT* 15 (1973), p. 306.

41. *Rer. Div. Her.* 3-7. It is appropriate for the wise (*sophoi*) to talk in the presence of God (*Rer. Div. Her.* 5.21). The wise speak in order to ask questions of God and learn from God (*Rer. Div. Her.* 5.18-19). The spiritual person speaks to God in full recognition of God's transcendent sovereignty, and as the recipient of God-given speech. Here Philo uses Exod. 4.12: 'I will open thy mouth and teach thee what thou shalt speak'. Free speech for the spiritual person expresses humble confidence in God and is used, at God's initiative, to learn about, and proclaim the things of God (*Rer. Div. Her.* 6).

42. It is noteworthy that both authors use the imagery of music to make their point. Philo speaks of the mind's music being apprehended by the mind's musician, i.e., by God alone (*Rer. Div. Her.* 4.15). The mind's music is a divine gift separate from the senses. The mind's music is intelligible in a private revelatory experience between an individual and God. Paul uses the imagery of music (1 Cor. 14.7-8) to argue the opposite. If the music which results from God's spiritual gifts does not communicate with other believers, it is unintelligible and consequently an inappropriate manifestation of the spirit of God.

43. Paul is concerned throughout ch. 14 to distinguish Christian prophecy from other types of prophecy, both Graeco-Roman and Jewish (see T. Callan who recognizes that one of Paul's concerns in 1 Cor. 14 is proving that Christian prophecy is not ecstatic, unlike Greek and Hellenistic Jewish prophecy that understood a trance-like state as a necessary accompaniment of prophecy ['Prophecy and Ecstasy in Greco-Roman Religion and in 1 Corinthians', *NovT* 27 (1985), pp.

Spiritual speech is not an expression of an individual in search of truth, but is the expression of those who already know the power of God (2.5) for the purpose of building up the church (14.12).

Philo distinguishes between ordinary speech and speech which expresses truth. Ordinary speech is one of the faculties (along with the body and the senses) from which it is necessary to be freed in order to inherit the things of God.[44] Ordinary speech too readily seeks to give expression to the inexpressible and steers the seeker away from the truth.[45] Only when the mind is 'no longer in its own keeping, but is stirred to its depths and maddened by heavenward yearning' can the things of God be realized by an individual.[46] True understanding comes from a mind dedicated to God.[47] Philo's wise man is the one whose mind has been united with God, the one who has been gifted with seeing the things of God.[48] He considers that spiritual speech is essentially supra-rational[49] even though its goal is to understand and express with the mind.

125-40, p. 139]). The Hellenistic world considered that prophecy was properly accompanied by an inactive mind (see D.E. Aune, *Prophecy in Early Christianity and the Mediterranean World* [Grand Rapids: Eerdmans, 1983], p. 21). Aune notes that in the mystery cults 'the basic assumption was that if a god was actually speaking through an individual, that person's own mind must become inactive in order that his speech organs might become instruments of the divinity' (p. 47). See also L.H. Feldman on Josephus's description of prophets for a pagan audience, which emphasizes that the prophet has a god within causing him to speak with a strange voice ('Prophets and Prophecy in Josephus', *JTS* NS 41 [1990], pp. 386-422, p. 412); and H. Krämer, '*prophētēs ktl*', *TDNT*, VI, pp. 790-91. See R. Meyer, '*propētēs ktl*', *TDNT*, VI, pp. 819-21 for instances of ecstatic experiences of Jewish prophets. Paul stresses that the gift of prophecy is capable of subordination for the purpose of peace in the assembly (14.32) and is subject to the law of love, thereby making Christian prophecy distinctive. See M.E. Boring: 'There is tension between Paul's understanding of prophecy and the understanding of *pneuma* held by the Corinthians, in that theirs tends toward individualism, while Paul rejects an individualistic anthropology in favor of the community, the new eschatological people of God, as the bearer of the Spirit' (*Sayings of the Risen Jesus: Christian Prophecy in the Synoptic Tradition* [Cambridge: Cambridge University Press, 1982], p. 60).

44. *Rer. Div. Her.* 9. See *Migr. Abr.* 24.137.
45. *Rer. Div. Her.* 14.
46. *Rer. Div. Her.* 14.70.
47. *Rer. Div. Her.* 14.74.
48. *Migr. Abr.* 9.
49. *Rer. Div. Her.* 14.70.

Only when speech is sentenced to long speechlessness can it eventually speak intelligibly.[50] Speechlessness is a necessary aspect of the spiritual journey. It is only possible to listen to God in silence—the silence of the tongue and of the soul.[51] In this regard Philo refers to Deut. 27.9, 'be silent and hear'. Only in peace and tranquillity can an individual hear the things of God. It is especially important for those who have nothing worth hearing to be silent in the presence of God. Philo stresses the value of silence in the spiritual journey and expands the meaning of listening.[52]

In light of Philo's words, Paul's concern about the Corinthians' worship in 1 Cor. 14.34-35 may be more fully appreciated. Paul's concern about 'the women' at Corinth appears to be that, while they considered themselves spiritual, and therefore free to speak during prophecy,[53] Paul thought their speech was actually 'aspiritual'.[54] 'The women' probably understood themselves as having the wisdom that comes from revelation and consequently complete freedom of speech in the assembly. Paul considers that his task is to disabuse these women (and perhaps the whole assembly)[55] of the perception that 'the women's' contribution during prophecy was 'spiritual'. Paul's reference to 'the women's' desire to learn (v. 35) may be his implicit acknowledgment of their self-understanding that their speaking and asking questions was the discernment of prophecy.[56] As noted, however, Paul

50. *Rer. Div. Her.* 14.

51. *Rer. Div. Her.* 3.

52. 'Whereas the voice of mortal beings is judged by hearing, the sacred oracles intimate that the words of God are seen as light is seen...words spoken by God are interpreted by the power of sight residing in the soul' (*Migr. Abr.* 9.47, 49).

53. As mentioned above, the most reasonable accounting for the location of Paul's gloss is that the speaking he finds reprehensible occurred during prophetic utterance.

54. This is a different reading from that of Wire who thinks that Paul regarded the women as prophets (*The Corinthian Women Prophets*, pp. 152-58), and is also different from that of J. Sevenster who does not think that the women considered themselves particularly spiritual, but rather suggests that they were expressing their emancipation in Christ and so engaging in 'heated argument' with their husbands (*Paul and Seneca* [Leiden: Brill, 1961], p. 198).

55. He does not address 'the women' in the second person, thereby suggesting that he directs his instruction to the whole assembly.

56. There appears to have been a widespread understanding in early Christianity that the prophet was a teacher. See D. Hill, *New Testament Prophecy* (Atlanta: John Knox, 1979), pp. 126-27; and E.E. Ellis, *Prophecy and Hermeneutic in Early*

does not choose the word *diakrinō* to describe 'the women's' questions, which suggests that, according to Paul, 'the women's' speaking was not the discerning of prophecies.

Paul's Diagnosis and Remedies

Paul prescribes for the women three remedies: silence, asking their men at home, and submission. Did Paul prescribe silence not just because it was the obvious antidote to disruptive speech but also because his readers might recognize silence as having spiritual value? It is feasible that, if the Corinthians shared a spiritual perspective similar to that of Philo, they might have understood silence (as Paul might have intended them to) in the sense both of suppression of speech and of stillness, repose, peace and receptivity. The tone of Paul's command may have been far less restrictive than later readers have assumed. This proposal is supported by the fact that in the immediate context Paul commands silence in an analogous way. In the direction that some in the community are to be silent so that the gifts of God may benefit all (vv. 28, 30) silence is a temporary state in which individuals suppress their speech for the good order of the Christian community. The silence (suppression of speech) of some results in appropriate peace and calm for the whole community. This interpretation goes a long way towards explaining how in one letter Paul could both accept women's praying and prophesying (1 Cor. 11.2-16) and instruct women to be silent in the assembly.

Another remedy Paul dispenses for the women is 'asking their men at home'. Here we should notice the connection between silence and learning. As we have seen, Philo understands that silence is the necessary prelude to learning and wisdom. The true seeker, the one who is truly spiritual, understands both the value of learning and the necessity of silence to that process. Paul appeals to such an understanding when he entreats the Corinthian prophets to prophesy 'one by one'[57] (while the rest are silent, v. 30) by saying that only in this way can they learn

---

Christianity: New Testament Essays (Grand Rapids: Eerdmans, 1978), p. 141. See also G.F. Hawthorne, 'The Role of the Christian Prophets in the Gospel Tradition', in *idem* with O. Betz (eds.), *Tradition and Interpretation in the New Testament: Essays in Honor of E. Earle Ellis* (Grand Rapids: Eerdmans, 1987), pp. 119-33, p. 120.

57. C.F.D. Moule translates *kath' hena* as 'one by one' (*Idiom Book of New Testament Greek* [Cambridge: Cambridge University Press, 1977], p. 60).

from one another (v. 31). When Paul's commands to 'ask' and to 'be silent' are seen in relation to one another we find that the latter wears a more positive face than is usually recognized. By being silent 'the women' not only contribute to the good functioning of the assembly's spiritual worship but also adopt the posture of learners.[58] The command to ask questions (v. 35) is then in part an affirmation of 'the women's' right to learn.[59]

In this context Paul's other prescription that 'the women' be in submission would entail both the submission of their speaking for the good of the assembly and the submission of the learner.[60] Traditionally the command to be 'in submission' has been understood as 'in submission to the men',[61] an interpretation which seems particularly reasonable if the 'law' is understood to be Gen. 3.16. Yet as we have already noted, no law is specified in the text. It should further be noticed that the verb *hupotassō* in v. 34 is not followed by an object. We are not told to whom the women are to be in submission. Given the chief concern of 1 Corinthians 14—that the expression of oral spiritual gifts be done so as to build up the church (14.12) and witness to the character of God (14.25)—it is as likely that the mysterious law to which Paul alludes underlined this concern than that it was a law about wifely submission.[62] In fact, the larger context of the passage makes it more

58. See A. Besançon Spencer's helpful presentation of texts from Judaism and the early church that speak of the importance of silence for learning (*Beyond the Curse: Women Called to Ministry* [Nashville: Nelson, 1985], pp. 77-81).

59. Calvin noticed the positive nature of Paul's mention of learning: 'So that he might not give the impression, by speaking like this, of closing the door on learning on women, he instructs them to make their inquiries in private' (*Corinthians*, p. 307).

60. See Philo's words about the humility and submission of the learner in *Rer. Div. Her.* 21.102-104. 1 Tim. 2.11 expresses a similar understanding: learning involves silence and submission. The similarity between 1 Cor. 14.34-35 and 1 Tim. 2.11 is due to the common recognition that learning involves quiet and subordination.

61. Often such an interpretation also understands *hai gunaikes* as 'wives' and argues that Paul thought it unseemly that wives should speak in public (for example Calvin, *Corinthians*, p. 306). However, Wire argues that a reference to submission 'is appropriate not only for wives, since daughters, widows, and women slaves are just as subordinate to the man of the house' (*The Corinthian Women Prophets*, p. 156).

62. The suggestion that Paul's reference to 'law' may be an allusion to a common Graeco-Roman concern about the morality of orgiastic cults and the

than reasonable to suppose that the women are to be in submission in a general way; to the cause of the good functioning of the Christian assembly. As speakers in tongues are to control the expression of their gift for the good of all (vv. 27-28) and the prophets are to submit (*hupotassō*) the spirits of prophecy for the sake of peace and order in the assembly (v. 32), for the same reason the women are to be in submission in regard to their speaking. The correlative *kathōs* clause then might refer to a law about curtailing and controlling inappropriate speech rather than to a law about wifely submission.[63]

presence of women at such gatherings (see for example Schüssler Fiorenza, *In Memory of Her*, p. 232) is far-fetched. For this proposition rests on several shaky assumptions. The first assumption is that Paul would use *nomos* to refer to a Graeco-Roman moral concern. While other Jewish thinkers like Ben Sira and Philo might speak of the Jewish law as equivalent to universal wisdom or the law of nature (Sir. 24; *Op. Mund.* 3; *Spec. Leg.* 2.13) the vast majority of Paul's references to the law mean 'the sum of specific divine requirements given to Israel through Moses' (Westerholm, *Israel's Law*, p. 108). The second premise is that the context in which to understand vv. 34-35 is Paul's concern that his converts not be mistaken for an orgiastic cult. There are several aspects of the text which tell against this. First, 1 Cor. 14.34-35 does not ask the women to leave but only to be quiet. So, while the presence of women at 'secret' religious gatherings was suspect in the mainstream culture, Paul does not ask his converts to subscribe to what is respectable in that regard. Secondly, when Paul does express a concern that outsiders might think his converts 'mad' (*mainomai*, v. 23) he refers to speakers in tongues, not specifically the speaking of women. If he had referred to the speaking of women in vv. 34-35 as a problem because outsiders might think them 'mad', there would be more reason to suggest that his concern was that outsiders might wrongly identify his converts (for instance, for worshippers of Dionysus [see Euripides' *Bacchae*]). It is more likely that in the earlier text Paul deliberately used the word *mainomai* to critique a preconception on the part of the Corinthian Christians that it was necessary for them to act as if they were mad (see Philo, *Rer. Div. Her.* 14.70: 'Like persons possessed and corybants, be filled with inspired frenzy, even as the prophets are inspired'). Thirdly, the context suggests that Paul's concern is focused positively (that the Christian assembly manifest the true character of God) rather than negatively (that they not be mistaken for a morally subversive cult). Chapters 12–14 do not evidence a protective stance. The larger context suggests not that Paul wanted his converts to be careful to differentiate themselves from other ecstatic groups but that his converts might recognize that their spiritual gifts should demonstrate the character of God (vv. 25, 33).

63. It is more likely that the 'law' to which Paul refers (v. 34) might have been one such as Philo also uses in discussing appropriate speech and silence (i.e., Deut. 27.9 or Exod. 4.12)—texts which assert the need for silence in order to hear God and that true speech comes from divine not human initiative—rather than a law like Gen.

The upshot of this nuancing of the type of speech Paul censures and the nature of his advice is the proposal that Paul limits speech in the assembly when it consists of questions which detract from prophecy and its interpretation. Paul's advice is that 'the women' who do this should be silent, be in submission and ask questions of their men at home. To modern readers in search of an inclusive Paul this is relatively good news, for it renders Paul's words a limitation on free speech in only a very specialized situation. We should not, however, be too ready to include Paul in a pantheon of egalitarian heroes. What about v. 35b, where Paul writes that it is shameful for a woman to speak in church? It appears that here, as at 1 Cor. 11.6, Paul appeals to shame on the basis of his society's acceptance of the connection between women and shame.[64] In 1 Cor. 11.6 Paul stated what was culturally obvious: women should not be shorn or shaven, for such is shameful. It appears that he uses the same strategy at 1 Cor. 14.35. This suggests that Paul shared his culture's patriarchal attitude to women and is here exhibiting it.

There are, however, reasons to be cautious about too readily deciding that Paul imported wholesale his society's (both the broadly Graeco-Roman and his more narrowly Jewish) patriarchy into the church. The immediate difficulty encountered by a proposition that Paul was comfortable with his society's positioning of women is the extent of evidence for Paul's contrary views and practices.[65] On the basis of the fact that Paul's standard practice was inclusive of women it is certainly reasonable to propose that, despite his use of an appeal to shame at

3.16. (I am not here suggesting any direct dependence of Paul [or the Corinthians] on Philo.)

64. Malina points out that the ancient Mediterranean world connected women and shame (*The New Testament World*, pp. 25-50).

65. Paul clearly accepted women's speaking in the assembly (for example, Euodia and Syntyche [Phil. 4.2] and Prisca [1 Cor. 16.19] and the women mentioned in Rom. 16.1-16; see E. Schüssler Fiorenza, 'The Apostleship of Women in Early Christianity', in L. Swidler and A. Swidler (eds.), *Women Priests: A Catholic Commentary* [New York: Paulist Press, 1977], pp. 135-40; *idem*, 'Missionaries, Apostles, Coworkers: Romans 16 and the Reconstruction of Women's Early Christian History', *WW* 6.4 (1986), pp. 420-33; and P. Richardson, 'From Apostles to Virgins: Romans 16 and the Roles of Women in the Early Church', *Toronto Journal of Theology* 2.2 [1986], pp. 232-61) and in fact even relied on it (Phoebe's commission was most likely to elaborate on Paul's letter to the Roman house churches, like Timothy's in 1 Cor. 4.17 [see R. Jewett, 'Paul, Phoebe, and the Spanish Mission', in J. Neusner (ed.), *Social World of Formative Christianity and Judaism* (Philadelphia: Fortress Press, 1988), pp. 142-61, p. 149]).

14.35, he censured the women speaking on the basis of their behaviour rather than their gender.

How then do we understand the appeal to shame? What seems obvious is that by appealing to shame Paul hoped to communicate effectively with people who understood and responded to the value system in which that appeal worked.[66] And therein lies the rub. While Paul may not have limited the free speech of women *because* of their gender, he was willing to get them (and the Corinthian community) to change their behaviour by appealing to a value system in which women were obliged to accept the social control of men. This fact is both clear and, for modern readers hoping for a Paul untarnished with chauvinism, it is disappointing. But it should not be a fact that bears more significance than is appropriate. Paul appeals to shame for the purpose of persuasion. This reflects Paul's concern that his readers hear and respond to his directive. It does not indicate that Paul called for silence because he thought it wrong that women *qua* women should speak publicly.

It is also important to see that Paul's appeal to shame has a more positive function in light of his teaching on spiritual gifts. When Paul first described the proper functioning of spiritual gifts he used the category of 'honour' to extol the unity of the body (12.22-23). In the context of Paul's teaching on spiritual gifts it is shameful to cause disunity in the body of Christ.

Even with these nuances, however, the passage does not readily commend itself to our gender-sensitive ears. We are still left with the fact that Paul says specifically that at home 'the women' are to ask questions of their men. This suggests that Paul accepted the patriarchal ordering of Christians' home life (they are not told to ask their questions of the other women) and therefore the social subordination of women.[67] Yet as we have seen, a proposition that Paul limited women's speaking in the assembly on the basis of their gender yields problems of its own.[68] We

66. P. Marshall demonstrates that throughout 1 Corinthians Paul uses to his advantage his readers' acceptance of their society's honour and shame values (*Enmity in Corinth: Social Conventions in Paul's Relations with the Corinthians* [Tübingen: Mohr (Paul Siebeck), 1987], esp. pp. 389-95).

67. Col. 3.18-19 and Eph. 5.22-33, if authentic, provide corroborating evidence that Paul held this view.

68. See n. 65. It is important to distinguish between Paul's advice concerning the assembly and his advice about home life. The often noted conventional nature of the 'Haustafeln' may indicate that Paul did not feel authorized to give much specific or

might choose to solve the problematic tensions left by such a proposition by suggesting either that at this point Paul compromised his principles[69] or that he could not be expected to have egalitarian views.[70] The problem with the first of these solutions is that there is no corroborating evidence: nowhere else do we see Paul advocating a limitation on women's speech in the assembly.[71] A proposition of compromise in this regard must then rest solely on the passage under discussion. The problem with the second solution is that, while Paul does not advocate changing society's structures in a manner which might suit modern liberal sensibilities,[72] for those 'in Christ' he did propound a fairly non-conformist set of social relations tending towards egalitarianism.[73] So slaves were to be treated as family in Christ, and the marriage relationship was to be mutual.[74] The fact that Paul accepted and encouraged

original advice on family relations, unless a particular case arose (for example, 1 Cor. 5.1-2). He did, however, consider he had authority to organize relationships at worship. The 'love-patriarchalism' proposed by G. Theissen (*The Social Setting of Pauline Christianity: Essays on Corinth* [Philadelphia: Fortress Press, 1982], esp. pp. 107-108) as Paul's ethical pattern better describes Paul's ethic of the household than his ethic for the gathered community. There is, in fact, little evidence that Paul took social differences for granted or required subordination in accordance with social status in the gathered community.

69. For instance, R.N. Longenecker suggests that here Paul accommodated himself to his old religious mindset (*New Testament Social Ethics for Today* [Grand Rapids: Eerdmans, 1984], p. 87); and M. Hayter proposes that Paul accommodated himself to the social mores of the day (*The New Eve in Christ: The Use and Abuse of the Bible in the Debate about Women in the Church* [Grand Rapids: Eerdmans, 1987], pp. 130-31).

70. So Tomson: 'the conception of civil emancipation' is chronologically anomalous (*Paul and the Jewish Law*, p. 273).

71. Note that Eph. 5.22-33 and Col. 3.18-19 (if considered evidence for Paul's views) deal only with intra-household behaviour and, furthermore, that they do not concern women speaking.

72. For instance, he appears to be able to live with the fact of slavery.

73. See V.L. Wimbush: 'The Pauline Christians came to reject the ways of cultic markers or separatism and pneumatic-elitist renunciation as models of spirituality. The former they rejected because their communities were to be open to all, irrespective of ethnic-religious origins, the latter because the "things of the world" are in the final analysis not evil, not to be renounced, only relativized and reprioritized under the concern for the "things of the Lord"' (*Paul the Worldly Ascetic: Response to the World and Self-Understanding according to 1 Corinthians 7* [Macon, GA: Mercer University Press, 1987], p. 93). Also Verhey, *The Great Reversal*, p. 117.

74. To gain a sense of just how different Paul's advice on family relations was

counter-cultural attitudes such as discouraging divorce,[75] the possibility of celibacy,[76] and mixed-gender gatherings[77] is further evidence that Paul sought to establish a distinctive (rather than conformist) set of social standards for Christians. This leads us to distinguish between Paul's prescription and his diagnosis. That is, it cautions us against presuming that Paul uncritically accepted his society's social attitudes and so reading his prescription in vv. 34-35, which is undeniably patriarchal, as synonymous with his diagnosis (which may not have been). In light of Paul's other views, the most suitable scenario for 1 Cor. 14.34-35 is that Paul saw a problem with the type of speaking 'the women' engaged in, rather than with them as the speakers. A distinction between problem and remedy allows us to hold 1 Cor. 14.34-35 in creative tension with other passages in Paul. Paul evidently singled out 'the women' here simply

from his social world it is instructive to read Plutarch's *Advice on Marriage* or Musonius Rufus (see the helpful article by R.B. Ward, 'Musonius and Paul on Marriage', *NTS* 36 [1990], pp. 281-89).

75. J. McNamara notes that Justin Martyr contrasts Christians to society on the grounds that Christians do not divorce ('Wives and Widows in Early Christian Thought', *International Journal of Women's Studies* 2 [1979], pp. 575-92, p. 580). See also P. Perkins, 'Marriage in the New Testament and its World', in W.P. Roberts (ed.), *Commitment to Partnership: Explorations of the Theology of Marriage* (New York: Paulist Press, 1987), pp. 5-30, p. 26. P. Brown notes how radical some of Paul's sexual mores were for both Jews and Gentiles (*The Body and Society: Men, Women and Sexual Renunciation in Early Christianity* [New York: Columbia University Press, 1988], pp. 51-52).

76. Paul's allowance for celibacy was a threat both to Jewish attitudes (see J.D.M. Derret, 'The Disposal of Virgins', in *Studies in the New Testament* [Leiden: Brill, 1977], pp. 184-92; and G. Anderson who notes that *Gen. R.* 34.14 compares the celibate individual to 'one who impairs God's image and, even worse, to a murderer' ['Celibacy or Consummation in the Garden? Reflections on Early Jewish and Christian Interpretations of the Garden of Eden', *HTR* 82.2 (1982), pp. 121-48, p. 122]) and to the broader Graeco-Roman society (so Brown, *Body and Society*, p. 32). See McNamara, 'Wives and Widows in Early Christian Thought', p. 584. The words of Musonius Rufus reveal the importance attached to procreation: 'Is it not then plain that he [the creator] wished the two [male and female] to be united and live together, and by their joint efforts to devise a way of life in common and to produce and rear children together, so that the race might never die?' (C.E. Lutz, 'Musonius Rufus: The Roman Socrates', in A.R. Bellinger [ed.], *Yale Classical Studies* [New Haven: Yale University Press, 1947], pp. 3-147, p. 93).

77. There were of course other religious or philosophical groups in which both men and women met together, for example the Bacchae and the Epicureans. But these assemblies were considered counter-cultural.

because in his eyes, they were the culprits in the situation.[78]

We are left with a complex picture of Paul's motivation and attitudes in 1 Cor. 14.34-35. I have argued that Paul responded to 'the women' alone because their speaking, rather than that done by any of the men, was disrupting the communal expression of prophecy. Yet in the process of convincing his converts to change their behaviour he was willing to resort to the patriarchal values of his society. The resulting complexity is best understood, as mentioned above, by distinguishing between Paul's diagnosis and his remedy. It is the former, Paul's diagnosis, which opens a window to his fundamental concern about 'the women's' speaking. And it is Paul's primary concern which should be the focus of our interpretation and control our appropriation of his words.

Putting 1 Corinthians 14.34-35 in Context
The context in which our passage is situated indicates that Paul's foremost consideration is the peaceful expression of prophecy. Throughout chs. 12–14 he sets forth his case that the varied manifestations of

78. It is possible that it was more often women than men who were prone to disruptive or insensitive speech during ecstatic gatherings. The special intensity of religious commitment and experience for those who have been socially deprived is well known (see C.Y. Glock, 'The Role of Deprivation in the Origin and Evolution of Religious Groups', in R. Lee and M.E. Marty [eds.], *Religion and Social Conflict* [New York: Oxford University Press, 1964], pp. 24-36). Many have commented that Christianity must have been especially liberating for women. E. Pagels notes that one of the chief developments of Christianity was 'a new vision of the basis of social and political order—an order no longer founded upon the divine claims of the ruler of the state, but upon qualities that Christians believed were inherent within every man, and, some dared insist, within every woman as well, through our common creation "in God's image"' (*Adam, Eve, and the Serpent* [New York: Random House, 1988], p. 55; see also R.S. Kraemer, *Her Share of the Blessings: Women's Religions among Pagans, Jews and Christians in the Greco-Roman World* [New York: Oxford University Press, 1992], p. 156). After a lifetime of being under the authority either of their fathers or their husbands many women must have felt a wondrous sense of freedom at being able to act independently in church (often in the presence of those to whom they were otherwise socially subordinated). Paul evidently felt that 'the women' at Corinth misunderstood how their freedom should be expressed. On the basis of Paul's appeal to patriarchal values (shame) and his patriarchal remedy (ask their men at home) we may want to conjecture that if men had asked questions during prophecy Paul would not have so readily quashed them. But that must remain a conjecture. He certainly silences men's free speech earlier in ch. 14.

spirituality (including prophecy) should be subject to the law of love.[79] This fact is most clearly seen by noticing that Paul interrupts his practical directives in chs. 12–14 with the love poem of ch. 13. As J. Smit has shown, this poem serves to demonstrate Paul's main point throughout chs. 12–14, that *charismata* are to be subsumed under love.[80] If Paul's fundamental concern in chs. 12–14 (and indeed throughout his letter)[81] is to insist that his readers act lovingly towards one another, then it is very likely that such a concern also undergirds 14.34-35.

Conclusion

The broader perspective afforded by looking at vv. 34-35 in context confirms the preceding interpretation. Evidently Paul wrote these words out of concern that some women's speech was detrimental to the Corinthian assembly's exercise of prophecy, not because it was spoken by women, but because it was self-focused rather than loving. As such it did not belong in church. Paul considered it necessary that in this instance free speech be curtailed. In order for the Corinthians' prophecy to be truly a manifestation of God, Paul decided that those who were speaking in this way ('the women') had to be silent, for their speaking was injurious to the peace, order and loving concern which should mark Christian prophecy.

Paul's means of persuasion ought not to detract us from his central concern, nor serve to legitimate anything other than a corresponding concern that believers' sensitivity and love for each other be the cardinal testimony to the Christian God. His closing words to the Corinthians reiterate the point: 'Let all that you do be done in love' (16.14).

79. See Boring, *Sayings of the Risen Jesus*, p. 35.

80. 'The Genre of 1 Corinthians 13 in the Light of Classical Rhetoric', *NovT* 33 (1991), pp. 193-216, p. 215. See W. Meeks, *The First Urban Christians* (New Haven: Yale University Press, 1983), p. 90. J. Painter writes that 'chapter 13 places all the gifts under the criterion of love' ('Paul and the *pneumatikoi* at Corinth', in M.D. Hooker and S.G. Wilson [eds.], *Paul and Paulinism: Essays in Honour of C.K Barrett* [London: SPCK, 1982], pp. 237-50, p. 244).

81. M.M. Mitchell demonstrates that 1 Corinthians is an example of deliberative rhetoric in which 'love is the unifying, concordant power which Paul urges on his divided church' (*Paul and the Rhetoric of Reconciliation: An Exegetical Investigation of the Language and Composition of 1 Corinthians* [Tübingen: Mohr (Paul Siebeck), 1991], p. 171 n. 646).

'FOR ME TO LIVE IS CHRIST':
PAULINE SPIRITUALITY AS A BASIS FOR MINISTRY

Christopher D. Marshall

1. *Preliminary Comments*

A reawakening of interest in spirituality and spiritual experience is increasingly apparent in contemporary Western society. Pervasive secularism has created a spiritual vacuum into which all manner of spiritual traditions have streamed, to the point where Christian faith is only one of several options available in the market place. This diversity of spiritualities prompts the question: What are the distinguishing characteristics of a genuinely Christian approach to spiritual experience? In our pluralistic age, this question is of pressing importance to all Christians, not least to those who, like Bishop Penny, are charged with guarding and tending the flock of God (1 Pet. 5.2; Acts 20.28). Christians may be immensely grateful for the enrichment that has come in recent years from the cross-fertilization of the various spiritual traditions within Christianity. But what makes a spiritual tradition Christian? How are we to test the spirits at work in our world (1 Cor. 12.3, 10; see also 2.12-14; 7.40; 1 Thess. 5.19-22; 2 Thess. 2.2; 1 Jn 4.1)?[1]

Any attempt to formulate an authentically Christian spirituality must take its bearings from the teaching of the Christian Scriptures, in particular the New Testament. Within the New Testament, the writings of Paul are of singular importance, for spirituality is central to the apostle's own life and thought[2] and 'no other person has had a greater influence on

1. See J.S. Ukpong, 'Pluralism and the Problem of the Discernment of Spirits', *Ecumenical Revue* 41 (1989), pp. 416-25.
2. G.D. Fee, 'Some Reflections on Pauline Spirituality', in J.I. Packer and L. Wilkins (eds.), *Alive to God: Studies in Spirituality Presented to James Houston* (Downers Grove, IL: Inter-Varsity Press, 1992), pp. 96-98.

Christian spirituality than Paul'.[3] It was Paul who virtually coined the term 'spiritual' (*pneumatikos*) for Christian use.[4] The word occurs 26 times in the New Testament and, with the exception of 1 Pet. 2.5 (although see also Rev. 11.8), is found only in the Pauline corpus.[5] The term is not widely attested in ancient literature, and it is possible that Paul himself was the first to use it in a specifically religious connection.[6]

Paul also provides our earliest written testimony to the spiritual temper of first-generation Christianity, and arguably it was his own personality and experience that was the single greatest influence in shaping the spirituality of the Christian movement at its most formative stage. Paul's letters are manifestly spiritual documents,[7] from their opening greetings ('grace to you and peace from God our Father and the Lord Jesus Christ')[8] to their closing benedictions ('may the grace of the Lord Jesus

3.   R.P. Meye, 'Spirituality', in G.F. Hawthorne and R.P. Martin (eds.), *Dictionary of Paul and his Letters* (Downers Grove, IL: Inter-Varsity Press, 1993), p. 907.

4.   Paul uses the term in three main ways: as an adjective, for example, 'spiritual blessing'; as a masculine noun, 'spiritual people'; and as a neuter plural noun, 'spiritual things'. See further J.D.G. Dunn, *Jesus and the Spirit: A Study of the Religious and Charismatic Experience of Jesus and the First Christians as Reflected in the New Testament* (London: SCM Press, 1975), pp. 207-209; G.D. Fee, *God's Empowering Presence: The Holy Spirit in the Letters of Paul* (Peabody, MA: Hendrickson, 1994), pp. 28-32; E.G. Selwyn, *The First Epistle of St Peter* (London: Macmillan, 1947), pp. 281-85.

5.   Rom. 1.11; 7.14; 15.27; 1 Cor. 2.13, 14, 15; 3.1; 9.11; 10.3, 4; 12.1; 14.1, 37; 15.44, 46; Gal. 6.1; Eph. 1.3; 5.19; 6.12; Col. 1.9; 3.16; see also 1 Pet. 2.5; Rev. 11.8.

6.   The term was already entrenched in Christian vocabulary by the time of the writing of 1 Corinthians. Selwyn suggests that Paul coined the word 'spiritual' for Christian use during his Ephesian ministry, 52–55 CE (*First Peter*, p. 284). See also W.D. Stacey: 'All the light of Paul's Christian experience is concentrated in this term...the word is Paul's word...', *The Pauline View of Man in Relation to its Judaic and Hellenistic Background* (London: Macmillan, 1956), p. 153. Others have attempted to source the term in Gnosticism, Hellenistic mystery cults, Jewish wisdom tradition and apocalypticism, or in the theology of Paul's Corinthian opponents. For a brief review, see J. Painter, 'Paul and the *Pneumatikoi* at Corinth', in M.D. Hooker and S.G. Wilson (eds.), *Paul and Paulinism: FS for C.K. Barrett* (London: SPCK, 1982), pp. 237-50.

7.   For this essay, Pauline authorship is assumed for all the documents in the New Testament bearing his name, with the exception of the Pastorals. Where relevant, references to the Pastorals are included for comparative purposes.

8.   2 Cor. 1.2; see also Rom. 1.7; 1 Cor. 1.3; Gal. 1.3; Phil. 1.2; 1 Thess. 1.1;

Christ be with your spirit, brothers and sisters. Amen').[9] Their content reveals the intensity of Paul's own religious convictions and experiences, as well as those of the communities to which he wrote.

Yet these letters are not esoteric treatises on the inner life. They deal with the mundane issues that confront believers in the hurly-burly of everyday life. Spirituality, for Paul, is not confined to private meditation or to sacramental worship or to supranormal manifestations of the Holy Spirit. Spiritual experience embraces the whole of life and works itself out in all the manifold activities of life. Spiritual progress may well mean dying to the world and the flesh in terms of allegiance (see for example Rom. 8.12-13; Gal. 5.16-17; 6.14). But it does not mean a monastic withdrawal from the world, nor an ascetic disdain of bodily life. 'His is not a spirituality of the monastery but of the road.'[10] Because Christ came into the world (Rom. 8.3; Gal. 4.4; 2 Cor. 5.19; see also 1 Tim. 1.15) and lived 'in a body of flesh' (Col. 1.22; see also Rom. 8.3), a spirituality that owns Christ's name must also be lived in the world (1 Cor. 5.10; Phil. 2.15) and in the flesh (Gal. 2.20), while simultaneously setting its sights on the things of the Spirit (Rom. 8.5-9).

This, for Paul, is what it means to be a 'spiritual' person—someone who lives in this world consciously under the dominion of the Holy Spirit. Paul does not use the word 'spiritual' simply to denote a person's interior life: in every case the term has some reference to the Spirit of God, giving Paul's reflections on the topic an inherently trinitarian character.[11] All believers, by definition, possess the Spirit; all are therefore Spirit-people (Rom. 8.9, 14; Gal. 3.2, 14; 4.6). Yet Paul still calls Christians to be spiritual, to 'keep in step with the Spirit' (Gal. 5.16; Rom. 8.4), in the sense of consciously allowing the Spirit of God to dictate their behaviour patterns. This is Paul's primary imperative. By contrast Paul's antagonists in Corinth considered there to be two distinct classes of Christians—those who possessed the Spirit fully and those who did not. Those who were truly possessed of the Spirit apparently called themselves *hoi pneumatikoi* ('the people of the spirit' or 'spiritual

---

2 Thess. 1.2; Phlm. 3; Eph. 1.2; Col. 1.2. See also 1 Tim. 1.2; 2 Tim. 2.2; Tit. 1.4.

9.　Gal. 6.18; see also Rom. 16.27; 1 Cor. 16.23; 2 Cor. 13.14; Phil. 4.23; 1 Thess. 5.28; 2 Thess. 3.18; Phlm. 25; Eph. 6.23-24; also 2 Tim. 4.22

10.　D.J. Bosch, *A Spirituality of the Road* (Scottdale, PA: Herald Press, 1979), p. 20.

11.　So Fee, 'Pauline Spirituality', pp. 96-97; also, *God's Empowering Presence*, pp. 829-45.

specialists'), and they derided the non-spiritual members of the church as 'the carnal or fleshly ones', 'the weak', 'the babes in Christ' (1 Cor. 3.1-4; 8.7-13). Their unique endowment with the Spirit, attested in powerful ecstatic experiences and possession of esoteric 'wisdom' and 'knowledge', freed them from the moral, religious and cultural constraints that cramped ordinary, earth-bound believers. Paul's response to this élitist, other-worldly Corinthian spirituality affords us considerable insight into the distinctive contours of Pauline spirituality.

For these reasons, then, Pauline spirituality is foundational to the study of Christian spirituality in general. In turning to examine Paul's perspective it is not easy to limit the scope of our inquiry, for 'St Paul's deepest spiritual teaching flows from, and is of a piece with, his fundamental theology'.[12] We must confine ourselves to a few of the perspectives that shaped his reflections on the spiritual life.

2. The Balance of Experience and Tradition

It is simply not possible to understand the life and ministry of Paul or to do justice to his theology without recognizing the creative power of his own spiritual experience. 'He is, perhaps, the prime example of how religious experience can creatively and permanently change the direction of a religious tradition.'[13] Yet Paul's theology is not merely the product of experience; it is, more precisely, the outcome of an interaction between personal experience and communal tradition. His spirituality consists of an initial and ongoing experience of the grace of God in Christ, comprehended and articulated within the interpretive framework of Jewish and Christian tradition. In other words, there is a constant interplay in the spirituality of Paul between the subjective and objective aspects of revelation (Gal. 1.12 and 1 Cor. 15.3; also 1 Cor. 11.2, 23).[14]

The framework of Paul's religious outlook was the theology of first-century Judaism. In several places Paul lays claim to a superior Jewish pedigree (Phil. 3.5-6; 2 Cor. 11.22; Rom. 11.1; see also Acts 23.6). He was evidently born into a strictly observant Jewish family in Tarsus

12. C.P.M. Jones, 'The New Testament', in C. Jones, G. Wainwright and E. Yarnold (eds.), *The Study of Spirituality* (London: SPCK, 1986), p. 75.

13. T.H. Tobin, *The Spirituality of Paul* (Wilmington, DE: Michael Glazier, 1987), p. 59.

14. See also R.Y.K. Fung, 'Revelation and Tradition: The Origins of Paul's Gospel', *EvQ* 57 (1985), pp. 23-41.

(Acts 21.39; 23.6; 26.5), but, according to Acts, spent his formative years as a young Pharisee in Jerusalem (22.3). He was so zealous for the law and his ancestral traditions that he advanced in learning beyond his colleagues (Gal. 1.14), and could count himself as 'blameless' with respect to legal piety (Phil. 3.6). As a Jerusalem-trained Pharisee with roots in the Jewish Diaspora, Paul would have been well acquainted with the major currents in contemporary Judaism. From this Jewish heritage Paul derived his fundamental religious convictions which remained with him throughout his life. These included the belief that there is but one true God (Gal. 4.3, 9; 1 Cor. 8.4-6; 1 Thess. 1.9-10; Eph. 4.6); that God is revealed in the Hebrew Scriptures (Rom. 4.23-24; 15.4; 1 Cor. 10.11; see also 9.10);[15] and that God stands in unique covenantal relationship with Israel, his chosen people (Rom. 3.1-8; 9.1-5; 11.1-2, 25-31).

After his acceptance of Christ, Paul was also deeply influenced by the traditions of early Christianity. Paul mentions his indebtedness to Christian tradition in several places (1 Cor. 11.2, 23-26; 15.3-7, 11; see also 1 Thess. 2.13; 2 Thess. 2.15; 3.6; Gal. 1.9; Phil. 4.9; Rom. 6.17), and often incorporates fragments of Christian hymns, prayers, liturgies, creeds and instruction in his epistles.[16] Pre-eminent among the Christian convictions Paul inherited were the absolute centrality of Jesus Christ in God's purposes for humanity,[17] the saving significance of his life, death and resurrection (Rom. 3.21-26; 1 Cor. 15.3-5), and his expected return in glory to consummate salvation (1 Thess. 5.1-11; Rom. 13.11-14; 1 Cor. 7.29-30).

Paul was also indebted to Hellenistic tradition, mediated in part through Hellenized Judaism, for some of the terminology and concepts he uses to express his religious convictions. Paul uses Greek political, commercial and legal terminology in his letters (for example, Gal. 3.15; 4.1-2; Rom. 7.1-3; Phil. 3.20; Col. 2.14) and employs imagery drawn from the emperor cult (1 Thess. 2.19), the sporting arena (Phil. 2.16; 3.14; 1 Cor. 9.24-27; 2 Cor. 4.8-9; see also 1 Tim. 1.18; 6.12), and the

15. See, e.g., R.B. Hays, *Echoes of Scripture in the Letters of Paul* (New Haven: Yale University Press, 1989).

16. See, for example, Rom. 1.2-4; 8.15; 10.8-9; Phil. 2.6-11; 4.20; 1 Cor. 6.9; 11.23-25; 15.3-7; 16.22; Gal. 6.18; Eph. 3.21; and Col. 1.15-20.

17. '*Solus Christus*, Christ alone, is the primary motto of Paul's theology, and most of the errors which he fights can be regarded as in some form or other qualifications of that *solus*'; C.K. Barrett, *Paul: An Introduction to his Thought* (Louisville, KY: Westminster/John Knox Press, 1994), p. 44.

Hellenistic slave-trade (1 Cor. 7.22; Rom. 7.14). His literary style reveals the influence of Greek rhetoric and philosophical practice (such as the Cynic-Stoic diatribe), and he makes use of popular Stoic concepts such as conscience, nature, freedom, duty, excellence, spending and being spent, and so on.

Pauline spirituality is therefore located firmly in a particular Jewish-Christian religious tradition, set within a Hellenistic social, cultural and political milieu. But it was Paul's personal *experience* of God in Christ that led him to interpret those traditional elements in new ways and to give them new emphases. Clearly the most life-changing and enduring of all Paul's spiritual experiences was his encounter with the risen Jesus on the road to Damascus (Gal. 1.11-17; 1 Cor. 15.8-11).[18] The enormous significance of this event never seems to have left Paul. He was to have other visionary and revelatory experiences (2 Cor. 12.1-13, see also Acts 16.6-10) but nothing comparable to this one. It was a unique Christophany, whose only possible analogies were the resurrection appearances of Jesus to the earlier apostles (1 Cor. 9.1; 15.5-10).[19] He speaks of no further such appearances either to himself or to others after him.[20] It was therefore an extraordinary rather than a typical component of Paul's spiritual journey.

The uniqueness of the experience is seen further in the three things Paul traces back directly to it. The first is his commitment to Christ (Phil. 3.12). It is true that Paul does not speak of the Damascus road event as a 'conversion' to the Christian faith; he describes it rather as a 'revelation' and 'call' (compare Gal. 1.15-16 and Isa. 49.1, 5-6; Jer. 1.5). In one sense the word 'conversion' is quite inappropriate since Paul did not see his commitment to Christ as either a change of religion or a reformation of his moral character.[21] Yet, in another sense, Paul's

18. Luke records the Damascus road event three times (Acts 9.1-19; 22.3-21; 26.2-18), and Paul refers to it at length twice (Gal. 1.11-17; 1 Cor. 15.8-11) and alludes to it on many other occasions (for example, 1 Cor. 9.1; 2 Cor. 4.6; Phil. 3.4-11). See also S. Kim, *The Origin of Paul's Gospel* (Tübingen: Mohr [Paul Siebeck]; Grand Rapids: Eerdmans, 1981), pp. 3-31.

19. See P.R. Jones, '1 Corinthians 15.8: Paul the Last Apostle', *TynBul* 36 (1985), pp. 3-34.

20. See Dunn, *Jesus and the Spirit*, pp. 95-114.

21. On this, see the seminal essay by K. Stendahl, 'The Apostle Paul and the Introspective Conscience of the West', in *Paul among Jews and Gentiles* (Philadelphia: Fortress Press, 1976), pp. 78-96 (also in *HTR* 56 [1963], pp. 199-215).

response to Christ did constitute a thoroughgoing conversion, for it produced a fundamental change in some of his most deeply held religious convictions.[22] Paul completely reversed his previous human judgment on Jesus (2 Cor. 5.16) and now accepted him as God's Son, Messiah and Lord. This in turn led to a radical re-evaluation of the status and meaning of the Torah, to which he had been passionately committed. It was also a conversion insofar as it set Paul in a theological direction that eventually resulted in the separation of Christianity from Judaism as a new and distinct religion.[23]

Secondly, Paul grounded his much-contested claim to be an apostle on his Damascus road experience (1 Cor. 9.1; 15.8-11) which, he insisted, placed him on a par with the apostles in Jerusalem (Gal. 1.11-17). His apostolic appointment was simultaneously a commission 'to preach [Christ] among the Gentiles' (Gal. 1.16; see also Acts 9.15),[24] a task which Paul considered to be of eschatological significance (Rom. 11.13-16; 15.15-21; Gal. 2.7-9; Eph. 3.1-13). That the rigorist young Pharisee, who had actively persecuted the Jesus movement for its blasphemies against God (1 Cor. 15.9; Gal. 1.13, 23; see also Acts 6.11-14; 9.1, 21; 26.9-11), was ready to proclaim the crucified Jesus as Lord and Messiah, and to do so among the 'lawless' Gentiles, is a measure of the extent to which individual religious experience can change the direction of a whole religious tradition.

Paul claims, thirdly, to have received his understanding of the gospel from his experience outside Damascus. 'For I want you to know, brothers and sisters, that the gospel which was preached by me is not a human gospel. For I did not receive it from a human source, nor was I taught it, but I received it through a revelation of Jesus Christ' (Gal. 1.11-12). This surely does not mean that the great themes of Paul's

22. A.F. Segal takes issue with Stendahl and insists that Paul's 'wrenching and decisive change' (p. 6) on the Damascus road *is* best spoken of as a 'conversion'. He observes that 'the central theme of Paul's autobiographical sections is the contrast between his previous life and his present one', *Paul the Convert: The Apostolate and Apostasy of Saul the Pharisee* (New Haven: Yale University Press, 1990), p. 12.

23. Tobin, *Spirituality of Paul*, pp. 43-49. See also J.D.G. Dunn, *The Parting of the Ways between Christianity and Judaism and their Significance for the Character of Christianity* (London: SCM Press, 1991).

24. See Fung, 'Revelation and Tradition', pp. 30-33. For a different estimate of the timing and significance of Paul's Gentile commission, see F. Watson, *Paul, Judaism and the Gentiles: A Sociological Approach* (SNTSMS, 56; Cambridge: Cambridge University Press, 1986).

theology were implanted directly into his brain at the moment of encounter with Christ, or dictated from heaven over subsequent days. It presumably means that the essential truths of the gospel were encompassed in the whole manner in which Christ appeared to him. The event was not a content-less experience of the Divine Other. It had a definite, undeniable christological content and a range of eschatological and soteriological corollaries that unfolded over time into the characteristic Pauline expression of the gospel. In this sense Paul's gospel was essentially an 'unpacking' of the inner logic of his personal experience of Jesus Christ on the Damascus road. But this unpacking took place in dialogue with, and in submission to the constraints of, Jewish and Christian tradition and was articulated in traditional categories. Elsewhere Paul emphasizes that his version of the gospel corresponds fully with that of primitive Christian tradition (1 Cor. 15.3-11; Gal. 1.9; 2.1-10).

The interdependence of tradition and experience is therefore central to Pauline spirituality. Plainly for Paul tradition is not an unbending norm. It may be legitimately reshaped in light of new experience. Yet that experience does not enjoy autonomy from or sovereignty over tradition. Paul sought to comprehend and to communicate his religious experience in the language and concepts of pre-existing tradition. He felt obliged to examine spiritual experience in light of the 'givens' of Jewish and Christian tradition to ensure it was compatible with the testimony of past revelation. He strove to hold the experiential and the traditional poles of revelation in creative tension. There is an important lesson in this, for it is only by sustaining such a tension that contemporary expressions of spirituality can avoid the traps of rigidity on the one hand, and total subjectivism on the other.

3. *Christ-Mysticism*

One of Paul's favourite ways for describing the present position of believers is 'in Christ' or 'in the Lord'.[25] Some form of this phrase occurs in every letter of the Pauline corpus except Titus,[26] and the same

---

25. Paul's treatment of union with Christ is distinctive but not unique. See, for example, S.S. Smalley, 'The Christ–Christian Relationship in Paul and John', in D.A. Hagner and M.J. Harris (eds.), *Pauline Studies: FS F.F. Bruce* (Exeter: Paternoster Press; Grand Rapids: Eerdmans, 1980), pp. 95-105.

26. The variant forms are: 'in Christ Jesus' (43 times), 'in the Lord' (38), 'in

idea is also present in a network of other participatory expressions Paul uses.[27] There is a whole stream of Pauline scholarship, from Adolf Deissmann[28] and Albert Schweitzer[29] to W.D. Davies[30] and E.P. Sanders,[31] that maintains that Paul's emphasis on the incorporation of the believer in Christ is the centre of Paul's theology and the heart of his spirituality. This is not the place to enter the debate over the centrality of Christ-mysticism in Paul's thought, or its relationship to the other metaphors Paul uses for the experience of salvation, in particular the legal metaphor of justification.[32] But from the point of view of spirituality two comments are worth making.

First, the word 'mysticism' is probably not the best term to capture what Paul means by union with Christ. Mysticism is a diverse phenomenon but the term is usually applied to those expressions of religious life that consciously seek the way to God through inner experience without the mediation of rational thought. Understood in this way, 'mysticism' scarcely does justice to Paul's perspective. The way to God

---

[the] Christ' (33), 'in him' (19), 'in whom' (11), 'in Christ Jesus our Lord' (5), 'in the Lord Jesus' (4), 'in the Lord Jesus Christ' (3), 'in Jesus' (1), and 'in the beloved' (1). The distribution of the formula is as follows: Romans (21), 1 Corinthians (22), 2 Corinthians (11), Galatians (34), Philippians (20), Colossians (18), 1 Thessalonians (7), 2 Thessalonians (4), Philemon (4), 1 Timothy (2), 2 Timothy (7), Titus (0).

27. See A. Schweitzer, *The Mysticism of Paul the Apostle* (trans. W. Montgomery; London: A. & C. Black, 1931), pp. 119-27; E.P. Sanders, *Paul and Palestinian Judaism* (London: SCM Press, 1977), pp. 456-63. See also M. Parsons, '"In Christ" in Paul', *Vox Evangelica* 8 (1988), pp. 25-44.

28. According to Deissmann, 'Paul's communion with Christ…[is] no small detail of his teaching, but the very centre of his religion'; A. Deissmann, *The Religion of Jesus and the Faith of Paul* (trans. W.E. Wilson; New York: George H. Doran, 1923), p. 153. See also *idem*, *St Paul: A Study in Social and Religious History* (trans. L.R.M. Strachan; London: Hodder & Stoughton, 1927).

29. For Schweitzer, '"This being-in-Christ" is the prime enigma of the Pauline teaching; once grasped it gives the clue to the whole', *Mysticism*, p. 3.

30. W.D. Davies, *Paul and Rabbinic Judaism: Some Rabbinic Elements in Pauline Theology* (London: SPCK, 4th edn, 1981), pp. 221-22.

31. Sanders, *Paul*, pp. 438-42.

32. See, for example, J. Plevnik, 'The Center of Paul's Theology', *CBQ* 51 (1989), pp. 461-78; D.N. Howell, Jr, 'The Center of Pauline Theology', *BSac* 151 (1994), pp. 61-70. See also J.C. Beker's several presentations of his 'contingency-coherence' model, for example recently in 'Recasting Pauline Theology: The Coherence-Contingency Scheme as Interpretive Model', in J.M. Bassler (ed.), *Pauline Theology* (Minneapolis: Fortress Press, 1991), I, pp. 15-24.

for him was not found through any human technique to establish relation with the Absolute, but through God's gracious initiative in the 'objective' events of the cross and resurrection of Christ. And while the apostle underwent intense religious experiences these were, as we have seen, mediated through the existing structures of his thought. Mysticism also tends to evoke the idea of individualistic, subjective experience, whereas for Paul being 'in Christ' primarily denotes an objective, communal or ecclesiological reality.[33] To be in Christ means to participate, as members of the church, Christ's body, in the benefits of his death and resurrection through baptism.[34] Paul advocates a 'spirituality of ecclesial dedication', which has been deemed his unique contribution to spirituality.[35] To speak of Pauline mysticism is, therefore, potentially misleading.[36]

But—to make the second point—this fact must not be allowed to eclipse the experiential dimension of being 'in Christ', nor the mystery or mystical reality of the relationship. Paul speaks not only of congregations being in Christ (for example Gal. 1.22; Phil. 1.1; 1 Thess. 1.1; 2.14; 2 Thess. 1.1; Col. 1.2) but also of individuals being in Christ (for example Rom. 8.1; 16.7; 2 Cor. 5.17; Phil. 3.8; Eph. 3.11-12). It is both an objective social reality and a personal subjective experience, and even the metaphors Paul uses for the social reality, such as family, body and temple, evoke a sense of intimate bonding with the Lord. Paul's very attraction for the language of indwelling is itself powerful testimony to how he experienced his own relatedness to Christ—as an intimate participation in the very being of Christ and a profound consciousness of Christ's presence in all aspects of his life, as well as in the lives of other believers. This was not a matter of impersonal absorption in the divine essence, but of a deeply personal relationship of love (see 1 Cor. 6.15-20) with One who is personal yet more than individual. It was this experience of Christ as an 'inclusive' personality, Moule suggests, that

33. So, for example, F.F. Bruce, *Paul: Apostle of the Heart Set Free* (Grand Rapids: Eerdmans, 1977), p. 138; H. Ridderbos, *Paul: An Outline of his Theology* (Grand Rapids: Eerdmans, 1975), pp. 59-60; H. Conzelmann, *An Outline of the Theology of the New Testament* (London: SCM Press, 1969), pp. 209-11.

34. See C.F.D. Moule, *The Origin of Christology* (Cambridge: Cambridge University Press, 1977), pp. 54-69.

35. H. Doohan, *Paul's Vision of the Church* (Wilmington, DE: Michael Glazier, 1989), pp. 170-93.

36. According to Sanders, the evaluation of Schweitzer's work has been afflicted by misunderstanding of what he meant by 'mysticism', *Paul*, p. 434.

led Paul 'to conceive of Christ as any theist conceives of God: personal indeed, but transcending the individual category'.[37]

For Paul, the corollary of believers being 'in' Christ is the awareness of the Spirit of Christ being 'in' believers (Rom. 8.11), both individually (1 Cor. 6.19) and corporately (1 Cor. 3.16-17). This was an experiential reality. 'And unless we understand this experience', explains Dunn, 'we will never begin to understand whole tracts of Paul's theology...'[38] We turn therefore to consider the place of the Holy Spirit in Pauline spirituality.

4. *Life in the Spirit*

Above all else, Paul is a theologian of the Spirit.[39] Not only does he refer to the Spirit through all his epistles (except Philemon), but what he says of the Spirit is so thoroughly integrated with the other features of his theology that it is impossible to treat the subject in isolation. Almost everything Paul says about new life in Christ he at some point attributes to the Spirit (see 1 Cor. 6.11). True knowledge of God, insight into divine wisdom in its profoundest sense—the essential goal of all spirituality—is only possible, Paul declares, through the impartation of God's Spirit (1 Cor. 2.6-16; see also 12.3; 14.2). So fundamental is the Spirit that A.M. Hunter once quipped, 'one might as well try to explain Paul's Christianity without the Spirit as modern civilization without electricity'.[40] I cannot hope to summarize all that Paul says about the Spirit; I will confine myself once again to a few observations pertinent to spirituality.

We have already noted the primacy of intense experience in Paul's doctrine of the Spirit. Such was the quality of that experience that the presence or absence of the Spirit in a person's (or community's) life was directly perceptible. So-called 'Christian assurance' rested not on accepting theological propositions or undergoing ritual initiation but on the manifest presence of the Spirit in one's life (Gal. 3.1-5).[41] This

---

37. Moule, *Origin of Christology*, p.95.

38. J.D.G. Dunn, 'Rediscovering the Spirit (1)', *ExpTim* 84 (1972), p. 9.

39. See now the massive study on the Spirit in Pauline theology by Fee, *God's Empowering Presence*.

40. A.M. Hunter, *The Gospel according to St Paul* (London: SCM Press, 1954), p. 108.

41. C.F.D. Moule, *The Holy Spirit* (London: Mowbrays, 1978), p. 74.

experience, Paul suggests, is proof-positive that the new age has dawned (Gal. 3.14; 2 Cor. 3.1-18; Rom. 7.6). It is the eschatological counterpart to Moses' experience of God's glory on Mount Sinai (Exod. 33–34). That immediacy of relationship with God which Moses only fitfully enjoyed has now become the permanent blessing of every believer through the gift of the Spirit (2 Cor. 3.3-13).

According to Paul, the presence of the eschatological Spirit in a person's life is manifested in a wide variety of ways. The Spirit brings insight into divine truth (1 Cor. 2.10-12; 2 Cor. 3.14-17; 4.6; Eph. 1.17; 3.5; see also Gal. 1.12, 15); liberation from the power of law, sin, and the desires of the flesh (Rom. 7.6; 8.2; Gal. 3.3-5; 5.1, 16; 2 Cor. 3.17);[42] justifying power (1 Cor. 6.11; Gal. 3.2-4, 14)[43] and moral transformation of character (1 Cor. 6.9-11; 2 Cor. 3.18; Gal. 5.16-23, see also Rom. 8.28-30; 9.1; 14.17; 2 Cor. 6.6; Gal. 6.1); filial consciousness (Rom. 8.14-17; Gal. 4.6-7) marked by an overwhelming awareness of divine love (Rom. 5.5; 15.30; see also Col. 1.8), joy (Rom. 14.17; 15.13; 1 Thess. 1.6; see also Gal. 5.22), and acceptance by God (Eph. 1.17-18); and charismatic capacities of various kinds (1 Cor. 1.4-7; 2.4-5; 12–14; Gal. 3.5; Rom. 1.11; 15.19). The Spirit is, in particular, the Spirit of power, enabling believers to accomplish things beyond their natural abilities (1 Cor. 2.4-5; 2 Cor. 12.12; Rom. 1.4; 14.17; 15.13; 1 Thess. 1.5; Eph. 2.18; 3.5, 16; see also 2 Tim. 1.7). Pauline ethics is predicated upon the availability of this power (Rom. 8.2-3). It is not so much that Christians live by entirely different standards of conduct as that they live by a new and different power that enables them to put into practice those standards of conduct which even pagan wisdom recognized to be virtuous.[44]

This does not mean that the accomplishment of the Spirit's work in the world is an easy or instantaneous thing. The powerful activity of the Spirit is evidence the eschaton has dawned, but Paul recognizes that the future age has still not come in its fullness. Indeed it is a key role of the Spirit to sustain the tension between salvation already realized in the present yet still to be consummated in the future. The Spirit does this in both a positive and a negative way. Positively the Spirit grants believers an experiential foretaste of the blessedness of the coming age that keeps

---

42. See J.D.G. Dunn, *Christian Liberty: A New Testament Perspective* (Carlisle: Paternoster Press, 1993), pp. 53-77.

43. See also S.K. Williams, 'Justification and the Spirit in Galatians', *JSNT* 29 (1987), pp. 91-100.

44. Tobin, *Spirituality of Paul*, pp. 102, 117.

alive their hope of the future (Rom. 8.16-17, 23; 2 Cor. 1.22; 5.5; Eph. 1.13-14). Negatively the Spirit—as the Spirit of the Crucified One— makes believers conscious of the incompleteness of redemption, and ever sensitive to the sufferings of creation (Rom. 8.12-17). As Schweizer puts it, 'the Spirit bestows on the Christian community a solidarity with the suffering creation and makes them able to hear clearly that God has a purpose for it too'.[45]

The Spirit is that power, then, which begins the process of eschatological renewal and will carry it through to completion (2 Cor. 3.18; 2 Thess. 2.13; see also Rom. 8.28; Gal. 6.8; Phil. 1.16; Eph. 3.16-17). This process is not a matter of gradual, steady improvement over time but of a constant struggle between 'flesh' and 'Spirit' (Rom. 8.3-17; Gal. 5.13-26), between the forces and values of the old age and the power of the new age, a battle which, because of human weakness, is also played out in the internal lives of believers, though the sufficiency of the Spirit to live obediently in the present age is always stressed by Paul.[46]

This brings us to a highly significant facet of Pauline spirituality: because Christian existence is lived in the context of the 'already/not yet' of salvation, paradox and conflict are inevitable aspects of the spiritual pilgrimage. Even though the passage most often cited to substantiate this point, Rom. 7.14-25, is, in my opinion, a description of life outside Christ,[47] Paul makes it abundantly clear elsewhere that

45. E. Schweizer, 'On Distinguishing Between Spirits', *Ecumenical Revue* 41 (1989), pp. 408-409.

46. Fee insists that Paul portrays the struggle between Flesh and Spirit in eschatological rather than anthropological terms (i.e., as an opposition between two aeons; not as a continuous, internal struggle in the believer's heart); *God's Empowering Presence*, pp. 816-26. Of course, insofar as believers remain vulnerable to temptation to return to the values of the old age, as Pauline paraenesis shows, an internal struggle is present at least by implication.

47. The literature on Rom. 7.14-24 is vast. The main issues at stake are whether Paul's use of the personal pronoun 'I' is autobiographical or rhetorical, and whether the shift from the past to the present tense in vv. 14-25 is intended to denote present Christian experience or to add vividness and immediacy to what is still the plight of Paul's non-Christian Jewish contemporaries. In my view, while the passage is not strictly autobiographical, Paul's own experience is still reflected in the account (see also G. Theissen, *Psychological Aspects of Pauline Theology* [trans. J.P. Galvin; Philadelphia: Fortress Press, 1987], pp. 177-265); and Paul intends to depict life under the law as opposed to life in Christ (see also W. Russell, 'Insights from Postmodernism's Emphasis on Interpretive Communities in the Interpretation of

Christian life is a life in tension (for example, Rom. 6.12-23; 8.22-27; Gal. 5.16-26). Believers may be freed from the moral defeat of Romans 7; but they are freed precisely in order to join battle with sin and the flesh, as Romans 6 and 8 stress. Intense struggle in one's spiritual journey is not therefore a cause for alarm; it is the mark of a healthy spiritual experience, and evidence that the Spirit is engaged in shaping our character, a character which is still affected by the realities of the old age.

Among the actions of the Spirit that Paul accepts and values are non-rational or ecstatic phenomena. By this I mean forms of speech and behaviour that express an awareness of being constrained or compelled by a power beyond oneself.[48] Recent scholarship has rediscovered the importance of this dimension in early Christianity, at the same time as numerous believers have discovered it through renewal movements like the Charismatic Movement. Paul himself experienced visions (2 Cor. 12.6-9), worked miracles (Rom. 15.18), and spoke in tongues (1 Cor. 14.18). It is striking that when he was confronted in Corinth by an uncontrolled passion for ecstatic experiences resulting in chaos, Paul did not respond by forbidding or devaluing such phenomena (1 Cor. 14.39). Instead he affirmed the private, devotional value of even such a troublesome gift as tongues-speaking (14.2, 18, 28), while seeking to ensure that effective controls were in force in the public display of charismatic phenomena.

These controls involved, on the one hand, practical advice for the orderly conduct of worship services, such as taking stock of the various ministries that existed in the congregation (1 Cor. 12.1-31); linking together counter-balancing gifts, like glossolalia and interpretation (12.10, 30; 14.13, 27-28), prophecy and discernment (12.10; 14.29); encouraging people to exercise gifts one at a time while others keep silent (14.29-31); forbidding disruptive behaviour from women (if 14.33b-35 is Pauline);[49] and reminding those of ecstatic disposition that 'the spirits of prophets are subject to the prophets' (14.32). Such advice was aimed at

Romans 7', *JETS* 37.4 [1994], pp. 511-27). Yet Romans 6 and 8 make it clear enough that Christian experience still entails struggle against the temptation to walk 'according to the flesh'.

48. For a helpful 'rehabilitation' of ecstasy, see J.D.G. Dunn, 'Rediscovering the Spirit (2)', *ExpTim* 94 (1982), p. 9.

49. On the textual status of this unit, see G.D. Fee, *The First Epistle to the Corinthians* (Grand Rapids: Eerdmans, 1987), pp. 699-708. See also R.W. Allison, 'Let Women be Silent in the Churches (1 Cor. 14.33b-36): What did Paul Really Say and What Does it Mean?', *JSNT* 32 (1988), pp. 27-60.

eliminating confusion and inculcating mutual respect and interdependence in the community.

On the other hand, Paul strongly encouraged the congregation to exercise critical discernment of spiritual phenomena in the assembly (1 Cor. 12.3; 14.29, 38; see also 2.12-14; 1 Thess. 5.19-22; 2 Thess. 2.2). According to 1 Cor. 12.10, distinguishing or differentiating between the Spirit of God and other spirits is itself a gift of the Holy Spirit. But there are important yardsticks the Spirit uses in the task of discernment.[50] One crucial yardstick is, once again, conformity to received tradition. If a spiritual manifestation is of God, it will confess dependence on the lordship of the crucified Christ (1 Cor. 12.3; see also 8.6; Gal. 1.6-9; Rom. 10.9; 2 Cor. 11.4).[51] Another essential yardstick is the impact of spiritual manifestations on the gathered community. Paul explains in 1 Corinthians 13 that extravagant manifestations of spirituality which do not promote love are wholly without value. It is not enough for a charisma to be a manifestation of divine energy or spiritual insight; it must also be an act of loving service to God's people. Accordingly throughout 1 Corinthians 14 Paul employs the ethical concept of 'edification' as a criterion of spiritual discernment.[52] Whether a spiritual activity appears outwardly impressive or completely unpretentious is entirely irrelevant. The key question is whether it benefits the whole congregation (14.1-5, 12, 17, 24). It is right to 'earnestly desire spiritual things' (14.1), but only so long as one also 'strives to excel in them for building up the church' (14.12).

What this system of controls amounts to is a recognition by Paul that all spiritual manifestations and disciplines are inherently ambiguous. Ecstatic phenomena are also attested in non-Christian religions, both in antiquity and today, and within the biblical tradition may be associated with false prophets as well as true (Mk 13.6, 22-23 par.; 1 Cor. 12.2; 2 Cor. 12.11-12). Even within the Christian community, spiritual phenomena may operate in a sub-Christian way. Dunn suggests that when

50. See also Dunn, 'Rediscovering the Spirit, 2', pp. 13-14; *Jesus and the Spirit*, pp. 293-97.

51. 'Among the many spirits that buffeted man (1 Cor. 2.12; 12.10; 2 Cor. 11.4), among the many forces that pressed upon him and shaped his consciousness, the Spirit of God identified itself by causing people to become dependent on the crucified Jesus as their Lord'; L. Goppelt, *Theology of the New Testament* (Grand Rapids: Eerdmans, 1982), II, p. 122.

52. See also G.R. O'Day, 'The Ethical Shape of Pauline Spirituality', *Brethren Life and Thought* 32 (1987), p. 86.

Paul wants to mark off his own religious experience or that of his
converts from a less-than-Christian spirituality, it is essentially the 'Jesus-
character' of Christian experience he seizes upon (Rom. 8.14-17;
Gal. 4.6; 1 Cor. 4.15-16; 11.1; 12.3; 2 Cor. 3.18; Phil. 2.5-11; 3.12-17;
1 Thess. 1.6).[53] Only that power which reproduces the imprint of Jesus
Christ in its recipients is to be recognized as the power of God.

Now if the moral character of Jesus is the distinguishing mark of the
Spirit of God, the distinguishing mark of the character of Jesus is, above
all else, the way of the cross. True spirituality, for Paul, is a spirituality of
the cross.

5. *Spirituality of the Cross*

I have commented already on the role that 'power' plays in Paul's
understanding of the spiritual life. God is 'eternal power' (Rom. 1.20)
and Christ is 'the power of God and wisdom of God' revealed to the
world (1 Cor. 1.18-25). The gospel is 'the power of God unto salvation'
(Rom. 1.16; 1 Cor. 1.18) and Paul is willing to count all as loss for the
privilege of knowing Christ 'and the power of his resurrection' (Phil.
3.10-11). The consummation of salvation is when Christ returns in power
to subjugate his enemies and complete his dominion (1 Cor. 15.20-28;
1 Thess. 4.16-18).

Paul's understanding of the character of divine power underwent a
radical transformation as a result of his Christian experience. That God
accomplished the salvation of the world through the ignominy and
'defeat' of the cross indicated to Paul that God is most powerful at the
nadir of human weakness (1 Cor. 1.18-25).[54] Paul accordingly resolved,
'I will all the more gladly boast of my weaknesses that the power of
Christ may rest upon me' (2 Cor. 12.9-10; see also 1 Cor. 2.1-5). Paul
came to prize highly his experience of weakness, hardship, suffering and

---

53. Dunn, *Jesus and the Spirit*, pp. 254, 324-25. The extent and nature of Paul's
knowledge of the Jesus-tradition has been much debated. For an excellent survey,
see J.M.G. Barclay, 'Jesus and Paul', in Hawthorne and Martin (eds.), *Dictionary of
Paul and his Letters*, pp. 492-503. Two recent studies, M. Thompson, *Clothed with
Christ: The Example and Teaching of Jesus in Romans 12.1–15.13* (JSNTSup, 59;
Sheffield: JSOT Press, 1991), and D. Wenham, *Paul: Follower of Jesus or
Founder of Christianity?* (Grand Rapids: Eerdmans, 1995), argue for substantial
continuity between Paul and the Jesus-tradition.

54. For a brief survey of Paul's weakness motif, see D.A. Black, 'Paulus
Infirmus: The Pauline Concept of Weakness', *GTJ* 5 (1984), pp. 77-94.

decay (see for example Rom. 5.3; 1 Cor. 4.8-13; 2 Cor. 1.5-7; 2.14-15; 4.7-12; 6.3-10; 11.23–12.10). Whereas the Corinthian pneumatics saw weakness and suffering as signifying the absence of the Spirit of Power, Paul saw them as the necessary context for the operation of life-giving power (2 Cor. 12.1-5). Why? Because transformation into the image of Christ, which is the Spirit's pre-eminent task (2 Cor. 3.17-18), entails conformity to the suffering and death of Christ, as well as to his risen life and power.

Paul's understanding of this matter stems, once again, from the interaction of personal experience and received tradition, in this case the kerygma of Christ crucified (1 Cor. 1.18; 2.2; 15.3-4). His frequent references to suffering are not armchair reflections: they are attempts, at least in part, to make sense out of painful experience—both his own and those of other believers. Yet his theology of suffering is more than the product of rational reflection on personal hardship. It stems primarily from an experiential awareness of 'mystical' inclusion in the sufferings of Jesus attested in the kerygma. Paul was so conscious of the presence of the crucified Christ in the midst of his own persecution and affliction, he was so aware of the sustaining power of the risen Lord as his own strength gave out, that he came to understand Christian suffering as a participation in the very passion and resurrection of Jesus himself (2 Cor. 4.7–5.5; 13.3-4; Rom. 6.3-14; Phil. 3.10).

This is not simply a matter of the believer's sufferings resembling those of Christ, as an imitation of them.[55] Rather they are an integral part or extension of Christ's own sufferings (see Col. 1.24). In some places Paul speaks of the believer's participation in the death of Jesus as a decisive event in the past (Rom. 6.2-4; Gal. 2.19a; Col. 2.11-14, 20; 3.3). But elsewhere he makes it clear that the 'dying' of conversion is only the beginning of an ongoing process of Christ's death working itself out existentially in the Christian's daily experience, so much so that Paul can speak of 'always carrying about in the body the death of Jesus' (2 Cor. 4.10; see Gal. 2.19-20; 6.14; Rom. 6.5). If this is so then, in a real sense, the sufferings of Christ himself continue on. As a saving act, the death of Christ is a finished event of the historical past. But insofar as the work of salvation is still not complete—for the old age lingers on—Christ continues to suffer. He suffers in, with and through his people, who find that their personal suffering is somehow comprehended by his.

---

55. Paul does sometimes speak in this way (for example, 1 Thess. 1.6), but elsewhere his thought runs deeper.

This notion that in their own sufferings believers 'share abundantly in Christ's sufferings' (2 Cor. 1.5) is one of the most profound elements of Paul's theology. Its implication for spirituality is plain: endurance of suffering is an inevitable part of a Christian's spiritual growth.[56] To know Christ is to know his power in the midst of weakness, life in the midst of death. They are simultaneous experiences. Suffering is not a temporary precondition for the infusion of transcendent power. The risen, cosmic Christ is also the crucified earthly Jesus, and any spirituality that bears his name must be conditioned by both dimensions of Christ's experience. According to Phil. 3.7-11, Paul's deepest spiritual yearning was to know Christ's resurrection power manifested in and through sustained fellowship in Christ's sufferings. Pauline spirituality is a spirituality of the cross.

6. The Role of Prayer

No study of spirituality would be complete without reference to prayer. This is particularly true of Pauline spirituality, for 'to live as a Christian was to Paul to live a life of prayer'.[57] His letters not only exhort readers to prayer and thanksgiving but contain accounts of his own prayers and are punctuated with spontaneous outbursts of praise (for example, 2 Cor. 11.31; Gal. 1.5; Rom. 1.25; 9.5; 11.33-36). Paul understood prayer as a natural expression of his relationship with God, and also a natural expression of the relationship between believers. Paul was constantly praying for his own converts, invariably asking for their continual growth as Spirit-people (Phil. 1.3-11; 1 Thess. 3.9-10; 2 Thess. 1.11-12; 2 Cor. 13.7-9; see also 2 Tim. 1.3, 4), and ever seeking their prayers for himself and specifically for his ministry in the gospel (2 Cor. 1.11; Phil. 1.19-20; Rom. 15.30-32; 2 Thess. 3.1-2; Phlm. 22; 2 Thess. 3.2; Eph. 6.18-20; Col. 4.2-4).

Several characteristics of Paul's prayer life emerge from his epistles. He prayed unceasingly and exhorted others to do likewise (Rom. 1.9, 10; 12.12; 1 Cor. 1.4; 1 Thess. 1.2-3; 2.13; 5.17; 2 Thess. 1.3, 11, 12; 2.13-15; Phil. 1.3-5; Eph. 1.15, 16; Col. 1.3, 9). 'For Paul, praying is like

---

56. M. Scott Peck insists that 'legitimate suffering' is essential to all personal and spiritual growth; *The Road Less Traveled* (New York: Simon & Schuster, 1978).

57. R.E. Speer, *Studies of the Man Paul* (London: Partridge & Company, n.d.), p. 279.

breathing. It cannot be interrupted without mortal danger.'[58] His prayers are saturated with expressions of gratitude to God, more often for people than for things or events (Rom. 1.8; 7.25; 1 Cor. 1.4; Phil. 1.3-5; 1 Thess. 1.2; 2.13; 2 Thess. 1.3, 4; 2.13; Eph. 1.16; Col. 1.3-5) and he enjoined his readers to be similarly thankful (Phil. 4.6; Eph. 5.4; Col. 2.7; 4.2; see also 1 Tim. 2.1). 'Thanksgiving—gratitude experienced and expressed—is the "heartbeat" of Pauline spirituality.'[59] Paul also prayed with great intensity and often experienced an overflowing of love and joy (Rom. 10.1; Phil. 1.4; Phlm. 4-7; 1 Thess. 3.9-10; Col. 4.12; see also 2 Tim. 1.3, 4). He speaks of 'groaning' in prayer, just as the Holy Spirit groans utterances on our behalf (2 Cor. 5.2-4; Rom. 8.26). Paul regarded nothing as beyond the scope of prayer. He prayed for the salvation of all Israel (Rom. 10.1), for the enlargement of his missionary work (Rom. 1.10; 1 Thess. 3.10), for the consummation of bodily redemption (2 Cor. 5.1-4), and for insight into God's ultimate plan for the universe (Eph. 1.15-23; 3.14-21; Col. 1.9-23). Having made his prayer he was content to accept the will of God (2 Cor. 12.8-10).

7. Conclusion

To conclude I will draw together some of the threads of our exploration of Pauline spirituality.

1. Paul's letters provide us with unparalleled insight into the emergence of Christian spirituality at its earliest stages, and Paul's own personality and religious experiences were major influences moulding the spiritual devotion of the young church. The term 'spirituality' belongs distinctively to Paul's theological vocabulary.

2. Spirituality is concerned with the whole of life. It is not one aspect of the wider experience of reality but underlies and penetrates one's entire life in the world. The spiritual Christian is one who lives his or her life in this world under the direction of the Holy Spirit.

3. Paul's spirituality is marked by an interaction between personal religious experience and the normative traditions of the

---

58. H.J.M. Nouwen, *Clowning in Rome: Reflections on Solitude, Celibacy, Prayer and Contemplation* (Garden City, NY: Image Books, 1979), p. 61.

59. Meye, 'Spirituality', p. 915.

community of faith. The watershed in Paul's religious pilgrimage and theological development was the Damascus road
event. He sought to understand and articulate this experience in
light of Jewish and Christian tradition, yet allowed that experience also to shape and change tradition.

4. Paul's spirituality is marked by an ability to hold in creative
    tension contrasting elements of experience, such as power and
    weakness, life and death, freedom and community, present and
    future, and so on. Paradox lies at the heart of Pauline spiri-
    tuality.[60]

5. One of Paul's favourite ways of characterizing Christian spiri-
    tual experience is to speak of believers being 'in Christ'. This
    phrase denotes a 'mystical' reality. This is not experienced as
    an impersonal absorption in the Divine Other, however, but as
    a personal relationship with the risen Christ mediated by the
    Holy Spirit.

6. Spirituality is in essence the experience of the Holy Spirit.
    Christ's saving work becomes an experienced reality through
    the gift of the Spirit. It is the Spirit that brings an immediacy of
    relationship with God and assures the believer of truly
    belonging to God. The Spirit's presence in the life of the
    believer is directly perceptible through such things as spiritual
    insight, filial consciousness, liberty, moral change and
    empowerment to live in obedience to God. Dreams, visions,
    prophecies, tongues, miracles and so on are also, as far as Paul
    is concerned, a natural part of Christian spirituality. But
    charismatic phenomena are inherently equivocal. It is only
    insofar as they manifest the love and moral character of Christ
    and strengthen the community that they are distinctively
    Christian or spiritually beneficial.

7. The Spirit's role is to initiate and supervise a lifelong process of
    spiritual renewal in the believer. This process or pilgrimage
    takes place in the context of an intense battle between the rival
    powers of the old age and of the new. This means that conflict
    and struggle are inevitable, and healthy, signs of spirituality.

8. Pauline spirituality always bears the stamp of the cross.
    Spiritual growth is a matter of suffering and death as much as
    it is a matter of life and renewal. Weakness and suffering are

60. Tobin, *Spirituality*, p. 16.

the necessary context for the experience of transforming power. More than that, Christian suffering is the means by which Christ himself continues to suffer with the world. True spirituality is to know the fellowship of Christ's sufferings *in order that* we might know the power of his resurrection (Phil. 3.10-11).

9.   The medium of spiritual growth is prayer. Paul's life was drenched in prayer, as the ubiquitous references to prayer in his epistles indicate. Prayer is the natural expression of the believer's relatedness to God in the Spirit, while intercessory prayer is the natural expression of relationship between believers. Permeating both are expressions of gratitude to God. As an expression of creaturely humility and dependence, gratitude is the primary mark of a healthy spirituality.

Our study of Pauline spirituality has been largely descriptive. Far more important than describing Paul's reflections on the spiritual life is of course sharing in its reality. That reality, for Paul, is, above all else, a consciousness of the person and presence of Christ, who embodies the graciousness of God.[61] Paul's awareness of Christ was so all-encompassing, 'the unique, global qualification of his entire life',[62] that whether he lived or died was inconsequential to him, for both life and death were subsumed in the experiential reality of knowing Christ. 'For me to live is Christ and to die is gain' (Phil. 1.21). This is the bottom line of Pauline spirituality and of Christian ministry.

---

61. Dunn, *Jesus and the Spirit*, p. 340.
62. T.F. Dailey, 'To Live or Die: Paul's Eschatological Dilemma in Philippians 1.19-26', *Int* 44 (1990), p. 23.

MINISTRY AND CHURCH LEADERSHIP IN THE GOSPEL OF JOHN

Ruth B. Edwards

Introduction

The Fourth Gospel's attitude to church leadership is something of an enigma. On the one hand, John seems in many ways to be the least ecclesiastical of all the Gospels. The word *ecclēsia*, 'congregation' or 'church', never appears; the term *apostolos*—so frequently associated by theologians with the beginnings of an ordained ministry—occurs only once. Unlike the Synoptics, John never lists the Twelve, and only rarely mentions them as a group. In his account of Jesus' active ministry he never describes them preaching, teaching, healing, or exorcizing. His favourite term for those closest to Jesus is *mathētai*, literally 'learners'. A key note in this Gospel is 'witness' (*marturia*), seemingly borne by women and men alike in delightful informality. The emphasis here is on individual faith, obedience and love, and on the role of the Spirit. It is no wonder that this Gospel has been seen as one of free, charismatic individualism.[1]

On the other hand, John's Gospel also contains passages which have been interpreted as sanctioning a highly authoritative view of the church's ministry. Chapters 13–17 are seen as showing the apostles' preparation for their future role as church leaders, and certain parts of chs. 20 and 21 are understood as formally commissioning a male apostolic band, who were to be the fountainhead of a hierarchical, ordained ministry with the power to forgive or to retain sins, and clearly

---

1. See, for example, E. Schweizer, *Church Order in the New Testament* (trans. F. Clarke; London: SCM Press, 1961), pp. 127-28; J.D.G. Dunn, *Unity and Diversity in the New Testament* (London: SCM Press, 1977), pp. 118-19, 131; G. Burge, *The Anointed Community: The Holy Spirit in the Johannine Tradition* (Grand Rapids: Eerdmans, 1987).

distinguished from the ordinary members of the church. Those who take this view often point out that there were no women present at these commissionings, and that women's ministry in John is hence informal and private, rather than public and officially authorized.[2]

A reconsideration of these issues seems opportune at the present time, when old hierarchical patterns of ministry are being challenged and new collaborative models are emerging. It is also of special relevance to current controversies arising from the ordination of women as ministers of Word and Sacrament and, in the Anglican communion, as bishops, priests and deacons. But before we embark on our study, we need to outline a few basic principles that may guide our methodology.

It is not the purpose of any of the Gospels to describe the organization of the early church. However, all four Evangelists, consciously or unconsciously, reveal details about the Christian communities in which they lived. Great care needs to be exercised in using this as evidence for early church organization and ministry, and we must guard against assuming that John and his contemporaries were already engaged in ecclesiastical and theological controversies that belong to later times. In what follows I shall take it for granted that John's Gospel is the result of a long literary process and profound theological reflection. Whether or not the author used the other Gospels among his sources, he shows familiarity with many of the traditions lying behind them, and he may also have had access to independent oral or written sources. Certain parts seem likely to have been added to the original work at a later stage, but any attempt to disentangle the different strands in what is now a stylistically homogeneous writing, and to identify them with different ecclesiastical situations, would be perilous indeed. I therefore propose to approach the Gospel as a whole, and will seek to read it with fresh eyes to see what can be learnt about its author's attitudes to ministry and to Christian leadership.

---

2. For example, the Vatican Declaration *Inter Insigniores* (1976), esp. §2; J. Galot, *Theology of the Priesthood* (trans. R. Balducelli; San Francisco: Ignatius Press, 1985), esp. pp. 255-60; P. Toon, *Let Women be Women* (Leominster: Gracewing, 1990), p. 73. For a detailed attempt to root a hierarchical understanding of ministry in the New Testament see K.E. Kirk (ed.), *The Apostolic Ministry* (London: Hodder & Stoughton, 1946), esp. p. 108 and p. 125 for comments on John.

1. *The Disciples and Jesus*

A striking feature about the Fourth Gospel is its emphasis on discipleship. Those who were to emerge as community leaders—Peter, the Twelve, and others close to Jesus—appear here as *learners*. The different ways in which the Evangelist refers to them—as 'disciples' (*mathētai*), 'little children', 'friends', 'brothers', and, indirectly, as 'servants'—all emphasize their subordination to Jesus or their community with him, but not their role as teachers, missionaries or leaders.[3] This humble role, as learners in a community of love, is further brought out by the verbs of following, hearing, remembering and obeying which are associated with them. This fits in with the high Christology of this Gospel, in which Jesus is not only Teacher and Prophet, but also King, 'Son', pre-existent Word, Revealer of Truth, and in perfect unity with the Father, whom he uniquely represents. John seems deliberately to avoid expressions which might foster the idea of the disciples as authoritative leaders, especially the term 'apostle'.[4] This image of potential church leaders as learners has important implications for our study, since the disciples in John's Gospel stand not just for church *leaders*, but even more so for church *members*. As our study progresses we shall find increasingly that their primary role is to be the nucleus of the future ecclesial community as a whole, rather than merely its leadership.

It is widely recognized that the Gospel of John falls into two parts. The first, chs. 1–12, is concerned with Jesus' public ministry, and is sometimes called 'the Book of Signs' (so Dodd and Brown), because it focuses on Jesus' miracles which are themselves seen as signs (*sēmeia*) that reveal his divine sonship and messiahship. These chapters also

---

3. *mathētēs* occurs 74 times in John of Jesus' disciples (44 times in Mark; 37 times in Luke; 69 times in Matthew; 29 times in Acts, including once in the feminine). 'Little children' occurs twice in John (*teknia*, 13.33; *paidia*, 21.5); 'friends' (*philoi*) also twice (15.14, 15); 'brothers' (*adelphoi*) once (20.17). Jesus never directly calls his followers 'servants', but note the use of *diakonos* in 12.26, *doulos* in 13.16 and 15.20, and *hupēretai* in 18.36.

4. *apostolos* occurs only at 13.16 in the general sense of 'envoy': see C.C. Black, 'Christian Ministry in Johannine Perspective', *Int* 28 (1986), p. 34. Here John is close to both Mark and Matthew (each once); contrast Luke–Acts and Paul (each 34 times). See further C.K. Barrett, *The Signs of an Apostle* (London: Epworth Press, 1970), with H.K. Rengstorf, *TDNT*, I, *s.v.*, and D. Müller, *NIDNTT*, I, *s.v.*

include a series of dramatic dialogues with individuals (for example, with Nicodemus), and with 'the Jews', a term used collectively for the Jewish leaders. The second part of the Gospel, chs. 13–21, deals with Jesus' passion, death and resurrection. This is sometimes called 'the Book of Glory' (so Brown and Quast), because of its distinctive Johannine insight that the whole of Jesus' suffering and exaltation is a process of glorification. In 'the Book of Glory' Jesus seems to change his relationship with the disciples. This part of the Gospel is believed by many to rest on different sources from the earlier part.[5] It will, therefore, be helpful in our discussion to begin by treating these two parts of the Gospel separately. We consider first the role of the disciples during Jesus' public ministry in 'the Book of Signs'.

2. *The Disciples in 'the Book of Signs' (John 1–12)*

The Disciples as Those Called by Jesus (1.18-51)

John's account of the disciples' calling contains some distinctive features. The first disciples, we are told, were originally followers of John the Baptist. They take the initiative in deciding to follow Jesus, and seek out further companions to be with him. This contrasts quite sharply with the Synoptic pattern of an authoritative summons by Jesus to pairs or individuals to leave their normal occupations and follow him, and seems closer to the rabbinic model whereby a pupil seeks out his master. Jesus is called 'rabbi' more frequently in this Gospel than in any other.[6] This, too, serves to emphasize the disciples' role as pupils.

But although at first sight the disciples appear to be taking the initiative, we soon realize that John sees these events as part of the divine plan: Jesus makes it clear that it is God who has entrusted him with the disciples and he, in fact, chose them (see 15.16; 17.12). The calls described in ch. 1 are therefore only 'sample' calls. Interestingly, they do not lead to a prompt sending-out in active ministry (in contrast to the Synoptics). John firmly places the sending after Jesus' resurrection in ch. 20, though there are hints that he knew traditions of an earlier mission (see, for example, 4.38).

---

5.   For a discussion of John's sources see B. Lindars, *John* (NTG; Sheffield: JSOT Press, 1990), pp. 31-36.

6.   John uses *rabbi/rabbouni* nine times of Jesus; contrast Matthew twice; Mark four times; Luke none.

Even in ch. 1, however, the disciples already function as witnesses: every person called gives some kind of testimony about Jesus (for instance, as 'Messiah', 'King of Israel', 'Son of God'). Historically, such affirmations are improbable at this stage (contrast again the Synoptic pattern, where the disciples only gradually come to realize who Jesus is). Even John the Baptist acts as a spokesman for the Christian church (1.29). In all this we have to recognize John's literary art and theological purpose. He wants his readers to know Jesus' identity from the start. But the christological confessions also fit in with the central function of the disciples as witnesses.

The Disciples as Companions of Jesus
Throughout the Gospel the disciples regularly appear as companions of Jesus. They are mentioned in association with him at the wedding at Cana (2.2), at Capernaum (2.12), in Jerusalem when he cleanses the Temple (2.17), in Judaea (3.22), in Samaria (4.8, etc.), in Galilee at the feeding miracle (6.3-13), in Jerusalem at the healing of the man born blind (9.1), at the raising of Lazarus (11.7), at the anointing at Bethany, and at the triumphal entry (12.4, 16). In Samaria they baptize with Jesus (an activity never hinted at in the Synoptics), and at the feeding miracle they gather up the fragments. At the climax of Jesus' active ministry, in ch. 12, Philip and Andrew bring some Greeks to Jesus. We note especially the motifs of service and mission. With hindsight we might see in these activities models for the church's future ministry, but the theme is not explicit, and we are never told precisely on what basis they do these things. There are also occasions when the disciples are not mentioned. This does not mean that the Evangelist does not picture them as present, but he is focusing on different issues.

The disciples constantly listen to Jesus' teaching, but they do not always understand it. In John, just as in the Synoptics (especially Mark), we find the repeated motif of their slowness of comprehension. In ch. 4 they cannot fathom why Jesus should be talking to a woman (4.27); they do not understand when he says, 'I have food to eat of which you know nothing' (4.31-34). They cannot comprehend why he should wish to return to Jerusalem when the Jews are threatening to stone him (11.8). They misunderstand when he says that Lazarus is 'asleep' (11.12). Some grumble and fall away after his teaching about the bread of heaven (6.66-67). In all this they might seem poor examples for imitation, whether by Christian believers or church leaders. But we have to bear in mind that, first, historically the disciples were 'only human', and the Evangelists may be faithfully recording their failings; and that, secondly, John regularly makes use of the literary device of an ambiguous saying by Jesus, which is misunderstod by his listener(s) and later clarified by him. Several of the examples listed above may fall into this category.

Faithful Disciples as Witnesses

Anthony Harvey has drawn attention to the importance of the theme of 'witness' in the Gospel of John.[7] It is as if Jesus is on trial for his divine sonship, and the various characters are appearing as witnesses, prominent among whom are the faithful disciples. This includes both those who appear among the Twelve in the Synoptic tradition— Andrew, Peter, Philip and Thomas—and those who do not. In some cases it is not clear whether or not an individual is pictured as among the Twelve (for instance, Nathanael and the so-called Beloved Disciple).[8] We find disciples, named and unnamed, fulfilling the function of faithful witness in Jerusalem, in Samaria and in Galilee—sometimes travelling round with Jesus, more often remaining in their own homes. Prominent among those who are not members of the Twelve are the blind man in Jerusalem, the woman of Samaria, the officer whose son was cured, Martha, and Mary Magdalene. All of these make some kind of profession of faith. The blind man who was healed responds to Jesus' question, 'Have you faith in the Son of Man?', with the words 'Lord, I believe', and he falls on his knees before him in worship (9.38).[9] The Samaritan woman is more hesitant, expressing her faith in a question, 'Could this be the Messiah?' (4.29), but the Evangelist tells us that 'many believe' because of her word. In spite of the limited validity of a woman's legal testimony at this time, the Evangelist expressly describes her as 'witnessing' (*marturein*) to Jesus (4.39). The official in 4.46-53

7.   A. E. Harvey, *Jesus on Trial* (London: SPCK, 1976); see also A. Trites, *The New Testament Concept of Witness* (Cambridge: Cambridge University Press, 1977), pp. 78-124.

8.   The evidence for identifying Nathaniel with Bartholomew is very slight; the Beloved Disciple was probably not one of the Twelve: see O. Cullmann, *The Johannine Circle* (London: SCM Press, 1975), pp. 71-85; both Schnackenburg and Brown have retracted their earlier views that this figure is to be identified with the apostle John.

9.   'The Jews' spoke more truly than they realized when they abused him with the words 'You are that man's disciple' (9.28).

has such faith in Jesus that he trusts his child will be healed without Jesus even coming to his house: the climax of this episode is his 'believing' (*pisteuein*) together with all his household.[10]

The little family at Bethany, near Jerusalem, should also be mentioned here. John expressly says that Jesus 'loved' Martha, Mary and Lazarus (11.5), and refers to Lazarus as 'his friend' (11.11). In Christian usage this term implies discipleship.[11] One can hardly doubt that Lazarus's two sisters were also disciples in a real sense of the term. We note especially Martha's confession of faith: 'I believe that you are the Messiah, the Son of God, who was to come into the world' (11.27). This closely rivals Peter's confession in 6.69 for its insight (and yet how much more frequently do we see Peter's cited and commemorated in the church!). Mary, too, symbolically displays her faith in her prophetic anointing of Jesus, and when she is criticized, Jesus affirms her action, connecting it with his burial (12.1-8). The other women from Galilee form a special category. We do not know whether John pictured them as regularly travelling around with Jesus, since he lacks the note given in Lk. 8.1-3 about their ministry, but he does make it clear that they had followed Jesus from Galilee to Jerusalem on his last visit, and were present at the cross. They, and Jesus' mother, surely also feature here as faithful witnesses[12] (we shall return to the women below).

The evidence so far reviewed suggests that during Jesus' 'active' ministry the disciples functioned chiefly as companions of Jesus, as learners and as witnesses. While being imperfect in understanding, these figures—which include women as well as men—are Christian models or exemplars. There is little to suggest that they were thought of as church leaders: rather, they seem to serve as examples to all future believers. But this is not the whole picture: there are signs that the Fourth Evangelist saw a significant turning point in Jesus' ministry, and this evidence must now be considered.

10. We may note the similarities with stories of conversions in Acts.

11. C.K. Barrett, *The Gospel according to St John* (Philadelphia: Westminster Press, 2nd edn, 1978), p. 392.

12. For Mary as a disciple see R.E. Brown, *The Community of the Beloved Disciple* (New York: Paulist Press, 1979), pp. 192-97; F.J. Moloney, *Woman: First among the Faithful* (London: Dartman, Longman & Todd, 1984), pp. 87-92.

3. *The 'Coming of Jesus' Hour' and 'the Book of Glory' (John 13–19)*

At several points in the earlier part of his Gospel, John refers to the coming of Jesus' hour, but says it is 'not yet' (see 2.4; 7.30; 8.20). In ch. 12 the Gospel reaches a watershed: Jesus says, 'The hour has come for the Son of Man to be glorified' (12.23), and he speaks of the turmoil that is in his soul. In the following chapters we find Jesus in 'the circle of his own' (the phrase is Schnackenburg's), and we are conscious that he is preparing them for his imminent 'departure' (death, resurrection and return to God). But is he also 'grooming' the disciples here as future church leaders? The narrative falls into four parts.

The Footwashing

Chapter 13 both introduces and interprets Jesus' hour. It demonstrates Jesus' love for the disciples, and teaches them an essential lesson—the need for humility and love. At a more subtle level, it also shows them the absolute necessity for unity with their master. These lessons are brought home by a vivid 'acted parable'. Footwashing was usually carried out by the most menial of servants—Gentile slaves or women. It was also sometimes done, as an act of great devotion, by rabbinic pupils for their teachers. But now, at his last meal with them, Jesus performs this humble task for his pupils, and makes the lesson explicit: 'If I, your Lord and Teacher, have washed your feet, you ought also to wash one another's feet. I have set you an example: you are to do as I have done for you' (13.14-15).[13]

The parallel between Jesus and the disciples is further brought home by a pair of proverbial sayings: 'A servant is not greater than his master, nor a messenger (*apostolos*) than the one who sent him' (13.15). We should note the implication here that the disciples are being sent, an idea which is strengthened by the following aphorism that those who receive anyone whom Jesus sends receive him, and those who receive him receive the one that sent him (13.20). Both sayings demonstrate the paradox that the disciples are, at the same time, both totally subordinate

---

13. On the foot washing see esp. J.A.T. Robinson, 'The Significance of the Foot-Washing', in *Twelve More New Testament Studies* (London: SCM Press, 1984), pp. 77-80 (originally published in *Neotestamentica et Patristica: FS Oscar Cullmann* [Leiden: Brill, 1962], pp. 144-47), comparing Mk 10.45; also J.C. Thomas, *Footwashing in John 13 and the Johannine Community* (JSNTSup, 61; Sheffield: JSOT Press, 1991).

to Jesus (as a slave to a master) and to be identified with him. Lest we get this out of proportion, it is worth remembering that in the Synoptics Jesus also taught that whoever receives a child receives him, and whoever shows kindness to the least of his 'brothers' in need shows it to him (Mk 9.7; Mt. 24.45).

Many scholars believe that in the footwashing there is also a veiled allusion to Jesus humbling himself in death—a fate voluntarily undertaken on behalf of those he loves (see Jn 10.11, 15).[14] Such an understanding helps to make sense of the episode when Peter at first refuses to have his feet washed and Jesus says, 'If I do not wash you, you have no part with me' (13.8). Being washed by Jesus means accepting his sacrifice, becoming part of him, and being prepared to follow his path of total dedication, even unto death.

This chapter also links discipleship with showing love. Jesus says: 'I give you a new commandment: love one another; as I have loved you, so you are to love one another. If there is this love among you, then everyone will know that you are my disciples' (13.34). We observe here the grounding of the disciples' love for one another in Jesus' own love, and the results of it—that people will know by their love that they are truly disciples. One could hardly have a clearer statement than this that love and service are essential qualifications for discipleship. The implications for future church leaders are plain, but the teaching applies equally to all believers.

The Supper Discourses
Following this episode are two discourses (chs. 14 and 15–16), which may originally have belonged to different editions of the Gospel. Their themes are essentially the same. Each prepares the disciples for Jesus' departure. Jesus reassures them that he is going to prepare a place for them, and that he will come to them again. He also promises that he will send 'the Paraclete', or Spirit of Truth, to teach them everything and to remind them of what he has told them (14.26; 16.13). An important function of the disciples after the resurrection will be to remember what Jesus has taught them (see 2.17, 22; 12.16; 13.7). Just as the Paraclete bears witness to Jesus, so too will the disciples, because they have been with Jesus from the first (15.27; see also Acts 1.8). The Spirit will take

14. I have developed this theme in 'The Christological Basis of the Johannine Footwashing', in J.B. Green and M. Turner (eds.), *Jesus of Nazareth: Lord and Christ* (Grand Rapids: Eerdmans; Carlisle: Paternoster Press, 1994), pp. 367-83.

Jesus' place as their teacher and thus the disciples will continue to be learners as well as witnesses. Jesus also warns the disciples that they must suffer for his sake (16.1-4), but promises them that whoever has faith will do even greater works than his (14.12). These verses look forward to future mission, and the 'greater' works may well include the idea of miracles.

The second discourse features the allegory of the vine. Its chief function is to bring out the essential unity between Jesus and true believers—they are as much a part of him as branches are of a vine. Those that dwell in Jesus will bear fruit, if they remain united with him. Amazing promises are made: 'If you dwell in me, and my words dwell in you, ask whatever you want, and you shall have it...You are to bear fruit in plenty and so be my disciples'. The reference to 'fruit' may well imply suffering. We may compare 12.24-25, where Jesus says that if a grain of wheat falls into the ground and dies, it will bring forth fruit.[15]

Both discourses reiterate the need for love and obedience, and the concept is enriched by the thought that there can be no greater love than laying down one's life for one's friends (15.11-17). It is at this point that Jesus says, 'You are my friends, if you do what I command you. I no longer call you servants [*douloi*, literally 'slaves'], but friends'. Some have seen here a change in status in the disciples, in contrast to Jesus' allusion to them as 'slaves' in 13.16. The point, however, is not that they have suddenly become Jesus' equals. Friendship, which was much prized in the ancient world, need not imply precise reciprocity. One could be a 'friend' of a king, and still be his subject. The emphasis is, rather, on the fact that they share the truth which Jesus has brought from God, as the continuation makes plain: 'I have called you friends, because I have disclosed to you everything that I heard from my Father'. They are Jesus' friends because of their knowledge of his teaching. The discourse ends with the disciples' making a communal profession of faith: 'We are now certain that you know everything, and do not need to be asked; because of this we believe that you have come from God' (16.30).

---

15. There has been some debate as to whom Jesus intends by his references in this discourse. The solemn language of 'choosing' and 'appointing' in 15.16 might suggest that he has singled out the disciples for leadership. But the continuation makes it clear that Jesus has chosen them out of 'the world', which hates them, as it has hated him (15.18-21). The contrast is between the disciples and the hostile world, not between the disciples and other Christians. This also fits in with the more general application of the similar saying in 12.25.

Jesus' Prayer of Consecration

The whole of ch. 17 is taken up with Jesus' farewell prayer, often known as 'the high-priestly prayer', in which he consecrates himself, and intercedes both for the disciples and for future believers. There are many literary parallels to this in the 'testaments' or final charges of other great leaders. The prayer moves through three phases to a conclusion: (1) Jesus announces again that his 'hour' has come, and prays to the Father to 'glorify' him. He has accomplished what the Father gave him to do (vv. 1-5). (2) He prays for those whom he has taught, that they may be one, as Jesus and the Father are one: for their sake he consecrates himself, so that they too may be consecrated by the truth (vv. 6-19). And (3) he prays for all who believe through them (vv. 20-23). He then sums up the results of his own ministry: the world has not known God, but those whom God has given him know that God sent him. Jesus has made God known and will continue to do so, so that the love with which God loved Jesus may be in them and he in them (vv. 24-26).

Several features in this prayer are important to questions of ministry and church leadership: the perception that God gave the disciples to Jesus; the stress on Jesus teaching them what he learned from God, their knowledge of this, and their obedience to it; the negative attitude to 'the world'; the fact that Jesus prays for *the consecration* of the disciples in precisely the same language as he prays for his own consecration; Jesus' reference to the disciples' *mission*; and his prayer that those who believe through them may be perfectly one, through a mutual indwelling with him.

In all this is John referring to the future church as an organization? There can be little doubt that he does envisage a *community*.[16] But whether he is talking about an organizational unity, as is often supposed by those who quote Jesus' prayer as an ecumenical rallying-call, is more doubtful. Rather, the author envisages a unity of purpose in those engaged in Christian mission and witness. It is possible that the text presupposes divisions among Christians at the time of the Gospel's composition, but it is speculative to seek references to any known

---

16. See R.E. Brown, *The Gospel according to John* (2 vols.; Garden City, NY: Doubleday, 1966, 1970), II, pp. 773-79, comparing the concept of 'oneness' (*yahad*) at Qumran. On the church in John see further A. Corell, *Consummatum Est: Eschatology and Church in the Gospel of St John* (London: SPCK, 1958), ch. 2; and R. Schnackenburg, *The Gospel according to St John* (trans. D. Smith and G.A. Kon; 3 vols.; New York: Crossroad, 1982), III, pp. 203-17.

divisions.[17] Perhaps we may sum up here by saying that there is a general reference to the church, but no specific reference to its organization or government.

And what of the disciples? It is almost impossible here to distinguish between their role as future church leaders and their role as models for all who would follow Jesus. Nothing is said of them that could not be applied to all believers and, as we saw earlier, the primary distinction is between the disciples as believers and 'the world', not between the disciples as leaders and the rest of the faithful. One passage might seem to contradict this, that is, when Jesus speaks of the 'consecration' of the disciples (vv. 17-18). The word *hagiazein* used here means placing in the realm of the holy (compare the Hebrew *qdš*), and it can involve the notions of both sacrifice and sanctification. In the Hebrew Bible the verb from this root is associated with both prophetic and priestly ministry.[18] Yet it is very doubtful whether we should argue from this basis that here the disciples are consecrated in a way that other Christians are not. The Johannine account of the cleansing of the Temple implies the idea of the church as Jesus' body (1.19, 21), and other New Testament writers affirm the concept of the company of believers as a consecrated, priestly people (for example, 1 Pet . 2.9; see also Rom. 6.3-5).

As for 'succession', the word *diadochos*, used so often by the Church Fathers for bishops as the apostles' successors, does not appear in John's narrative. This term is never used of Christians in the New Testament (and even in the LXX it is very rare). The true successor of Jesus in the supper discourses is the Paraclete, whom Jesus sends only when he has returned to the Father. It is the Paraclete who takes what belongs to Jesus and declares it to his continuing disciples, leading them into all truth. Thus the Paraclete is the teacher *par excellence*, and the true successor of Jesus.

Yet there is a sense in which Jesus' disciples are also his successors, at least for the interim period between Jesus' departure and his final return.[19] They have been told that they will do even greater works than Jesus; that they will be hated as he was hated; that whatever they ask in prayer will be granted; and, in ch. 20, that the sins they pronounce

17. For a hypothetical reconstruction of divisions in the Johannine church, see Brown, *Community*.

18. See, for example, Exod. 28.41; Jer. 1.5; compare also Sir. 45.4.

19. See D.B. Woll, *Johannine Christianity in Conflict* (Chico, CA: Scholars Press, 1981), esp. p. 127.

forgiven are forgiven. But are these functions granted them as future leaders of an organized church, or merely as faithful believers? To answer this we need to look in more detail at the crucial passages in chs. 20 and 21. First, however, we must briefly consider the role of the disciples in the narrative of the passion itself.

The Passion

In chs. 18–19 the tone changes. There is a move from the more reflective style of the supper discourses and prayer, back to a taut narrative. It is probable that John is using different sources from those of the discourses—sources closer to those of the Synoptic tradition, but with distinctive features. The role of the disciples is again instructive. Once again they appear as companions of Jesus, going with him to the garden (18.1). At the arrest Peter attempts to defend Jesus with his sword, and is rebuked. This is a lively example of Peter's mistaken impetuosity and loyalty, and has parallels in incidents described in the Synoptics. John lacks Mark's poignant reference to the disciples all forsaking their master and fleeing (Mk 14.50), but he shows Jesus' concern for their safety, as he says: 'I am the man you want; let these others go' (Jn 18.8). One recalls Jesus' earlier words: 'I warn you...you are to be scattered, each to his own home, leaving me alone' (16.32; see also Mk 14.27). But the scattering is not total: Peter and 'another disciple' (almost certainly the Beloved Disciple) follow Jesus to the high priest's house, where Peter is to deny Jesus three times.

In the account of the crucifixion (19.17-30) we hear nothing of any male disciple, except the Beloved Disciple. But John singles out for special mention four women who stand near the cross: Mary the mother of Jesus, his mother's sister, Mary wife of Clopas, and Mary Magdalene (v. 5). The women at the cross and the tomb are also a persistent feature of the Synoptic tradition (Mark tells us that they had followed Jesus from Galilee and ministered to him).[20]

4. *Jesus' Return, and Commission to 'Those God has Given Him'*

Chapter 20 begins a new phase in the role of the disciples. At the arrest of Jesus they dispersed, though we have noted the presence of the women and the Beloved Disciple at the cross. Now Jesus returns to both

---

20. Mk 15.40-41, where the verbs (*akolouthein* and *diakonein*) imply discipleship; see Mt. 27.55; Lk. 8.1-3, 23-49.

his male and female disciples, and actively commissions them in a series
of three resurrection appearances.

The Resurrection Appearances of Chapter 20

The first appearance occurs at the tomb. Two distinct elements are
interwoven in the narrative: the story of Peter and the Beloved Disciple
(vv. 2-9), and Jesus' encounter with Mary Magdalene (vv. 1-2, 10-18). A
salient feature of the first episode is the witness of both Peter and the
Beloved Disciple to the empty tomb, and the faith of the latter who 'sees
and believes', even though he has not yet encountered the risen Jesus.
The moving story of Jesus' meeting with Mary needs no retelling. We
note how she recognizes Jesus as he calls her by name (recalling Jesus'
earlier words about the good shepherd and his sheep: see 10.3-16). She
acknowledges him as 'Teacher' (*Rabbouni*, a variant form of Rabbi).
Jesus gives her a message to go to his 'brothers'[21] and tell them that he
is ascending to 'his God and theirs'. Mary goes off immediately to give
Jesus' message to the disciples, boldly proclaiming 'I have seen the
Lord' (20.18). We may contrast this with the apparent reticence of the
two male disciples, who simply return to their own homes (20.10), and
with the silence of the women in Mark (16.8). There can be no doubt
that in this important narrative a woman functions as a witness of the
resurrection—indeed a primary witness, since she actually sees Jesus,
whereas Peter and the Beloved Disciple do not: possibly John is counter-
balancing here an early tradition that Jesus appeared first to Peter (see
1 Cor. 15.5).

The Appearance on Easter Evening (20.19-23)

Later that day Jesus appears to 'the disciples'. We are not told precisely
who is present. The narrative is close to that of Lk. 24.33-49, which
mentions as present 'the eleven and their companions' (possibly
including some women), but we should not necessarily presume the
presence of the same group in John. Jesus gives the group a greeting of
peace, and one is reminded of his words in the supper discourse (14.27)
where peace was described as his parting gift to them. He then utters the
words of commission: 'As the Father has sent me, so I send you.' He
breathes on them, and gives them the authority to forgive or to retain
sins. At last we have Jesus' authoritative commission to the disciples to

---

21. 'Brothers' in Greek may be used of men and women together, or of men
alone. It is clear that disciples are intended here, not Jesus' biological family.

carry on his work. The lines of the narrative are simple and stark, compared with the parallel commissionings in Matthew (28.16-20) and Luke (24.44-49): Jesus simply 'sends', gives the Spirit, and assigns the authority to forgive. We now examine these critical acts in more detail:

1. The 'sending': we are not told what the disciples are being sent to do. Yet the 'sending' is totally authoritative, being paralleled by Jesus' own sending: 'As the Father has sent me, so I send you.'[22]

2. The 'insufflation': Jesus breathes into (the verb used is *emphusan*) those present and says, 'Receive (the) Holy Spirit'.[23] There has been much debate about the nature of this prophetic symbolism. Some have suggested that it marks an ordination rite (for instance, Lohse), but there is no evidence that breathing on or into people formed part of the ceremony of either Jewish or early Christian ordination.[24] Others have seen the breathing of the Spirit as a sign of new creation, possibly marking the disciples' 'baptism in the Holy Spirit', or the beginning of the church.[25] But it is doubtful if these ideas exhaust the symbolism. If— as seems highly probable—the 'insufflation' (v. 22) is to be linked with what follows (v. 23), as well as with what precedes (v. 21), then it must symbolize an empowering of the disciples for the work they have to do. Is this the giving of the Paraclete promised in the supper discourses? Moreover, how does it relate to the gift of the Spirit at Pentecost, described in ch. 2 of Acts?

Some have argued that there were two differentiated gifts of the Spirit; one on Easter Day and one at Pentecost.[26] Others have suggested that Jn 20.22 refers only to a *promise* of the Spirit.[27] The most plausible hypothesis proposed, however, is that Jn 20.21-23 is the Johannine

---

22. There is no distinction in meaning between the two Greek words used here (*pempein* and *apostellein*).

23. There is no definite article with 'Spirit' in the Greek.

24. See A. Ehrhardt, 'Jewish and Christian Ordination', *JEH* 5 (1954), pp. 125-38, with criticisms of Lohse.

25. See the commentaries of E.C. Hoskyns (*The Fourth Gospel* [ed. F.N. Davey; London: Faber & Faber, 1947]) and Lindars (*John*), *ad loc.*; also J.D.G. Dunn, *Baptism in the Holy Spirit* (London: SCM Press, 1970), pp. 177-78.

26. See M.M.B. Turner, 'The Concept of Receiving the Spirit in John's Gospel', *Vox Evangelica* 10 (1976), pp. 24-42.

27. See D.A. Carson, *The Gospel according to John* (Grand Rapids: Eerdmans, 1991), pp. 649-55, arguing, improbably, that *emphusan* means merely 'exhale', rather then 'breathe into'.

equivalent of Pentecost, when Jesus imparts the actual gift of the Paraclete who has been promised earlier (so Dodd and Brown).[28]

3. The command to declare the forgiveness of sins: only one specific commission is given—to let go (*aphienai*) and to hold back (*kratein*) sins: 'Whose soever sins ye forgive, they are forgiven unto them; whose soever sins ye retain, they are retained' (20.23, AV). The saying is paralleled at two different points in Matthew: the first is when Jesus gives Peter authority 'to bind' and 'to loose' on earth (Mt. 16.19), and the second when he gives similar authority to a wider group of disciples when dealing with a 'brother' who has sinned (Mt. 18.18). It is likely that all three versions go back to the same original saying, probably based itself on Isa. 22.22.[29] Two opposing interpretations have been argued in the past for John's meaning here: (1) that the passage refers to the forgiveness (or retention) of post-baptismal sins in the sacrament of 'penance'; or (2) that it refers to the preaching of the gospel. Both these interpretations, however, are unsatisfactory.

The first view is traditional in Roman Catholicism. The Council of Trent declared:

> If anyone say that these words of the Saviour...are not to be understood of the power of remitting and retaining sins in the sacrament of Penance, as the Catholic Church has from the beginning understood, but shall twist their meaning so as to apply them to the authority of preaching the Gospel, and not to the institution of this sacrament, let him be anathema.

This interpretation has been defended by some modern scholars,[30] but it is open to the strong objection that it reads back into the text ideas of priesthood and church discipline which did not exist at the time Jesus spoke, or John wrote. Increasingly, both Anglican and Roman Catholic interpreters (such as Brown and Schnackenburg) are recognizing that it is anachronistic to suppose that John thought in terms of an institutionalized sacrament of penance or reconciliation (to use the modern term).

The second interpretation, namely, that this passage refers to the preaching of the gospel, was argued by a number of Reformers (hence

---

28. C.H. Dodd, *The Interpretation of the Fourth Gospel* (Cambridge: Cambridge University Press, 1953), p. 430; Brown, *Gospel according to John*, pp. 1037-39.

29. See R.B. Edwards, *The Case for Women's Ministry* (London: SPCK, 1989), pp. 77-78.

30. For example P. Niewalda, *Sakramentssymbolik im Johannesevangelium?* (Limburg: Lahn, 1958), pp. 6-7; for Trent, see Hoskyns, *The Fourth Gospel*, p. 545.

the polemical tone of the Council of Trent), and in recent times has been defended as at least part of the meaning by many Protestant and Evangelical interpreters. But this view is open to the objection that it involves reading into John the purposes of the commissions found in the other Gospels, especially that of Matthew.

A growing number of scholars, therefore, now argue that the commission is both to preach and to declare the forgiveness of sins (whether pre- or post-baptismal), but that the authority to do this is being given, *not to a special priestly class, but to the church or Christian community as a whole.* They rest their case on strong contextual arguments. Those who receive the Spirit in this passage are simply called 'the disciples'; they are not described as a limited, specific group (such as 'the apostles' or 'the Twelve'). Moreover, the Gospel of John shows no interest elsewhere in the concept of a priestly class, but it does frequently use the disciples to represent faithful believers, i.e., the future church *in nuce*. The whole Johannine Gospel is about making a decision of faith, which leads either to eternal life, or to loss and exclusion from God's presence. Preaching and baptizing, though not explicitly mentioned, may be inferred from the 'sending' of 20.21 and the gift of the Spirit-Paraclete, who will aid the disciples in witness and mission. Thus, R. Hanson concludes: 'When in John 20 Jesus breathes upon the disciples...and confers on them the power of forgiving or retaining sins, this power is conferred on the whole church, not upon the ministry as such.' H. von Campenhausen similarly affirms: 'It is the Church as a whole in which this great power is vested.'[31]

The Appearance a Week Later (20.24-29)
This is a peculiarly Johannine tradition, which follows somewhat uneasily after the appearance on Easter evening, when the absence of Thomas was not noted. Like the appearance to Mary Magdalene it has much of the character of a personal encounter, this time in the context of an appearance to the disciples in general. It is remarkable for Thomas's confession of faith: 'My Lord and my God', and Jesus' blessing on all

---

31. H. von Campenhausen, *Ecclesiastical Authority and Spiritual Power in the Church of the First Three Centuries* (trans. J.A. Baker; London: A. & C. Black, 1969), p. 128; see also R. Hanson, *Christian Priesthood Examined* (London: Lutterworth Press, 1979), p. 10. G.R. Beasley-Murray, similarly, writes of 20.21-23, 'All three sentences have to do with the whole church' (*John* [Waco, TX: Word Books, 1987], p. 381).

who may find faith without seeing him. Thus, Thomas's acknowledgment of Jesus' lordship, without actually verifying his identity by
touching his wounds, is clearly intended as a model for future believers,
and not specifically for church leaders.

The Appearance by the Lake (21.1-14)

Chapter 21 describes a further resurrection appearance of Jesus to seven
disciples, and focuses on the future fate of two of them. It is generally
acknowledged that the section comprises an afterthought or appendix to
the main narrative, as is indicated by the fresh start after 20.30-31, the
second conclusion (21.25), and numerous details of style and content.
Some scholars (such as Barrett) believe that this 'appendix' is by the
main author, but was added some time after the main composition.
More probably, the whole chapter is an editorial addition by a member
of the Johannine school who had stronger ecclesiastical interests than the
author of the main Gospel (so Schnackenburg).

The first part of the narrative (vv. 1-14) vividly tells of the disciples'
unsuccessful fishing through the night, and the miraculous draft of fish.
The detail of the number of fish caught, together with the symbolism of
fishing elsewhere (for example, Mk 1.17), has led many commentators
to see here an acted parable of mission, while the untorn net (contrast
Lk. 5.6) may be a symbol of the unity of the church (so Hoskyns and
Schnackenburg). Some have also argued that the invitation of Jesus to
breakfast reflects the Eucharist (so Cullmann). If this is so, it is worth
noting that the whole emphasis is on Jesus' role as the gracious host.
Once again, there is no hint of any special role for the disciples as priests
or church leaders.

The Commissioning of Peter (21.15-19)

After breakfast Jesus three times asks Peter whether he loves him. Three
times Peter protests his love, and three times Jesus bids him feed/tend his
lambs/sheep.[32] Most commentators rightly see in this scene a
'rehabilitation' of Peter after his threefold denial of Jesus (18.12-27). But
it is more than this. In language reminiscent of Jesus' image of himself as
the Good Shepherd (10.11), Peter is given an explicit pastoral
commission to care for Jesus' flock. The flock, of course, still belongs to
Jesus, as Augustine and others have noted.

---

32. Two different Greek words are used for love, feeding/tending and
sheep/lambs, but the variations do not appear to be significant.

This passage has also been the subject of much ecclesiastical controversy. The first time that Jesus asks Peter the question he does so in the form, 'Do you love me more than these [i.e. the other disciples]?', and Peter replies 'Yes'. Many commentators, including some early Fathers, have suggested that Peter is here being given a primacy over the other apostles. Thomas Aquinas even supposed that the passage referred to three grades of Christians under the guise of the sheep and lambs, over all of whom Peter was given supremacy. Cornelius a Lapide claimed that 'Christ here designates his Vicar upon earth and creates Peter Supreme Pontiff'. The First Vatican Council of 1870 similarly explained that here 'Peter the apostle was constituted by Christ the Lord as chief of all the apostles and as visible head of the Church on earth'.[33]

Since the Second Vatican Council, Roman Catholic commentators have had greater freedom in handling this text. While not repudiating the claims of the Papacy, scholars such as Brown and Schnackenburg have distinguished the original intention of the text from its later use in the church. They now agree with many Protestant commentators that the primary concern of the text is not Peter's superiority over other disciples—still less any succession of Supreme Pastors in his stead—but Peter's restoration in Jesus' love, and his commission to care for his Lord's flock. Such a view is supported by the application in the New Testament of the shepherding image to other church leaders besides Peter.[34] It is further pointed out that the only 'qualification' required of Peter is love.

Yet one cannot help feeling that Peter has been singled out here in a special way. Of no other member of the Twelve is such a personal commission recorded. Hence, those scholars are probably right who link this passage with the special commission in Mt. 16.16-19, where Peter is given 'the power of the keys'. But the terms of Jesus' commission are very different in the two passages, the language in John being much less juridical or legal in tone than Matthew's. A closer comparison is perhaps that with the personal commission in Lk. 22.32, when Jesus predicts Satan's testing of the disciples and Peter's threefold denial, and says to Peter, 'When you are restored, give strength to your brothers'. In neither John nor Luke is there any reference to binding authority:

33. Details are given in the commentaries by Hoskyns, Brown and Schnackenburg, *ad loc.*
34. For example, Eph. 4.11; Acts 20.28; 1 Pet. 5.2.

rather, the commission is to care for those who are already believers, Jesus' own 'sheep', who are Peter's brothers (and sisters).[35]

The commission to Peter is followed by an oblique prediction of his future (Jn 21.18-19), which may come from a separate fragment of tradition. While the details of the imagery are obscure to us, in the present context it seems to refer to Peter's future death by crucifixion. It reveals the obvious outcome of Peter's total dedication in discipleship, and picks up Jesus' words at the last supper, when he told Peter that he could not follow him now, but he would later (13.36-38). Thus Peter is assigned the role of martyr as well as pastor. Both roles are part of his discipleship, as is shown by Jesus' concluding words (21.19; compare 22), 'Follow me'. The words are the same as were used in the Synoptic calls of the first disciples, and of Philip in Jn 1.43. They poignantly remind us of Jesus' basic teaching: 'If any would become my followers, let them deny themselves, take up their cross and follow me' (Mk 8.34, NRSV). This summons to follow applies not just to Peter, but to all Christians.

But why should Peter be given such prominence in this final chapter? The other Gospels are content to recount his denials without an explicit restoration. The answer must lie in Peter's subsequent role in the church and his relationship to the Beloved Disciple, to which we now turn.

The Witness of the Beloved Disciple (21.20-24)

After the prediction of his death, Peter turns round and sees 'the disciple whom Jesus loved' following, and asks, 'Lord what about him?' Jesus replies, 'If it should be my will that he stay till I come, what is that to you?' The author explains that after this a saying went around that that disciple would never die, although Jesus had not actually said this. Even those scholars (such as Bultmann) who believe that the Beloved Disciple represents an ideal figure, now recognize that here he must stand for a real person—a leader of the Johannine community. This material must have been included to explain his recent death, which seemed to contradict a specific prediction by Jesus. The passage also guarantees the truth of this disciple's witness (see 19.35), and seems to understand him as the

---

35. On 'Petrine' texts and ministry see R.E. Brown, K.P. Donfried and J. Reumann (eds.), *Peter in the New Testament* (New York: Paulist Press, 1973); *Anglican–Roman Catholic International Commission: The Final Report, Windsor, September 1982* (London: SPCK/Catholic Truth Society, 1982), pp. 64-67; and J.F. O'Grady, *Disciples and Leaders* (New York: Paulist Press, 1991), pp. 114-25.

author of the Gospel: 'This is the disciple who is testifying to these things and has written them, and we know that his testimony is true' (v. 24, NRSV). Most scholars therefore agree that an important function of 21.15-24 must be to set the ministries of Peter and the Beloved Disciple into a relationship with one another.

One theory is that the Johannine Christians, who formed a distinct group somewhat separate from the main church, wished to defend the status and credibility of their leader over against Peter, who was the representative of the 'apostolic' or 'great church' (so Brown). This could help to explain why the role of the Twelve is so small in this Gospel, and perhaps even why the title 'apostle' is so rigorously avoided. Others suggest that the appendix in ch. 21 was added for precisely the opposite purpose—to redress a balance and to correct a tendency in the Johannine community towards sectarianism. On this view, the purpose of ch. 21 is to reinforce Peter's role as leader of the 'apostolic' Christians over against exaggerated claims which had been made for the Beloved Disciple (so Quast[36]).

Both these theories are speculative. We do not even know whether 'Peter' here represents the Jerusalem church (whose leadership was taken over by James long before this Gospel was written), the church at Rome, or some other Christian centre. Moreover, Peter was probably dead by this time. It would, in any case, be ironic if the Gospel that seems so little concerned with hierarchy and status should end on a note concerned with rank.

A more attractive theory is that outlined by C.K. Barrett and others that we have here two models of leadership—Peter, the martyr-pastor, and the Beloved Disciple, the witness. They are equally important: both serve as models for church leaders, and both as models for all Christians. For, as Barrett has stressed in a published sermon,

> All are in the positive, fundamental sense ministers, and the shape and basis of the ministry they acquire by being Christians are before us. Every Christian has a responsibility to his fellow-Christians...each has a duty to the rest: 'Feed my sheep'. And each bears witness to the truth that has created him. He does this, not by writing gospels, not by preaching sermons, but by being what the Word has made him.[37]

36. K. Quast, *Peter and the Beloved Disciple* (JSNTSup, 32; Sheffield: JSOT Press, 1989).
37. C.K. Barrett, *Essays on John* (Philadelphia: Westminster Press, 1982), pp. 166-67.

With an adjustment of the pronouns to include the feminine, it would be hard to find a better summing up of John's message on Christian ministry than this.

Conclusions

At the start of this essay I spoke of the 'enigma' of John's Gospel, which seemed to support two very different ideals of ministry. It is now clear that its emphasis is not on church leadership, but on *discipleship*, and any conclusions about church leadership must be deduced from this more fundamental teaching.

The first lesson to be drawn is that throughout the Gospel, even after the resurrection, the disciples are *learners*. They are the pupils and Jesus is the rabbi or authoritative teacher. Their task is to listen to him, to obey his commands, and 'to follow' him, even if this leads to death. Any Christian leader, consequently, must aspire to the same role, and must always remain at heart a learner. Moreover, those who would follow Jesus must be called by him and remain in unity with him. As the footwashing so vividly demonstrates, this means being prepared to serve others, even in the humblest of roles. John's Gospel places a special emphasis on love and service, in which all Christians are commanded to imitate their master. This applies as much to church leaders as to other members of the community. John never suggests that Jesus' followers should resemble him in his role as King and Judge (contrast Mt. 19.28; Lk. 22.30), but rather in his love, service and self-sacrifice.

A notable feature of this Gospel is its account of how, towards the end of his earthly life, Jesus prepared the disciples for his departure (chs. 13–17). But even here there is no hint of them as his successors in office. Jesus' successor as teacher is the Paraclete, who continues to teach and to guide Jesus' followers. A further requirement, then, for all who aspire to the Johannine pattern of discipleship, must be openness to the Spirit. This means receiving newness of life by being 'born' of the Spirit (3.3-5), worshipping God in Spirit and truth (4.23), and accepting the Spirit's guidance and teaching (14.25; 16.13). It is striking that John, in contrast to the Synoptics, describes no sending out of the disciples in mission until after they have been empowered for this work by Jesus' parting gift of the Spirit. There are strong reasons for believing that Jesus' breathing into the disciples on the evening of Easter Day (20.22) is the

Johannine equivalent of Pentecost. This is their authoritative commissioning, and it applies to the followers of Jesus collectively, not just to their would-be leaders.

The Easter gift of the Spirit also marks the birth of the church, for although John never uses the word *ecclēsia* in the Gospel,[38] he does have a strong sense of the fellowship of Jesus' disciples. The Good Shepherd discourse, with its reference to 'the one flock' (10.1-18), the allegory of the vine (15.1-11), and Jesus' great prayer for the unity of the disciples and all who will believe through their witness (ch. 17), all point to the fact that believers do not work as individuals, but as part of a community. This community is separated from 'the world'. Yet all its members are called to witness to the world that Jesus is God's Son and its Saviour, Messiah, King, and Judge, sent by God to demonstrate God's love for all humanity. No distinction is made between the witness of women and men, or between that of itinerant followers and those who remain in their homes.

Thus the Gospel of John gives no support to those who would argue that clergy are to be hierarchically distinguished from laity. When Jesus said 'If you ask the Father for anything in my name, he will give it to you' (16.23; see also Mk 11.24-25; Mt. 21.22), he made no such distinction. Many other places in the New Testament bid Christians to pray for others, even for the forgiveness of their sins (1 Jn 5.16; Jas 5.16). Passages such as Jn 20.20-23, which have sometimes been interpreted as giving clergy but not laity the power or authority to forgive sins, are more plausibly interpreted as referring to the church as a whole. It may be that, for reasons of order, certain denominations choose to restrict to clergy (or to certain classes of clergy) the privilege of declaring sins forgiven; but this practice cannot be rooted in the teaching of the Gospel itself, and must remain a matter of internal church discipline. Has the time now come for some of our churches to review their practice here?[39]

---

38. It lies outside the scope of this essay to treat ministry in the Johannine Epistles, where the word *ecclēsia* appears three times (3 Jn 6, 9, 10). Although these writings relate closely to the Johannine Gospel, there are differences in theological emphasis and style, in the underlying church situation, and in attitudes to church leadership. For these reasons they have not been used to interpret the Gospel. See further J. Lieu, *The Theology of the Johannine Epistles* (Cambridge: Cambridge University Press, 1991), ch. 3.

39. I have in mind in particular situations where lay leaders (or deacons) are exercising a pastoral ministry to congregations or individuals.

As for the role of women, the Gospel of John gives no support to those who would exclude them from ministry, containing as it does shining examples of their witness (for example the woman of Samaria, Martha and Mary Magdalene). Nor should the absence of women from the Twelve be pressed as justifying their restriction to an informal or private ministry. The Twelve play only a minor role in this Gospel, and no distinctions of rank or ontology are made between them and Jesus' wider circle of friends in Jerusalem and elsewhere. Both groups bear witness in confessions of faith, and it is often hard to tell whether or not certain individuals are to be numbered among the Twelve.

At the same time it is important to note that this Gospel also provides no explicit authority *for* women's ordination to ecclesial office. This is not because the author is against women's ordained ministry, but because he is simply not thinking in terms of the categories 'lay' and 'ordained'. He provides equally little support for *male* ordained ministry. There is indeed only one place in the Gospel where an individual is charged with a pastoral ministry, and that is the special commission to Peter to feed Jesus' sheep (21.15-18). As we have seen, this occurs in an appendix to the Gospel, and may well have been added to meet specific needs in the Johannine community. But, even here, the emphasis is on love for Jesus and care for fellow Christians, and not on authority to be exercised over them. Moreover, Peter's role as martyr-pastor is carefully balanced by that of the Beloved Disciple as witness. Any attempt to equate Peter's commission with the institution of the Papacy, or to see John 20–21 as justifying a special role for the episcopate as the 'essential' ministry of the church, is to go well beyond the author's intentions.

Here we meet a recurrent problem. Christians of later ages are naturally eager to search the New Testament for guidance about how ministry should be practised. But they do not always realize the limitations of its evidence. The biblical writers were not seeking to offer guidance—far less lay down a blueprint—for future Christian ministry. They were writing in particular historical contexts to meet particular needs. Hence, we cannot extrapolate rules from them. They knew many different patterns of ministry—some quite charismatic and informal, others more structured. In the Patristic period the threefold pattern of (male) bishops, priests and deacons became established. But side by side with this there were, at least for a time, other ministries—those of prophets, teachers, widows, virgins, women deacons, and so on. Since the Reformation, patterns of ministry have diversified, but usually a clear-cut distinction has been maintained between lay and ordained ministries. Today, however, in societies where laity are often as well educated as clergy, this distinction is becoming blurred, with a wide variety of ministries emerging—stipendiary and non-stipendiary, formal and informal. Some people are suspicious of these changes, and wish to hark back to the old patterns of an authoritative 'ordained' class, responsible for teaching and exercising discipline over fellow members in the body of Christ. I suspect, however, that eventually this pattern will disappear.

Certainly, the church will always need leaders. The New Testament teaches that not all people have the same gifts, and not all Christians are called to the same functions within the body of Christ (see 1 Cor. 12). There are dangers in charismatic, individualistic ministries as well as in rigid, hierarchical ones. All of us, therefore, under the guidance of the Spirit, need continually to renew our patterns of ministry, measuring them by the standards of love and service set in the New Testament, and making sure that they are fit to meet the needs of each fresh situation. And in this ongoing task, the distinctive perspectives of John's Gospel will continue to play a vital part.

MINISTRY IN MATTHEAN CHRISTIANITY

Graham N. Stanton

I am delighted to have been asked to contribute to this volume of essays
in honour of Bishop Penelope Jamieson. Although I have not met her
personally, I have a special interest in her ministry as Bishop of Dunedin.
I was brought up in Dunedin in the Salvation Army and I recall vividly
from the 1950s the ministry of several outstanding women who far
outshone their husbands as preachers and as pastors. Ever since those
formative years I have valued the ministry of women. In due course I
received my theological training in Dunedin for the ministry of the
Presbyterian Church of New Zealand. At that time Presbyterians were
slowly (and in some cases reluctantly) recognizing the ministry of
women, but at least we were then several steps ahead of Anglicans!

I also have a long-standing interest in the Anglican see of Dunedin.
My first piece of serious historical research was a MA thesis on one
aspect of the ministry of the first Bishop of Dunedin, Bishop Samuel
Nevill.[1] From 1885 to 1907 Bishop Nevill led, or was closely associated
with, various efforts to establish Anglican work on a firm footing in Fiji,
Samoa and Tonga.[2] I hope that, unlike Bishop Nevill, Bishop Jamieson
does not have to endure sniping from correspondents to the *Otago
Daily Times*. On 14 August 1885, just prior to Bishop Nevill's departure

1. The early years of the diocese of Dunedin were marred by the Jenner
controversy. Jenner had been precipitately consecrated as Bishop to a see in New
Zealand, but his claim to the see of Dunedin was not upheld and eventually Nevill
was recognized as the first Bishop of Dunedin.

2. On re-reading my thesis over thirty years later, I am grateful for the grounding in historical research, and especially in the use of unpublished material and other
primary sources, which I was given by the History Department at the University of
Otago. My supervisor was Angus Ross; my other teachers were W.P. Morrell,
Gordon Parsonson and Austin Mitchell.

for Tonga and Samoa, a correspondent claimed that the Bishop's task did not include either an attempt to convert the heathen in the Pacific Islands or to reconvert the Wesleyans: there was a vast mission field open for the Bishop's efforts in his own diocese!

More recently some of my research has focused on Matthew's Gospel and its setting in early Judaism and in early Christianity. Although Matthew's Gospel has often been dubbed the 'most ecclesiastical' of the four canonical Gospels, this is not the corner of early Christianity to which modern Christians interested in 'ministry' naturally turn. Nonetheless, I hope to show that Matthew provides the careful reader with a number of points to ponder.

I concede immediately that in the paragraphs which follow I am bringing some of the concerns of systematic theology to the text of Matthew's Gospel. Along with many contemporary theologians, I want to emphasize that 'ministry' should be not be confined to issues of 'office', to 'who does what, and on what authority'. The whole people of God is called to 'ministry': ministry to God in worship and in carrying out God's will; ministry to one another in the life of the Christian community; ministry in the name of Christ to the world, especially to those in need. The ordained ministry should be considered only in the light of these basic convictions.[3]

New Testament scholars are instinctively reluctant to read any early Christian writing from a standpoint which smacks of systematic theology. Many would go further and insist that they are not merely reluctant to do this: they are vehemently opposed to such a strategy. The text should not be forced artificially into a modern theological mould, we are told endlessly. On the other hand, a neutral, detached reading of a text is impossible: the reader always brings her or his initial assumptions and questions to the text. So why should a specifically theological starting point be ruled out? Problems arise only when an initial doctrinal stance *pre-determines* exegetical results. A reading of the text can be stimulated by theological concerns, and, of course, vice

---

3.   The important and influential WCC statement, *Baptism, Eucharist and Ministry* (Geneva: WCC, 1982), §7 (b), p. 21, correctly emphasizes the calling of the whole people of God to 'ministry': 'the word *ministry* in its broadest sense denotes the service to which the whole people of God is called, whether as individuals, as a local community, or as the universal Church'. However, the statement as a whole is lop-sided: far more discussion is devoted to the ordained ministry than to ministry in the broad sense.

versa. Surely systematic theology and New Testament studies can and should live with one another in a symbiotic relationship.

Matthew's Gospel comes to us from a quite specific religious and social setting, attention to which warns us against using the Gospel as a set of prooftexts to prop up our current theological concerns. The Evangelist wrote to communities which had recently parted painfully from Judaism, communities which were encouraged by the Evangelist to see themselves as a 'new people'. In some respects Matthew's Gospel reflects a 'sectarian' outlook. The Evangelist's instincts are those of a pastor rather than those of a theologian. His primary aim is to set out the story and significance of Jesus, to write a Gospel rather than a handbook on the nature of Christian ministry.[4] A careful reading of the text cannot bypass these various considerations.

If 'ministry' is understood in the broad way I have sketched, then almost the whole of Matthew's Gospel is relevant to the theme of this volume of essays. Since I cannot possibly discuss all the relevant passages in this paper, I have decided to focus on three central issues which are all distinctively Matthean. First, I hope to show that the Evangelist insists that the ministry of Jesus is a model for his followers. Secondly, I shall discuss passages which are (or have seemed to some to be) concerned with the ministry of the people of God to the world. Thirdly, and quite deliberately at the end rather than at the beginning, I shall turn to the Evangelist's hints concerning leadership roles within the Christian communities to which he is writing.

1. *Jesus and the Disciples*

Matthew's second major discourse plays at least as important a role in the Evangelist's story as the Sermon on the Mount.[5] In the mission discourse the twelve are given authority over unclean spirits to cast them out, and to cure every disease and sickness. They are told, 'Go, proclaim the good news, "the kingdom of heaven has come near". Cure

---

4.   See G.N. Stanton, *A Gospel for a New People: Studies in Matthew* (Edinburgh: T. & T. Clark, 1992); see also *idem*, 'Revisiting Matthew's Communities', in E.H. Lovering (ed.), *Society of Biblical Literature 1994 Seminar Papers* (Atlanta: Scholars Press, 1994), pp. 9-23.

5.   For a fine study of this discourse, see U. Luz, 'The Disciples in the Gospel according to Matthew', in G.N. Stanton (ed.), *The Interpretation of Matthew* (Edinburgh: T. & T. Clark, rev. edn, 1995), pp. 115-48.

the sick, raise the dead, cleanse the lepers, cast out demons' (10.1, 7-8).

In the important summary passage which introduces this discourse, the Evangelist notes that Jesus himself 'went about all the cities and villages...proclaiming the good news of the kingdom, and curing every disease and sickness' (9.35). The verbal correspondence is striking: the disciples of Jesus are sent to proclaim the *same message* of the good news of the kingdom which Jesus himself has proclaimed, and to carry out the *same acts* of healing as Jesus.

Matthew has had this crucial point in mind from a much earlier point in his Gospel. In fact it is no exaggeration to claim that in the opening eleven chapters he has radically re-shaped his primary source, Mark, to draw attention to the ways in which the ministry of the disciples (ch. 10) is to be modelled on that of Jesus as set out in chs. 5–9.[6]

The Evangelist's own summary of the proclamation and actions of Jesus in 4.23-24 is followed by extended examples of his proclamation in the Sermon on the Mount (chs. 5–7) and by a cycle of miracle stories in chs. 8 and 9 which illustrate the summary references to the healing activity of Jesus.

In the mission discourse in ch. 10 both the proclamation of the disciples and their healing actions are modelled closely on those of Jesus: they are to continue his ministry. But there is a crucial difference: although the disciples are sent out on their mission bearing the full authority of Jesus as his formal representatives (10.40), Jesus is the unique messiah, the Son of God. This is made clear in the Q pericope which immediately follows the mission discourse in 11.2-6. Here the actions and proclamation of Jesus are seen as the fulfilment of Isa. 35.5-6 and 61.1; they are messianic in the broad sense of that term. In 11.2 Matthew adds to his source a redactional phrase which is much more explicit and which differentiates Jesus and his disciples: the deeds (*erga*) of Jesus are those of the messiah.[7]

The reader is made aware of this close correspondence between the ministries of Jesus and the disciples at the point at which Matthew introduces his account of the ministry of Jesus in 4.12-22. The first pericope

6.   In his later chapters Matthew follows Mark's order very closely.

7.   The NRSV correctly translates *Christos* here by 'messiah' to make the point clear to modern readers. On Jesus as Son of God, note especially 3.17 and 4.1-11. Jesus is first presented as Son of God 'in a casual, almost inadvertent manner' in 2.15; so D. Verseput, 'The Role and Meaning of the "Son of God" Title in Matthew's Gospel', *NTS* 33 (1987), p. 537.

in this introductory section is not paralleled directly in the other Gospels. The journey of Jesus from Nazareth to his base in Capernaum is seen as the fulfilment of Isa. 8.23–9.1; 58.10: the coming of Jesus is the dawning of a 'great light' for the people of Galilee of the Gentiles. Matthew carefully presents Jesus as the light of the world.[8] In the Sermon of the Mount disciples of Jesus are called *to the same ministry*: 'You are the light of the world' (5.14).

The second pericope in this extended introduction is taken from Mark. James and John are called to follow Jesus, a call which is so urgent that their father Zebedee is left behind (4.22). First-century readers would recognize the radical nature of Jesus' demand more readily than their modern counterparts: in antiquity family ties were abandoned only in the most exceptional circumstances. Matthew's story has already implied that in this respect disciples also follow the pattern of the ministry of Jesus: the family circle of Jesus disappears from view at 2.21. When the mother and brothers of Jesus reappear at 12.46, Jesus pointedly notes that the 'new family' of the circle of disciples takes precedence over biological family ties.[9]

Several aspects of Matthew's portrait of Jesus are quite distinctive. His meekness and humility are stressed much more strongly than in Mark. The one born 'king of the Jews' is the *child* Jesus, the Davidic messiah (2.2-6). Jesus is the one who is 'meek and lowly in heart' (11.29), the self-effacing chosen Servant of God (12.17-21), 'the humble king' (21.5). All these passages bear the stamp of the Evangelist himself.

In several passages disciples of Jesus are urged to bear *the same character traits as Jesus himself*. As the Evangelist does in numerous other places in his Gospel, he takes over a logion from one of his primary sources and expands or repeats it elsewhere.[10] From Q Matthew takes the blessing on the poor in spirit (5.3); he repeats the saying with different wording in 5.5, where the very word 'meek' used of Jesus in 11.29 and 21.5 is used to describe the disciples.

At 26.26-28 Matthew takes over almost verbatim the striking Markan sayings (10.43-45) about true greatness and true service (or 'ministry' in

8.   See Jn 8.12 where Jesus himself claims to be the light of the world.

9.   See further the fine study by S. Barton, *Discipleship and Family Ties according to Mark and Matthew* (SNTSMS, 80; Cambridge: Cambridge University Press, 1994).

10.   For examples and full discussion of this distinctive Matthean literary technique, see Stanton, *A Gospel for a New People*, pp. 326-45.

the broad sense): 'whoever wishes to be great among you must be your servant...*just as the Son of Man came not to be served but to serve*, and to give his life as a ransom for many'. Matthew uses part of this material redactionally at 18.4, and again (more fully) at 23.11-12. In the latter passage there is an extended comparison between alleged patterns of ministry among the scribes and Pharisees on the one hand, and the disciples of Jesus on the other. I shall return to this passage below. My present point is that these verses provide a further example of the way Matthew emphasizes that the disciples are to model their ministry on that of Jesus himself. Once again there is also differentiation: unlike Jesus, the Son of Man, the disciples do not give their lives as a ransom for many.

One further example is particularly interesting. At 6.34 Mark refers to the compassion of Jesus on the crowd 'because they were like sheep without a shepherd', and then shows how Jesus himself expressed his compassion for them by 'teaching them many things' and by satisfying their hunger (Mk 6.34-44). Matthew takes over the reference to the compassion of Jesus (9.36), and to the crowd 'like sheep without a shepherd'.[11] But whereas in Mark Jesus himself acts as a compassionate shepherd to the crowd, by reordering his sources Matthew emphasizes that the compassion of Jesus is expressed through the ministry of the disciples (9.37 and 10.1-42). Elsewhere in Matthew there are plenty of references to the compassion of Jesus towards those in need (for example 11.28-30 and 14.14); at 9.36–10.1 followers of Jesus are called to model their ministry of compassion on his.

So far I have noted that in numerous redactional passages Matthew emphasizes that the proclamation, healing actions, meekness, humility and compassion of Jesus are all models for his disciples and, we may add, for his followers in later times. There is also a darker side to the lines of correspondence Matthew carefully draws between Jesus and his disciples. This is expressed most powerfully in the important redactional saying Matthew has added at 10.25b: 'If they have called the master of the house Beelzebul, how much more will they malign those of his household'. In the preceding verses the disciples have been warned that they are to expect rejection and persecution. Now they are told that they are to expect *even greater* abuse than that heaped upon Jesus himself,

---

11. Matthew adds a description of the crowd which is not found in Mark: they are 'harassed and helpless'.

abuse which has already been referred to explicitly at 9.34.[12]

Since the sayings in the second part of Matthew 10 refer so clearly to the post-Easter period,[13] 10.25 implies that the persecution of Christians in the Evangelist's own day will include this form of abuse. In other words, the accusation that both Jesus and his followers are in league with the prince of demons is not a matter of past history; for Matthew and his readers it is a present experience.

This theme is found both earlier and later in the Gospel. In Matthew 2 Jesus and the wise men flee for their very lives from persecution. In this chapter the implacable opposition of the religious authorities to Jesus is foreshadowed. The reader of the Gospel does not have to wait long to learn that disciples of Jesus are to expect the same fate. In the final beatitudes (5.1-12), where Matthew's own hand is once again evident, the disciples (and later readers) are promised that they will be blessed and rewarded by God when they are persecuted and reviled.

The theme returns in a different key towards the end of the catalogue of woes heaped upon the scribes and Pharisees in ch. 23, a chapter which embarrasses acutely readers today who do not appreciate its original social setting—and even those who do. The reader is told that some of the Christian prophets, sages and scribes sent to the religious leaders in the Evangelist's day will be killed and crucified; some will be flogged in synagogues and hounded from town to town (23.34). Since crucifixion was a Roman but not a Jewish form of capital punishment, this verse is not intended merely to allude to later Jewish persecution of followers of Jesus. The point is rather that disciples (and later followers) of Jesus must be prepared to share his ultimate fate, which may even include crucifixion. As we shall see below, in one key passage they too are promised vindication by God.

In the preceding paragraphs I have noted several ways in which the ministry of Jesus functions as a model for the disciples, even though Jesus is portrayed as the promised messiah, the Son of God. In many respects his story is their story. Since the reader readily identifies with the disciples, the pattern of their ministry is clearly intended to be a model for later readers of the Gospel.

12. For a full discussion of the threefold accusation that Jesus is in league with the prince of demons (Mt. 9.34; 10.25; 12.24, 27), see Stanton, *A Gospel for a New People*, pp. 169-91.

13. See Luz, 'Disciples', pp. 98-128, especially p. 100.

2. *Ministry to the World*

The fourth of Matthew's five discourses is concerned with ministry within the community of followers of Jesus.[14] Only in this chapter (18.17 twice) and at 16.18 is the word 'church' used. Whereas in Lk. 15.3-7 the parable of the lost sheep speaks of God's love for those on the margins of society, tax collectors and sinners, in Mt. 18.12-14 the parable is used to encourage followers of Jesus to care for the 'straying' member of the community. In the same chapter 'regulations' for settling disputes within the community are set out (18.15-18).

Matthew's clear interest in ministry within the community is balanced by many passages in which disciples of Jesus are urged to exercise a ministry to the world. A number of examples have been noted in the preceding section; two further passages deserve close attention.

The Beatitudes, the first words Jesus addresses to his disciples, are concerned with the characteristics of discipleship (5.1-12). These qualities are to be shown both within the life of the community and in the disciples' relationships with those outside the community. The disciple is to be gentle, merciful and a peacemaker, for example, in both settings.

The carefully structured verses which follow the Beatitudes are concerned with the 'ministry' of followers of Jesus to the world: they are to be 'salt to the world', and 'light for all the world' (5.13-14). It is difficult to determine the precise sense in which the community is to be 'salt'. In antiquity salt was used as seasoning, for purification, for preservation (of meat, fish and vegetables), and also (in small quantities) as a fertilizer. Which quality is in view here? 'Salt' has been taken by ancient and modern interpreters to refer to the wisdom of the disciples, their proclamation, their willingness to sacrifice, and their manner of living.[15]

Since the most common use for salt has always been as seasoning for food, this is the probable sense here. The disciples do not exist for

---

14. 'Teaching about the kingdom' is the bland, unhelpful sub-heading which precedes Mt. 18 in the REB; NEB has an equally unhelpful header at the top of the page, 'Jesus and the Disciples'. The NRSV and NIB eschew headings at the top of the page and sub-headings within the text. In my view this is preferable to the misleading headings found in many places in the NEB and the REB. In many other respects, however, the NEB is excellent and the REB even better.

15. For details and a thorough discussion, see U. Luz, *Matthew 1–7* (ET; Edinburgh: T. & T. Clark, 1990).

themselves but for 'the world' beyond the community.[16] This line of interpretation is confirmed by the 'light' saying, and by 5.16, which brings both the 'salt' and the 'light' sayings to a climax. The characteristic qualities of disciples and their good works have a missionary function: followers of Jesus are called to minister to the world by their lives and their deeds.[17]

The concluding pericope in Matthew's fifth and final discourse (25.31-46) has often been taken to insist powerfully and dramatically that Christians (or men and women in general) will be separated like sheep and goats on the basis of their concern and care for the poor and needy. On this 'universalist' interpretation, *ministry to the world* is in view, and this passage is directly relevant to our present theme. It is hardly surprising that this interpretation has become one of the pillars of liberation theology.

However, an alternative interpretation is now winning the day among Matthean specialists: the non-Christian nations (among whom Israel may or may not be included) will be judged on the basis of their acceptance or rejection of Christians (or a particular group within Christian communities, such as missionaries or apostles).[18] 'The least of these my brothers' (25.40, 45) are not the poor and needy of the world, but Christians, who form a minority within society at large. If this 'particularist' interpretation is adopted, the pericope has the same general purpose as some apocalyptic writings: to offer consolation and encouragement to minority communities who are hard pressed by the dominant society which surrounds them and which is perceived to be threatening.[19] More specifically, the pericope functions as an answer to the question, 'Why are the enemies of the gospel allowed to trample over the followers of Jesus?' Or, 'Why do the nations triumph?' The Evangelist's answer to

16. So too Luz, *Matthew 1–7*.

17. REB translates 5.16 'Like the lamp, you must shed light among your fellows' (similarly, NEB). This is misleading, since to modern readers 'fellows' suggests fellow-followers of Jesus; this runs counter to the thrust of 5.13-16. The 'politically correct' NRSV changes RSV's 'Let your light so shine before men...' to 'let your light shine before others'. In this case the change is wholly welcome.

18. The history of interpretation has recently been fully documented by S.W. Gray, *The Least of My Brothers: Matthew 25.31-46: A History of Interpretation* (SBLDS, 114; Atlanta: Scholars Press, 1989). For a full discussion of this passage, see Stanton, *A Gospel for a New People*, pp. 207-31.

19. In my discussion of this passage (see the preceding note) I have emphasized the importance of these parallels.

his readers is that God will ultimately bring the nations to judgment. To their great surprise, those who have shown active caring concern for Christians will receive their reward, for in accepting the messengers and representatives of Jesus, the Son of Man, they will have accepted Jesus himself.

The nub of the exegetical dispute can be put quite simply. Is this pericope concerned with the attitude of the Christian community (or the world in general) to the needy (the 'universalist' interpretation), or is it, rather, the world's attitude to the church which is in view (the 'particularist' interpretation)? A decision depends very largely on answers given to two questions. Who are 'all the nations', gathered at the throne of the Son of Man for judgment (vv. 31 and 32)? Who are 'the least of these my brothers' (vv. 40 and 45), for whom deeds of mercy have been done?

Elsewhere in his Gospel (especially 24.9 and 14; 28.19) Matthew uses 'all the nations' to refer to Gentiles, over against Christians or Jews; the phrase is never used to refer to Christians (i.e. the *evangelized* nations) or even to Christians and non-Christians together. In this apocalyptic discourse it is the nations opposed to God's people who are to be assembled for judgment.

Who are 'the least of these my brothers'? Once again priority must be given to Matthean usage elsewhere. In Matthew 'the little ones' is a quite specific term for disciples (10.42; 18.10, 14). The phrase 'one of the least of these' in 25.40, 45 is very similar to the phrase in 10.42, 'one of these little ones', so we can be all but certain that it refers to disciples. Why is the superlative form of the adjective used in ch. 25? It can be argued that the superlative here has almost the same sense as the positive. In the New Testament 'true' superlatives are very rare; superlatives with an elative sense ('very') are much more common. The REB catches the nuance of the elative superlative here: 'one of these, however insignificant'. The difference between 'the little ones' (10.42) and 'the insignificant ones' (25.40, 45) is not great.[20]

The phrase 'my brothers' which is found in 25.40 (but not in v. 45) strengthens still further the conclusion that in our pericope the nations are to be judged on the basis of their acceptance or rejection of Christian disciples. Matthew uses 'brothers' 18 times to refer to fellow members

---

20. It is just possible that the superlative has been chosen to identify one particular group among the disciples. But if that was Matthew's intention, I think he would have been more specific about the group he had in mind.

of the Christian family; no fewer than 12 of the 18 are redactional. As in many other cases, Matthew has taken a word found in his sources and used it himself so frequently that it becomes part of his distinctive vocabulary.

There is a further consideration which strongly supports the interpretation I am defending. Perhaps the most startling aspect of this passage is the identification of the Son of Man, the King, with 'the least of these my brothers'. There are no other passages in Matthew, or in early Christian writings generally, which *identify* Jesus with the poor. It is, of course, just possible that Matthew did take a bold and unprecedented step. But from what we know of the Evangelist's methods elsewhere, it is much more likely that in the final pericope of his final discourse he would develop points made elsewhere in his Gospel rather than set out a wholly new idea.

On the other hand, if we take 'the least of these my brothers' to be a reference to followers of Jesus, then the identification of Jesus with them is not unexpected. The claim at the very opening of the Gospel that the birth of Jesus means that God is *with* his people (1.23) is matched by the closing promise of the Exalted Christ at the very end of the Gospel to be *with* his disciples to the end of the age (28.20). The closing logia of the missionary discourse, 10.40-42, foreshadow 25.31-46, the closing pericope of the final discourse.[21] In v. 40 Jesus identifies himself closely with his disciples: 'he who receives you, receives me'. Verse 42 is an extension of this theme: acceptance of 'one of these little ones' by giving a cup of cold water because he is a disciple is acceptance of Jesus himself.

I noted above several ways in which the ministry of Jesus is seen as a model for the ministry of his disciples. In 10.40-42 and in 25.31-46 their close relationship is taken further. Whereas early Christian writings do not identify Jesus with the poor and needy, the close identification of Jesus with his disciples is a thoroughly Matthean theme which is also found elsewhere.[22]

I accept without hesitation that many strands of both the Old and New Testaments exhort God's people to minister to the marginalized in

21. D. Marguerat, *Le jugement dans l'évangile de Matthieu* (Geneva: Labor et Fides, 1981), p. 485, notes that Mt. 10.40-42 is a 'hermeneutical canon' for the 'particularist' interpretation of 25.31-46.

22. See also 1 Cor. 8.12; Acts 9.4-5; 22.8; 26.15; *Ign., Eph.* 6.1; *Did.* 11.4; Justin, *I Apol.* 16.9-10; 63.5.

society, and I believe strongly that the church today is constrained to take this bias to the poor with the utmost seriousness. In short, on theological grounds I am predisposed to read Mt. 25.31-46 as a solemn exhortation to the church (and indeed, to all men and women) to give priority in ministry to the hungry, thirsty and needy of the world. As an exegete, however, I conclude with some reluctance that in Mt. 25.31-46 both the Evangelist's intentions, and the ways the first recipients understood this passage, were very different.

3. *Leadership Roles*

I turn finally to 'ministry' in the narrow sense, that is, to the patterns of leadership within Matthean Christianity. The reader of Matthew soon observes that the crowds play a much fuller and more clearly defined role in Matthew than in the other Gospels. Since the crowds are often positive in their response to Jesus, what is their relationship to the disciples? A reader of a story naturally identifies with one of the main characters—though the story-teller may spring surprises and force the reader to abandon an initial allegiance. With whom were the readers of Matthew's Gospel intended to identify, the crowds or the disciples?

In an influential article P.S. Minear claimed that when

> the modern reader finds Jesus speaking to the crowds, he may usually assume that Matthew was speaking to contemporary laymen. When he finds Jesus teaching the disciples, he may usually suppose that Matthew had in mind the vocation of contemporary leaders as stewards of Christ's household.[23]

The key word in these two sentences is 'usually'. Minear's theory accounts for some of the evidence (especially 14.13-21 and 15.32-9), but by no means all of it. In 26.47 the crowds oppose Jesus; in 12.46-50 and 13.10-17 they appear in a poor light in comparison with the disciples.[24]

A more nuanced view has recently been advanced by Warren Carter. He correctly notes that the crowds are

> recipients of Jesus' compassionate ministry, a ministry to be continued by disciples. At times crowds exhibit some perception that God is at work in

23. 'The Disciples and the Crowds in the Gospel of Matthew', *ATR Supplementary Series* 3 (1974), p. 41.

24. So too W. Carter, 'The Crowds in Matthew's Gospel', *CBQ* 55 (1993), p. 55.

a special way in Jesus, yet they lack both the faith and understanding manifested by the disciples and the hostility displayed by the Jewish leaders.[25]

In short, the disciples and the crowds do not foreshadow the later distinction between ordained and lay ministries. We must now ask whether the Gospel provides other evidence of patterns of ministry within Matthean Christianity.

From very early times right up to the present day many readers of the Gospel have concluded that in Mt. 16.13-20 Peter is singled out by Jesus and given supreme authority over the church. Modern scholars have interpreted this passage in diverse ways, but they all accept that it should not be considered in isolation from other evidence within the Gospel concerning Peter's role.

Some scholars conclude that Peter is presented by the Evangelist as the 'supreme rabbi' within the church, the 'guarantor' and 'transmitter' of its tradition of teaching. Other scholars see Peter's role very differently: he provides the individual member of Matthew's church with an example of what it means, both positively and negatively, to be a Christian.[26]

Two points are crucial. Although Peter plays a leading role in many passages in Matthew, in some he is less prominent than in the corresponding passage in Mark. Compare, for example, Mk 16.7 and Mt. 28.7; Mk 11.21 and Mt. 21.20. And secondly, and even more importantly, the authority to bind and loose which is given by Jesus to Peter in Mt. 16.19 is given to all the disciples in 18.18. By paying close attention to the ways Peter is first introduced to the reader, J.D. Kingsbury has shown that Peter is the 'rock', 'not by virtue of his being elevated to an office above, or apart from, the other disciples, but by reason of the fact that he was the "first" of the disciples whom Jesus called to follow him'.[27]

Of the terms used to refer to the disciples (or to some of them), 'the

25. W. Carter, 'The Crowds', p. 64.

26. For details and a full discussion with which I am largely in agrement, see J.D. Kingsbury, 'The Figure of Peter in Matthew's Gospel as a Theological Problem', *JBL* 98 (1979), pp. 67-83. See also R.E. Brown, K.P. Donfried and J. Reumann (eds.), *Peter in the New Testament* (Minneapolis: Augsburg; New York: Paulist Press, 1973), and T.V. Smith, *Petrine Controversies in Early Christianity* (Tübingen: Mohr [Paul Siebeck], 1985)

27. 'Peter in Matthew', p. 76.

little ones' is by far the most intriguing, as we have seen above. The phrase first appears at 10.42, the climax of a set of three sayings of Jesus at the end of the mission discourse. The opening saying (10.40), which is a Matthean development of a Q logion, draws an exact parallel between the authority given to Jesus by God and the authority given to (all) the disciples by Jesus: 'whoever receives you receives me, and whoever receives me receives the One who sent me'. 10.41, which is probably the Evangelist's own expansion of the preceding logion, refers to the rewards which will be given to those who welcome a prophet and a righteous person. 10.42 is Matthew's version of Mk 9.41; among the changes he makes is the introduction of the phrase 'the little ones' to refer to the disciples.[28] From the immediate context (and from Matthew's use of the phrase at 18.6, 10 and 14, and his use of the superlative at 25.40 and 45) it is clear that 'the little ones' is Matthew's characteristic way of referring to all the disciples, not to a special inner group.

The first reference to 'the little ones' in the fourth discourse in ch. 18 is striking. At 18.6 Mk 9.42 is expanded in order to state explicitly that 'the little ones' believe *in Jesus*—the only time such a phrase is used in the Synoptic traditions.[29] Here the Evangelist uses a post-Easter confessional phrase—a hint that readers in the Evangelist's own day are being addressed.

Who are the 'prophets' and the 'righteous', terms probably introduced in 10.41 by Matthew himself? The latter is the more difficult term, since it is not used elsewhere by Matthew to refer to disciples. As we shall see in a moment, 'prophets' are a particular group within the Matthean community. Hence it is likely that 'the righteous' are too; the reference to a reward appropriate for a 'righteous person' strongly suggests that this is the case. The verb 'receives' (and the wider context) implies 'welcome with hospitality', so both the prophets and the righteous are probably itinerant followers of Jesus. But it is impossible to say more about the role of 'the righteous' with any confidence.[30]

---

28. Matthew takes the phrase from Mk 9.42, the only place in Mark where it is used metaphorically of the disciples. As in many other passages, Matthew takes over a phrase from Mark and uses it himself several times in key passages. See Stanton, *A Gospel for a New People*, pp. 326-45.

29. A number of MSS do have 'believe in me' at Mk 9.42, but I take this reading to be a harmonization of the Matthean tradition.

30. Luz ('Disciples') speculates that at the pre-Matthean stage they may have been a special group of devout disciples, perhaps wandering ascetics, who were not prophets.

There is rather more evidence for prophets within Matthean Christianity. Matthew's warnings against the activity of false prophets in 7.18-23 presuppose the activity of true prophets, an activity which is referred to at 5.12 (implicitly); 10.41 and 23.34. Mt. 7.22 confirms that the false prophets prophesied, exorcized demons and performed healing miracles. Matthew does not indulge in polemic against these activities: prophets are rejected only when they fail to 'do the will of the heavenly Father'.

There is some evidence to suggest that prophecy was known in later Christian communities which also saw themselves as 'the little ones'. E. Schweizer has claimed that the Matthean church was 'the body of these little ones who are ready to follow Jesus', a group with an ascetic charismatic character, which found its continuation in the church of Syria, finally merging into the monastic movement of the Catholic church.[31] Part of this bold hypothesis received unexpected support from the Nag Hammadi *Apocalypse of Peter*. There is no doubt that this community saw itself as a group of 'these little ones' (the phrase recurs several times in a relatively short document). 'The little ones' joined issue with those 'who let themselves be called bishop, and also deacons, as if they had received authority from God, who recline at table after the law of the places of honour'.[32] Schweizer believes that the *Apocalypse of Peter* offers the first direct evidence of 'an ascetic Judaeo-Christian group of "these little ones" with no bishops or deacons, still experiencing heavenly visions and prophetic auditions'.[33]

I have argued that *5 Ezra* offers further support for this conclusion, for it too stems from a Judaeo–Christian community which sees itself as 'the little ones' and in which Christian prophecy continues.[34] In the final verse, which is very similar to the conclusion of the *Apocalypse of Peter*, Ezra is instructed by the angel of God to go and convey to the Christian community his prophetic vision (2.48); he is also commanded to take the *words* of the Lord to them (2.10). Ezra is portrayed as a prophet who speaks against Israel very much in the manner of Old

---

31. E. Schweizer, 'Observance of the Law and Charismatic Activity in Matthew', *NTS* 16 (1970), p. 229.

32. E. Schweizer, 'The "Matthean" Church', *NTS* 20 (1974), p. 216; there is a similar brief note in *ZNW* 65 (1974), p. 139. Schweizer refers to Mt. 23.6-10 and 18.10.

33. Schweizer, 'The "Matthean" Church', p. 216.

34. See Stanton, *A Gospel for a New People*, pp. 256-77.

Testament prophets (see for example 2.4, 8, 12, 15). Whereas Israel rejected the Old Testament prophets (and Ezra himself, 2.33), the clear implication is that the 'coming people' will not only obey the Old Testament prophets but will accept the prophetic words and visions given by God through Ezra. At 2.26 there is probably an explicit reference to Christian prophets: 'Not one of the servants whom I have given you will perish, for I will require them from among your number.'[35]

I have considered briefly evidence for two groups, prophets and the righteous, within the circle of 'the little ones'—a self-designation of followers of Jesus in the Evangelist's day. There is one further reference to a special group within Matthean Christianity. At 23.34 the scribes and Pharisees are told that they will reject and persecute the (Christian) 'prophets and wise men and scribes' who will be sent to them. The 'wise men' and the 'scribes' are almost certainly the same group.[36]

One other passage probably alludes to Christian scribes. Mt. 13.52 speaks of a scribe who has been 'discipled' for the kingdom of heaven. This may even be the Evangelist's own self-portrait at the centre-point of his Gospel—like an artist's signature in a corner of her or his painting.

Some scholars have claimed that Mt. 8.19 also points to the existence in the Evangelist's day of Christian scribes. However, a careful reading of the text rules out this interpretation. The eager scribe who seeks to follow Jesus merely on his own initiative and without a prior 'call' from Jesus is repudiated, but someone else, who is not a scribe, is portrayed as a disciple and reminded sharply of the radical nature of discipleship.[37] In typical Matthean fashion, the repudiated scribe addresses Jesus as 'teacher', while the true disciple addresses Jesus as 'Lord'.

Christian scribal activity is implied by the references to 'binding and loosing' at 16.19 and 18.18. Just as in Jewish communities one of the scribe's tasks was to pronounce on the interpretation of the law, that is,

35. The French recension of the Latin text has been quoted: the Spanish manuscripts do not differ significantly.

36. See the fine study by D.E. Orton, *The Understanding Scribe* (JSNTSup, 25; Sheffield: JSOT Press, 1988).

37. See J.D. Kingsbury, 'On Following Jesus: The "Eager" Scribe and the "Reluctant" Disciple (Matthew 8.18-22)', *NTS* 34 (1988), pp. 45-59. RSV translates 8.21 as 'another of the disciples', thereby implying that both men are scribes and are accepted by Jesus as true disciples. NEB and REB correctly translate 'another man, one of his disciples', thereby avoiding any suggestions that he is a scribe.

what is still binding and what is not, so too within Matthean Christian communities God's will (as expressed particularly in the sayings of Jesus) had to be discerned. In Mt. 16.19 and 18.18, however, authority to do this is given to Peter and to the whole community, not to one particular group.

I have suggested that within Matthean Christian communities special ministries were exercised by three groups: prophets, the righteous, and 'wise men and scribes'. No doubt these groups were not mutually exclusive: some prophets may also have been scribes. As E. Schweizer has noted, 'there is not the slightest indication of a specially emphasized ministry to which certain things are reserved that not every community member can do'.[38] In making that comment Schweizer referred to ch. 18, the 'church order' discourse. In my view his comments are a fair summary of the limited evidence Matthew's Gospel as a whole gives us concerning patterns of leadership.

In none of the passages referred to is there a suggestion that these groups enjoyed a particular status or used titles of honour. This observation is confirmed by Mt. 23.6-12. In contrast to synagogue communities, followers of Jesus are not to be concerned with status or titles of honour. 'The greatest among you must be your servant' (23.11).

I hope I hardly need to add that the absence in Matthew of bishops, deacons and elders is not significant. In historical studies it is always rash to build a case on the silence of one's sources. Matthew's primary purpose is to set out the story and significance of Jesus for his readers, not to give an account of ministry within the communities to which he is writing. We are given no more than a few hints concerning the self-understanding of Matthean communities and their patterns of ministry.

These hints provide us with several points to ponder. For Matthean Christians the story of Jesus offered a model of discipleship and ministry. His story is their story, even though Jesus is set apart as the Davidic messiah, the Son of God, the *Kurios*. Within Matthean communities special but not exclusive forms of ministry were certainly known, but status, rank and titles of honour were eschewed.

In the following generations the Matthean patterns of ministry seem to have survived in the circles in which the Nag Hammadi *Apocalypse of Peter* and *5 Ezra* were written. But by no stretch of the imagination were these circles prominent and influential in the second and later centuries. The future lay elsewhere.

38. 'Matthew's Church', in Stanton (ed.), *The Interpretation of Matthew*, p. 140.

Within a generation or so Matthew's Gospel was used by the author or compiler of the *Didache* and by Ignatius; in both cases there are very different patterns of ministry. The references in *Didache* 11–13 to itinerant teachers, apostles and prophets are intriguing. Are we to assume that these three groups were quite distinct? Or are we to assume that while all true apostles were prophets (as is implied in 11.4-5), the reverse was not the case? Were all prophets also teachers, as 13.2 implies?

Apostles appear only in 11.3-6. This passage refers briefly to their welcome, permitted short stay in the community, and their departure, but nothing is said about their role in community life. There is no suggestion (except in the later title of the *Didache*) that the apostles were identical with the twelve disciples of Jesus. In Paul's day apostles were primarily missionaries who established communities and then moved on to evangelize other areas (see Rom. 15.20; 2 Cor. 10.15-16). If this was still their primary role when the *Didache* was written, this would account for its failure to say anything in chs. 13–15 about their role in community life. Or perhaps by the time of the final compilation of the *Didache* the apostles' heyday was over: in contrast to the situations described in 1 Cor. 12.28-29 and Eph. 4.11, here they do not head the list of 'ministers'; they are less prominent than teachers and prophets.

In the *Didache* prophets are discussed much more fully than apostles and teachers. They can exercise freedom in leading worship (10.7). The marks of true and false prophets are set out at some length (11.7-12). Prophets are 'your high priests' (13.2) and are to be supported when they decide to settle in the community (13.1-7).

Did. 15.1 refers to the choice of 'bishops and deacons', who, apparently, are not itinerant. The same phrase is used in Phil. 1.1, but not otherwise in the New Testament. The community addressed by the *Didache* is encouraged strongly to be even-handed in its treatment of itinerant teachers, apostles and prophets on the one hand, and its own 'settled' bishops and deacons: both groups are to be given the same respect, for their ministry is similar. This may suggest that the choice of local 'settled' bishops and deacons is a recent innovation, perhaps to counter the influence of wandering charismatic prophets.

The *Didache* assumes that a Christian community may have several bishops who share leadership with teachers, apostles, prophets and deacons; there is no trace here of the single pre-eminent bishop whose importance is stressed strongly by Ignatius in about 100 CE.

These later developments within the *Didache* and the writings of Ignatius, two strands of later 'Matthean' Christianity, will be seen by some as inevitable, by others as highly desirable, and by others as retrogressions. But that is another agenda. I have chosen to focus my attention elsewhere, on the evidence of Matthew's Gospel itself, some of which has not received the attention it deserves in discussions of ministry within earliest Christianity. I hope I have shown that Matthew's Gospel is a rich source for contemporary reflection on the ministry of the people of God.

Part II

HISTORICAL AND THEOLOGICAL PERSPECTIVES ON MINISTRY

EMPOWERING MINISTRY:
THE PRAXIS OF PENTECOST

Ray S. Anderson

The title of this essay—'Empowering Ministry'—is deliberately ambiguous as to its intent. It includes both the sense of empowering the
ministry of the church and, at the same time, a ministry of the church
which empowers its members. The subtitle—'The Praxis of Pentecost'—
suggests the source of this empowerment and, as we shall see, the
formative concept for a theology of ministry which is empowered by the
Spirit of God, and which empowers God's people to do the ministry of
God. A great deal of attention has been devoted recently to the role of
the church in equipping its members for ministry. All too often,
however, members of the church who are equipped through the acqui-
sition of skills and techniques remain powerless. Thus, a theology of
empowerment is needed to send forth those who are equipped to carry
out the praxis of Christ's ministry in the world.

1. *The Praxis of God's Ministry in Christ*

The word 'praxis' as I will use it means something quite different from
the mere application of truth or theory. The word 'practice' ordinarily
refers to the methods and means by which we apply a skill or theory.
This tends to separate truth from method or action, so that one assumes
that what is true can be deduced or discovered apart from the action or
activity which applies it in practice. Hence, the faculties of theological
schools are often divided in this way, with academic theologians being
responsible for the pursuit of 'pure theology' and the truth of biblical
studies, while the practical department is assigned responsibility for

developing the skills and methods to which the truth can be applied. This is not praxis as I understand it.[1]

By 'praxis' I mean something of what Aristotle meant when he distinguished between *poiēsis* as an act of making something, where the *telos* lay outside of the act of making, and *praxis* as an action which includes its *telos* within itself. The *telos* of something is its final purpose, meaning or character.[2] Because praxis includes the *telos*, or final meaning and character, of truth, it is an action in and through which the truth is discovered, not merely applied, or 'practiced'. In praxis, one is not only guided in one's actions by the intention of realizing the *telos*, or purpose, but one discovers this *telos* through the action itself.

In the praxis of Christian ministry, God's truth is revealed through the structures of reality by which God's actions and presence are disclosed to us through our own actions. The truth of God's Word, for example, is not something which can be extracted from the Bible by the human

---

1. Christoph Schwöbel insightfully suggests: 'This essential interconnection between the practical questions of the life of the Church and the theoretical problems of the theological understanding of the Church, and their relation to the focal point of the nature of Christian faith and its constitution, is so important because we are today painfully aware of the gap between the factual existence of the Church in society and the theological formulae in which its nature is expressed. This leads to a situation in which the practical questions of day-to-day living in the Church are often decided on the basis of pragmatic and wholly untheological considerations, while the ecclesiology of academic theology, operating, as it seems, at one remove from the social reality of the Church, seems often unable to relate to the practical questions which face the Church in its struggle for survival in a society more and more shaped by a plurality of religious and quasi-religious world views. The challenge of the ecclesiology of the Reformers is the challenge of a theological reflection on the Church which is closely related to the practical problems of Christian life in the Church, and which is at the same time theoretically rigorous' ('The Creature of the Word: Recovering the Ecclesiology of the Reformers', in C.E. Gunton and D.W. Hardy [eds.], *On Being the Church: Essays on the Christian Community* [Edinburgh: T. & T. Clark, 1989], p. 117).

2. See *The Nichomachean Ethics* IX.vi. 5. The use of the term 'praxis' in contemporary theology has been greatly influenced by the quasi-Marxist connotation given to it by some Latin American liberation theologians. My own attempt in using the word is to recover the authentically biblical connotation of God's actions that reveal God's purpose and truth. I appreciate the concept of praxis as used by Orlando Costas; see *The Church and its Mission: A Shattering Critique from the Third World* (Wheaton: Tyndale House, 1974). I have discussed this further in my essay, 'Christopraxis: Competence as a Criterion for Theological Education', in *Theological Students Fellowship Bulletin* (Jan.–Feb. 1984), pp. 10-13.

mind so that one can 'possess' this truth as a formula or doctrine without regard to its purpose of bringing us 'into the truth'. There is also true doctrine as opposed to false doctrine. But God's truth does not end with our concept of truth, nor is the human mind the absolute criterion for God's truth. God is the authority for what is true of God. How could it be otherwise? 'Although every one is a liar', wrote Paul, 'let God be proved true' (Rom. 3.4).[3]

When Jesus experienced the work of God by effecting a miraculous healing on the sabbath (Jn 9), he argued that the truth of the sabbath was to be found in the restoration of humanity, not in 'keeping the law of sabbath'. When challenged by the Pharisees as to his view of the sabbath, he responded, 'The sabbath was made for humankind, not humankind for the sabbath; so the Son of Man is Lord even of the sabbath' (Mk 2.27). This is what is meant by praxis. The work of God in our midst discloses to us the Word of God, even as the Word of God reveals its truth in producing God's work. God's Word of truth reaches its *telos* in healing, making whole, and restoring God's created purpose. This is the praxis of God's Word as truth. The authority and power of the Word of God is contained as much in its effect as in its source—'so shall my word be that goes out from my mouth; it shall not return to me empty, but it shall accomplish that which I purpose, and succeed in the thing for which I sent it' (Isa. 55.11).

The continued presence and work of the Holy Spirit constitutes the praxis of Christ's resurrection. This means that the truth of resurrection is not only the fact of a historical event, but the presence and power of a resurrected person, Jesus Christ. Hence, Christ's work of making peace between humans and God does not take place through the application of methods, ideologies, or even theories derived from Scripture. It is Christ himself who 'makes peace' through the praxis of his Spirit in a dialogical relationship with our truth and methods.[4]

3.   All Scripture references are from the NRSV.
4.   James Will offers a helpful comment when he says, 'If incomplete and ideologically distorted persons nevertheless have the dignity of participation with their Creator in the preservation and completion of the creation, then praxis is a necessary dimension of theology. But praxis must not be misunderstood as practice. Practice has come to mean the use of external means to attain a theoretically defined end. It suggests that finite and sinful persons may so understand the meaning of God's peace as to be able to devise economic, political, diplomatic, and even military, means to attain it. The end of peace is thought to be a transcendent value that appropriate external means may effect. Praxis, on the other hand, is a dialectical

Pentecost, therefore, continues the praxis of Christ's reconciling death and resurrection through the empowering Holy Spirit. Those who are empowered by Pentecost carry out the mission of Christ in the theological task of informing the church of its nature and mission, and this from the perspective of the world as loved by and reconciled to God through Christ (2 Cor. 5.18-20).

2. *Pentecost and the Praxis of Christ through the Spirit*

I use the term 'Pentecost', on the one hand, in its historical sense, as the occasion on which the Spirit came upon the early believers (Acts 2), but also, on the other hand, to represent the contemporary actions of the Spirit of Christ disclosed and manifested in ways that are often experienced in discontinuity with historical and institutional antecedents.

The first Pentecost can be seen as the pivotal point from which we look back to the incarnation of God in Jesus of Nazareth, and forward into our contemporary life and witness to Jesus Christ in the world. It is my belief that Pentecost is more than a mere historical and instrumental link between a theology of the incarnation and a theology of the church. Pentecost can serve as a compass that performs two functions: (1) theologically, it orients us to the inner logic of God's incarnational manifestion in the world through Jesus Christ, and (2) experientially, it orients us to the eschatological vision of redemption for the world through Christ's presence and coming.[5]

First, theologically, Pentecost is the starting point for a theology of Jesus Christ, because the Holy Spirit reveals to us the inner life of God as the Father of Jesus and of Jesus as the Son of the Father. To receive the Spirit of God, wrote the apostle Paul, is to 'have the mind of Christ' (1 Cor. 2.10, 16). Jesus said, 'All things have been handed over to me

---

process of internally related events from which a result dynamically emerges. Given the finite and ideological character of our preconceptions of peace, they cannot be treated as sufficient definitions of an eternal value to guide our practice. Rather, we need a praxis; that is, peace must be allowed to emerge from a dialogical and dialectical process that may continuously correct our ideological tendencies. Praxis is thus a process of struggle, negotiation, and dialogue toward a genuinely voluntary consensus' (*A Christology of Peace* [Louisville, KY: Westminster/John Knox Press, 1989], pp. 24-25).

5. See my book, *Ministry on the Fireline: A Practical Theology of an Empowered Church* (Downers Grove, IL: IVP, 1993), esp. ch. 1, 'The Christ of Pentecost', pp. 21-40.

by my Father; and no one knows the Son except the Father, and no one knows the Father except the Son and anyone to whom the Son chooses to reveal him' (Mt. 11.27). The Holy Spirit is the revelation to us of the inner being of God as constituted by the relations between Father and Son. Secondly, experientially, Pentecost is the beginning point for our own relationship with God through Christ for, apart from the Spirit, we are alienated from the life of God. Paul wrote, 'any one who does not have the Spirit of Christ does not belong to him' (Rom. 8.9). Pentecost is thus both a theological and an experiential compass: without true knowledge of God (theology), our experience can slip into delusion and even become demonic; without authentic experience of Christ (faith), our theology can become vain and empty speculation.

Pentecost thus serves as a compass that orients both our theology and our experience to the inner logic of God's incarnational and eschatological vision of redemption for the world. Through God's embodiment in Jesus of Nazareth (the incarnation), the reality of humanity as created by God is grasped by God and retrieved from its fatal plunge into the abyss of eternal separation from God. But in becoming human, Jesus Christ assumed the human death which is the consequence of sin, and died that death, 'descending into hell', as the Apostles' Creed tells us. When God raised Jesus Christ from the dead that put an 'end' to the power of death and hell. This is the eschatological vision of the redemption of humanity, for the *eschatos*, or 'final event', has now already occurred in Christ. In Pentecost we view 'the inner logic' of incarnation and resurrection as the beginning and end of God's vision for humanity. This is true because the Spirit that descended at Pentecost is the Spirit of the resurrected Christ as well as of the incarnate Son, Jesus of Nazareth.

Without the incarnation of the divine Logos, who is the eternally begotten Son of God, Pentecost becomes 'glossolalia without logos'. It becomes a profusion of spirits without the unity of the Spirit. Jesus charged his opponents with failing to understand his speech (*lalia*) because they did not perceive his word (*logos*: so Jn 8.43). It is the incarnate Logos of God, as John clearly saw (1.11, 14), who maintains the unity of Spirit in its diversity.

Without the light of Pentecost as the empowerment of Spirit, the resurrection recedes into mere historical memory. The eschatological reality of the risen Christ as the *parousia*, or presence, empowering each contemporary event of faith and ministry, is replaced by historical theology on the one hand, and pragmatic principles for institutional life and growth on the other.

Pentecostal experience without incarnational theology is like a sailboat with neither oars nor rudder—it can only move when there is a wind though it cannot steer when it is moving. Incarnational theology without Pentecostal experience is like a coal-barge anchored to shore. It has fuel but no fire, and even if it should burn, it has no engine so as to turn water into steam, and steam into power. So, not being able to transport people, it takes on more coal!

> As Ernst Bloch has said, what we have now 'in the West is a patronizing, pluralistic boredom...It looks like a partial eclipse of the sun. Everything is remarkably grey and either the birds do not sing or they sing differently. Something is wrong in any case. The transcending being is weak'. Or else the dangerous memory has been extinguished and the eschatological memory has become exhausted.[6]

Without passion, Christian faith is pathetic. Without a praxis in which the presence of Christ takes hold of our faith, compelling us with a convicting sense of mission, our memory becomes sentimental and superficial. Christianity was once dangerous and subversive! For many it is now dull and deadly. Without being empowered by the praxis of the Spirit of Christ released at Pentecost, the church may be well equipped, but it is powerless to move. Pentecost empowers the church both as to its nature and its mission.

6.   J.B. Metz, *Faith in History: Toward a Practical Fundamental Theology* (trans. D. Smith; New York: Seabury Press, 1980), p. 92. The 'dangerous memory' to which Metz refers is the radical and eschatological contemporaneity of Jesus Christ breaking into our history. 'This definite memory breaks through the magic circle of the prevailing consciousness. It regards history as something more than a screen for contemporary interests. It mobilizes tradition as a dangerous tradition and therefore as a liberating force in respect of the one-dimensional character and certainty of the one whose "hour is always there" (Jn 7.6). It gives rise again and again to the suspicion that the plausible structures of a society may be relationships aimed to delude...Christian faith can and must, in my opinion, be seen in this way as a subversive memory...The criterion of its authentic Christianity is the liberating and redeeming danger with which it introduces the remembered freedom of Jesus into modern society and the forms of consciousness and praxis in that society...' (p. 90).

3. *A Mission Theology of the Church*

The nature of the church as the continuing mission of God through Jesus Christ is determined by its relation to Pentecost, not only to the Great Commission, given by Jesus prior to his crucifixion and resurrection. The command, 'Go and make disciples of all nations' (Mt. 28.19) anticipates the promise, 'you will receive power when the Holy Spirit has come upon you; and you will be my witnesses...' (Acts 1.8).

The Great Commission gives the church its instructions, Pentecost provides its initiation and power. 'At the beginning of the history of the New Testament Church stands the Pentecost event', writes Harry Boer. 'It does not stand *approximately* at the beginning, or as a first among several significant factors, but it stands *absolutely* at the beginning...It does not, however, stand in *isolation* from preceding and succeeding redemptive history.'[7] It is in this sense that one must speak of the nature of the church as revealed in its participation in the mission of God, and as empowered and directed by the Holy Spirit.

The church exists as the missionary people of God; that is its nature.[8] The mission of the church is to embody in its corporate life and ministry the continuing messianic and incarnational nature of the Son of God through the indwelling of the Holy Spirit. It is on this basis that I argue that the nature of the church is determined in its existence as the mission of God to the world. The church's nature, as well as its mission and ministry, have their source in the life of the triune God, Father, Son and Holy Spirit.

The mission and nature of the church have their common source in the mission of God through the incarnate messiah continuing in the world through Pentecost. This thesis requires that nature and mission be considered as a unity of thought and experience. This Paul was careful

---

7.   H.R. Boer, *Pentecost and Missions* (Grand Rapids: Eerdmans, 1961), p. 98. Boer argues persuasively that the Great Commission was not a conscious ingredient in the mission thinking of the early church, but rather it was the Pentecost event. This is set in contrast to much of modern mission emphasis which attempts to locate the mission imperative of the church in obedience to the Great Commission rather than to Pentecost. My own attempt goes beyond that of Boer, in saying that the very nature of the church is itself grounded in the Pentecost event so that mission, rather than missions, constitutes the ground of the church itself.

8.   See C. Van Engen, *God's Missionary People: Rethinking the Purpose of the Local Church* (Grand Rapids, MI: Baker, 1991).

to do in his formulation, 'one body, one Spirit; one Lord, one baptism' (Eph. 4.4, 5). Hence, Paul made it clear that the ministry of the Holy Spirit is essential to a knowledge of Jesus as the incarnate Lord. 'No one speaking by the Spirit of God ever says "Let Jesus be cursed!" and no one can say "Jesus is Lord" except by the Holy Spirit' (1 Cor. 12.3). He also warns, 'Anyone who does not have the Spirit of Christ does not belong to him' (Rom. 8.9).

The nature of the early church as the 'dwelling place of the Spirit' had already been established in the Pentecost experience and the subsequent manifestations of the Spirit through the early missionary work of Paul and others. Some within the New Testament church, apparently, attempted to take Paul's concept of the church as the 'body of Christ' and ground its nature in some kind of historical or institutional continuity with the incarnation. The church at Jerusalem had strong tendencies toward this kind of historical, apostolic and institutional continuity.[9]

Paul argued vehemently against this position on the ground that his own apostolic commission had come from the risen Christ, though he had never belonged to the community of the historical Jesus. Paul first experienced Jesus Christ as the resurrected Lord who ministered to him and who called him to become a minister of the gospel. The nature of the church, argued Paul, could not rest only upon a historical link with Jesus and the twelve disciples, but upon the Spirit of the resurrected Christ who has 'broken down the dividing wall of hostility', and created in himself 'one new humanity in place of the two' (Eph. 2.14, 15). The critical phrase for Paul with regard to the nature of the church is 'new

9. E. Brunner has argued the thesis that the earlier, Pauline ecclesiology, based on the ecclesial community under the direction of the Spirit, stands opposed in the New Testament to the Jerusalem form of 'the church'. He also argues that by the end of the New Testament period, the Pauline community had given way to the hierarchical and institutional form of the church: see his *Dogmatics. III. The Christian Doctrine of the Church, Faith and the Consummation* (London: Lutterworth, 1962). This thesis was presented earlier in *The Misunderstanding of the Church* (London: Lutterworth, 1952). Karl Barth's response and criticism of Brunner's thesis is found in *Church Dogmatics* (ET; Edinburgh: T. & T. Clark, 1962), 4.2, pp. 683-87. O. Weber, while not following Brunner's argument to its conclusion, also suggests that the New Testament 'always conceives of the *Ekklesia* as the "eschatological community of salvation"', and that this is based on the fact that the coming Christ is the present Christ in the community (*Foundation of Dogmatics* [Grand Rapids: Eerdmans, 1983], II, pp. 514-15).

creation'. This is 'from God, who reconciled us to himself through Christ, and has given us the ministry of reconciliation' (2 Cor. 5.17, 18).

4. *Eschatological Empowerment of the Apostolic Community*

The relation between the risen Christ and the historical Jesus is established by promise and fulfillment, and is a relation of election and grace. That is to say, the connection between the old covenant and the new covenant is a real one, but also one that is eschatological in nature. The relation is not predicated upon historical necessity, but upon covenant faithfulness on the part of God. The giving of the Holy Spirit through Pentecost is a testimony to God's faithfulness and the creation of continuity between the messianic community and the messiah.

Following the reading of the messianic promise of the anointing of the Spirit from Isaiah (61.1, 2; 58.6), Luke records Jesus as saying, 'Today this Scripture has been fulfilled in your hearing' (Lk. 4.18-21). Mission theology operates in the eternal present so that with the coming of the Spirit to each contemporary day, the 'today this is fulfilled' comes to pass. Because the Spirit is the Spirit of the resurrected Christ, and also the Spirit which forms the life and ministry of the church, there is continuity with both past and future.

This is the breakthrough which Jürgen Moltmann has contributed with his book, *The Church in the Power of the Spirit*, when he suggests that the messianic mission of Jesus is not entirely completed in his death and resurrection. Through the coming of the Spirit, his history becomes the church's gospel for the world. The church participates in his mission, becoming the messianic church of the coming kingdom. There is, says Moltmann, a 'conversion to the future' through which the church enters into the messianic proclamation of the coming of the kingdom.[10]

10. J. Moltmann, *The Church in the Power of the Spirit* (New York: Harper & Row, 1977), pp. 83, 80. Moltmann suggests that 'the sending of the Spirit' can be viewed as 'a sacrament of the Kingdom' (p. 199). 'In so far as Jesus as the Messiah is the mystery of the rule of God, the signs of the messianic era are also part of his mystery. In so far as the crucified and risen Jesus manifests the salvation of the world determined on by God, proclamation and faith and the outpouring of the Holy Spirit on the Gentiles are also part of this salvation...It also follows that a christological-ecclesiological rendering of the term—Christ and the church as the primal and fundamental sacrament of salvation—certainly touches on a further sphere covered by the New Testament but does not go far enough, especially if the church of Christ is only understood in its sacraments and not at the same time in the

When Paul was challenged as to the authority by which the Gentile churches were operating, he argued that with the death and resurrection of Jesus Christ a new age had broken into the old, so that these eras now overlapped. As David Ford puts it:

> The new is being realised now through the Holy Spirit, so the most urgent thing is to live according to the Spirit. It certainly involves present eschatological freedom, hope beyond death and the significance of the Church in history...But as regards contemporary ecclesiology there are two implications that seem most important. The first is that the determinisms of history are broken by the gift of the Spirit as the downpayment of what is to come. If God is free to open history from the future then the future need not mirror the past. In the Church this combines with the message of the cross to allow for discontinuities and innovations. The criterion for something is no longer whether that is how the Church has done it in the past or even whether Jesus said it (cf. Paul on his means of subsistence) but whether it embodies the new creation and its vision of love...For Paul the content of eschatology is christological and the final reality is face to face.[11]

While there was historical discontinuity between the community of Jesus Christ prior to his death and resurrection and the community of believers empowered at Pentecost, there was also a direct continuity through the identity of the Spirit given at Pentecost and the person of Jesus Christ. This was the distinctive reality of the early church and its source of empowerment. The continuity was one of the Spirit rather than the institutionalizing of historical precedence. The fact that this 'pneumatological' constitution of the church's life and mission did not last, has been noted by Edward Schillebeeckx.

---

context of the eschatology of world history' (pp. 204-205).

11. D.F. Ford, 'Faith in the Cities: Corinth and the Modern City', in Gunton and Hardy (eds.), *On Being the Church*, p. 248. Because Paul's concept of authority was grounded in the eschatological as well as the historical Christ, Ford says: 'Perhaps on no other area are Churches so subject to legalisms, bondage to the past, entanglement with distorting interests and idolatries than in that of authority. Paul's clarity about his ministry as helping to realise God's future and his refusal to absolutise past or present is a principle of liberation with wide relevance. At its heart is the great symbol of authority, the glory of God, enabling freedom and confidence, inspiring a whole community in energetic mutuality and glorifying of God, while recognising that the full transformation into the glory is to come (2 Cor. 3). And incarnating the glory of God is the fact of Christ, the ultimate embodiment of a persuasive, vulnerable authority, freely distributed through his Spirit' (p. 253).

> The continuity between Jesus Christ and the church is fundamentally based on the Spirit. The ministry is a specific sign of this, and not the substance itself. Whereas in the early church ministry was seen rather in the sign of the Spirit which fills the church, later, people began to see the ministry in terms of the ecclesiology which regards the church as the extension of the incarnation. People moved from a pneuma-christological view of ministry to a theology of ministry based directly on christology.[12]

Colin Gunton makes the same point when he calls for a renewed consideration and emphasis on the constitution of the church by the Spirit rather than an overstress on its institution by direct continuity with the past.

> What is required, therefore, is a reconsideration of the relation of pneumatology and christology, with a consequent reduction of stress on the Church's institution by Christ and a greater emphasis on its constitution by the Spirit. In such a way we may create fewer self-justifying and historicising links with the past and give more stress to the necessity for the present particularities of our churchly arrangements to be constituted by the Spirit...What is needed is, rather, a greater emphasis on the action of the Holy Spirit towards Jesus as the source of the *particularity* and so historicity of his humanity.[13]

The concept of apostolic authority as rooted in historical continuity with the twelve disciples and the first-century apostles has tended to institutionalize and to paralyze the church's order of ministry. The church, as Paul was to declare, is 'built upon the foundation of the apostles and prophets'. But what he also saw clearly was that it is a foundation with 'Christ Jesus himself as the cornerstone' (Eph. 2.20). There is a strong tendency in the theology of the church to ground the nature and ministry of the church in historical continuity with the foundation, with the incarnation as the 'cornerstone'. Because the first-century apostles are no longer 'living apostles', apostolic succession was instituted as the only link between the ruling bishop and the original apostles.

While the Reformers rejected this 'mechanical' succession of apostolic authority through the office, they tended to substitute in place of the concept of apostolic succession the notion of apostolic teaching, that is,

---

12. E. Schillebeeckx, *The Church with a Human Face: A New and Expanded Theology of Ministry* (New York: Crossroad, 1985), p. 206.

13. C. Gunton, 'The Church on Earth: The Roots of Community', in Gunton and Hardy (eds.), *On Being the Church*, pp. 62-63.

the content of the gospel of Christ bound with the canon of Holy Scripture.

In that Christ was the 'cornerstone', as Paul suggested, and the fact that this cornerstone is a 'living stone', as Peter reminds us (1 Pet. 2.4-5), the apostolic nature of the church is grounded in a 'living apostle', who is Jesus Christ. The book of Hebrews identifies Jesus as the 'apostle of our confession' (Heb. 3.1). The chief apostle of the church is Jesus Christ, and his apostleship continues through the age of the church until the end of the age.

In describing the sequence of events which will occur in connection with the day of resurrection, Paul argues that Christ, having been raised from the dead, constitutes the 'first fruits' of all who have died and who will be raised at his coming.

> But each in his own order: Christ the first fruits, then at his coming those who belong to Christ. Then comes the end, when he hands over the kingdom to God the Father after he has destroyed every ruler and every authority and power...When all things are subjected to him, then the Son himself will also be subjected to the one who put all things in subjection under him, so that God may be all in all (1 Cor. 15.23-24, 28).

This describes clearly the apostolic nature of Jesus' own ministry. As the Son of God, he was given the messianic task of inaugurating the kingdom of God to rule over all things. When this is completed, he will then be relieved of his apostolic mission and will continue in the eternal relation he has with the Father as the Son. Until then, Jesus continues to be the apostolic source of the church's life and mission in the world through his power and presence as Holy Spirit. Pentecost, therefore, is the eschatological manifestation of the apostolic nature of the church as the continuing praxis of Jesus' apostolic authority to the end of the age.

Wolfhart Pannenberg makes a significant contribution to this discussion when he suggests that the eschatological motif in the early church provides the criterion for an empowering concept of apostolicity which is centered on the resurrection of Christ and his coming to the world by the Holy Spirit. While continuing to hold to the apostolic foundation in the first century, Pannenberg suggests that there was an eschatological motif among these apostles lighting the way forward to the transforming power of the resurrection.

This is what I see: the apostolic nature of Christ's continuing ministry through the Spirit as a power that will increasingly transform the church itself into what it should be at the end. Pannenberg describes what this means in terms of the apostolic life of the church in this present age.

> It follows that the true *vita apostolica* is to be sought in the life of the church's leaders and in the life of individual Christians who let themselves be permeated by the final, all-encompassing, liberating, and transforming truth of Jesus. The *vita apostolica* does not mean copying the way of life of the apostolic age or what we think that way of life was, and it certainly cannot be lived by borrowing this or that form of life from the regulations of the apostles. That which was apostolic then may be irrelevant today or may even be a hindrance to our apostolic tasks. This insight enables the church to be free to live in its own historicity as opposed to that of the apostolic age and still remain in continuity with the mission of the apostles.[14]

Even as there was a 'first-century church', there will be a 'last-century church'. The church itself should seek to become the church which Christ desires to find when he comes, where distinctions of race, religion, ethnicity, economic and political status, and gender identity will no longer be found in the church and its apostolic life. This is what Paul clearly had in mind in writing to the Galatians: 'There is no longer Jew or Greek, there is no longer slave or free, there is no longer male and female; for all of you are one in Christ Jesus' (Gal. 3.28). This surely was not a description of the first-century church, but Paul believed that it should be a description of the 'last-century' church if it continued to grow into its own true nature under the apostolic ministry of Christ through the Spirit.

Some in the church today may feel compelled to deny the office of pastoral ministry to women either on traditional grounds or scriptural grounds in order to be apostolic. In fact, they may be placing a hindrance on the apostolic ministry of Christ in the church today. If the Spirit of the resurrected Jesus is present in the contemporary church, anointing and calling women as well as men to the office of pastoral ministry, then

---

14. W. Pannenberg, *The Church* (Philadelphia: Westminster Press, 1983), p. 57. 'In this age of historical consciousness, therefore, the church needs a new concept of apostolicity that will allow it to recognize without reservation the difference between the age of the apostles and its own day, without thereby losing its connection with the mission of the apostles. Attention to the eschatological motif in the early Christian apostolate can help us do this. The only criterion of apostolic teaching in this sense is whether and to what degree it is able to set forth the final truth and comprehensive universality of the person and work of Christ in the transforming and saving significance of his resurrection and the power that gives light to the world' (pp. 56-57).

this is surely an apostolic ministry as commissioned by Jesus as the living apostle.[15]

According to Paul, the baptism of the Spirit by which persons become part of the body of Christ removes historical discrimination between Jew and Gentile, male and female (1 Cor. 12.13; Gal. 3.27-28). Through baptism into Christ both men and women share in Christ's praxis of ministry through the Spirit. Edward Schillebeeckx makes this point emphatically when he says:

> The baptism of the Spirit removes historical discriminations. In principle, Christian baptism completely removes all these social and historical oppositions within the community of believers. Of course this is a performative and not a descriptive statement; however, it is a statement which expresses the hope which needs to be realized now, already, as a model in the community...According to Paul and the whole of the New Testament, at least within Christian communities of believers, relationships involving subjection are no longer to prevail. We find this principle throughout the New Testament, and it was also to determine strongly the New Testament view of ministry. This early-Christian egalitarian ecclesiology in no way excludes leadership and authority; but in that case authority must be one filled with the Spirit, from which no Christian, man or woman, is excluded in principle on the basis of the baptism of the Spirit.[16]

The church does not 'push' the kingdom into the world through its own institutional and pragmatic strategies. Rather, it is 'pulled' into the world as it follows the praxis of the Spirit. The church is thus constantly being 're-created' through the mission of the Spirit. At the same time, it has historical and ecclesial continuity and universality through its participation in the person and mission of Christ Jesus through the Spirit.

All apostolic authority and witness is grounded in the living and coming Christ, not only in the first-century Christ. The ministry of the church is apostolic when it recognizes the eschatological praxis of the Spirit in the present age, and interprets this in accordance with the Jesus Christ who is the same, yesterday, today and forever (Heb. 13.8). The author of Hebrews reveals the priestly nature of Jesus when he argues that Jesus is a priest after the order of Melchizedek, and not after that of Aaron (Heb. 6–7). Melchizedek was 'without genealogy, having neither

---

15. See my essay, 'The Resurrection of Jesus as Hermeneutical Criterion: A Case for Sexual Parity in Pastoral Ministry', in *Theological Students Fellowship Bulletin* (Mar.–Apr. 1986), pp. 15-20, and my *Ministry on the Fireline*, pp. 92-98.

16. E. Schillebeeckx, *The Church with a Human Face*, pp. 38-39.

beginning of days nor end of life' (Heb. 7.3). Apostolic authority is eschatological, not merely genealogical.

5. *The Empowering Ministry of Paraclesis*

The priestly nature of Christ's ministry through the power of the Spirit means that he comes alongside the church as the missionary people of God to be the advocate, or *paraclete*, by which those called to give leadership are empowered to empower the people for ministry. The church of Jesus Christ called forth by the Holy Spirit is an 'ordained' community, baptized into the ministry of Christ. The leadership of this community is a function of the community, and is empowered by the community: it is not a status over and against it.[17]

Baptism into Jesus Christ can be considered to be an 'ordination' into the ministry of Christ.[18] Thus, all those baptized into Christ by the one baptism and the one Spirit (1 Cor. 12.13) are summoned into the praxis of Christ's continuing ministry and are empowered for this ministry by the *paraclēsis* of the Holy Spirit. This 'baptism into ministry' by the Spirit breaks the historical determinism of an order of ministry with its precedents of race, gender and status.

The church has tended to stress two forms of the ministry of the Word of God: *kerygma*, the Word proclaimed; and *didachē*, the Word taught. This leaves *paraclēsis*, the ministry of encouragement or exhortation, to the Holy Spirit. Such a way of thinking separates the rational form of the Word from the relational. It tends towards a

17. 'Leadership is a function of the Christian community', says Werner Jeanrond, 'and not a status over against it' ('Community and Authority', in Gunton and Hardy [eds.], *On Being the Church*, p. 96). 'That the Christian community needs some form of leadership nobody doubts. That the Christian community needs an ordained ministry, however, cannot be taken for granted, but needs to be discussed with reference to both the theological demands of the Christian faith and the organisational demands of a contemporary human association. Given these requirements it seems rather odd that in some Churches the particular understanding of the ordained ministry is still focused on the now obsolete metaphysical understanding of past times and on the organisational needs of medieval congregations. Most urgently needed is a reassessment of the relationship between the ordained minister and the ordained community' (p. 98).

18. See R.S. Anderson (ed.), *Theological Foundations for Ministry* (Grand Rapids, MI: Eerdmans, 1979), 'Christ's Ministry through his Whole Church', ch. 15, pp. 430-57.

presentation of the gospel through preaching and teaching, as though the task is fully completed if one is faithful to the *content* of the Word. The human response to the Word of God is thus primarily a rational one, so that the emphasis is on what one understands as true, and not how one lives truthfully and authentically. If the Holy Spirit is considered at all as part of the gospel, it is to enlighten the mind, or to bend the will, rather than to complete the gospel of forgiveness through producing health and wholeness at the level of the emotional and relational self.

We can see the problem with this dichotomy between Word and Spirit in the pronouncement of absolution from sin, where the truth of forgiveness is upheld without regard for truthful forgiveness as measured in spiritual and psychological health and wholeness. Under this form of teaching and practice, Christians tend to have all sorts of emotional problems which are not dealt with as part of the praxis of the gospel of Christ. One can even go so far as to suggest that the proclamation of the gospel of Christ without regard to the affective, or feeling, level of those who hear and respond contributes to emotional disorder and dysfunction.

We need to see *paraclēsis* as critical to the praxis of the Word of Christ as proclaimed, taught and experienced. Word and Spirit must not be separated as though the Word is primarily mental and objective while the Spirit is primarily existential and subjective. A better way of looking at the praxis of *kerygma*, *didachē* and *paraclēsis* would be as follows: were God to come to me only in the mode of *kerygma*, that could mean 'God has come: be silent before him'—hence, my realities and interests do not really matter. The reality of the kingdom takes precedence. Were God to come only in the mode of *didachē*, that could mean 'God has come: the road on which life has brought me no longer is important; he has another way for me'. When God comes to me in the mode of *paraclēsis*, it dawns upon me: 'God has come and he wants to live in my place and my situation'. Thus, God enters my situation in its concrete historical reality, and appears in it for that very purpose. Through the paracletic presence of the Holy Spirit, Jesus himself takes up my cause as his own.[19]

Through this ministry of Christ in the power of the Holy Spirit, I am not simply addressed with the demands of the kingdom of God: I am

19. I am indebted to Jacob Firet for the substance of this paragraph: see his *Dynamics in Pastoring* (trans. J. Vriend; Grand Rapids, MI: Eerdmans, 1986 [1982]), p. 70.

grasped by the love of God as Father, upheld by the intercession of God as Son, and made to share in the inner life of Godself through the indwelling Holy Spirit. This paracletic ministry of Christ through the Spirit does not leave me as an individual, but incorporates me into the fellowship of the body of Christ, the missionary people of God. As part of this body and mission, I too share in the apostolic life of Christ in being 'sent' into the world.

From this we can see that the paracletic ministry of Jesus is grounded in the incarnation. Becoming truly human he became and is the advocate for all that is human, pledging his humanity on behalf of all others. This advocacy is more than an instrumental one, performed for the purpose of effecting legal atonement. Yes, he did die on the cross in full payment of the penalty of sin and so made atonement. But atonement without advocacy does not empower those for whom Christ died so as to recover their own humanity in full fellowship with God and each other. James Torrance put this point well when he wrote:

> Christ does not heal us by standing over against us, diagnosing our sickness, prescribing medicine for us to take, and then going away, to leave us to get better by obeying his instructions—as an ordinary doctor might. No, He becomes the patient! He assumes that very humanity which is in need of redemption, and by being anointed by the Spirit in our humanity, by a life of perfect obedience, by dying and rising again, for us, our humanity is healed *in him*. We are not just healed 'through Christ' because of the work of Christ but 'in and through Christ'.[20]

The advocacy of Christ for humans is the pledge of his humanity as the continuing representation of human persons to God, and the basis for the mode of paraclesis carried out by the Holy Spirit. The resurrection of Christ affirms his humanity and also ours as having an objective possibility of reconciliation to God. Thus, the Spirit has no incarnation of its own, nor does the Spirit become incarnate in the humanity of the church as the body of Christ. The church participates in the humanity of the risen Christ as the objective basis for its own fellowship with God. So also, the continuing humanity of Christ as the paraclete takes place through the life and humanity of the church in its apostolic mission.

The incarnation of God in Jesus is the pledge of the humanity of Jesus

---

20. J.B. Torrance, 'The Vicarious Humanity of Christ', in T.F. Torrance (ed.), *The Incarnation: Ecumenical Studies in the Nicene-Constantinopolitan Creed AD 381* (Edinburgh: Handsel Press, 1981), p. 141.

Christ on behalf of all human persons. Thus, Christ is the advocate of all persons; not only those who are 'in Christ'. 'Through Christ' all persons have an advocate with the Father. This enables Paul to say: 'All this is from God, who reconciled us to himself through Christ and has given us the ministry of reconciliation; that is, in Christ God was reconciling the world to himself, not counting their trespasses against them, and entrusting the message of reconciliation to us' (2 Cor. 5.18-19). The apostle John holds the same view. Immediately after writing that 'we have an advocate with the Father, Jesus Christ the righteous', he adds, 'and he is the atoning sacrifice for our sins, and not for ours only but also for the sins of the whole world' (1 Jn 2.1-2).

The praxis of Pentecost begins its theological reflection from the perspective of this paracletic ministry of the Spirit of Christ taking place in the world before it takes place in the church. That is to say, Christ is not first of all contained by the nature of the church, so that only when Christ is shared by the church does the world encounter him. Rather, as Thomas Torrance has put it, 'Christ clothed with His gospel meets with Christ clothed with the desperate needs of men'.[21]

This paracletic ministry of Jesus, of course, presupposes the *kerygma* as the announcement of this act of reconciliation. But even as the incarnation provides the basis for the *kerygma* in the humanity of Jesus Christ as the ground of reconciliation, so the continued humanity of Christ provides the ground for the paracletic ministry of the Holy Spirit and the kerygmatic message. Christ is present as the advocate of the people who have not yet heard the good news. The praxis of Christ is that of encouragement for those who need help and support in hearing and believing the gospel of forgiveness. The gospel of encouragement is the work of Christ through the power of the Holy Spirit, enabling and empowering persons to receive the gospel of forgiveness. Through the empowering of the Holy Spirit, released through Pentecost, the Spirit's ministry becomes 'Christopraxis'; the continued ministry of Christ for the reconciliation of the world to God.

6. *The Gospel of Forgiveness—Empowering Reconciliation*

The kerygmatic form of the gospel of forgiveness is that 'All this is from God, who through Christ reconciled us to himself and gave us the

---

21. T.F. Torrance, 'Service in Jesus Christ', in Anderson (ed.), *Theological Foundations for Ministry*, p. 724.

ministry of reconciliation; that is, in Christ God was reconciling the
world to himself, not counting their trespasses against them, and
entrusting to us the message of reconciliation' (2 Cor. 5.18-19). This is
the gospel of Christ's reconciliation accomplished through death and
resurrection. This is the gospel which is proclaimed as completed and
sealed as God's work of grace, to be received unconditionally and freely.

The paracletic form of this gospel of forgiveness is also described by
Paul when he wrote to the Thessalonians:

> Our message of the gospel came to you not in word only, but also in
> power and in the Holy Spirit and with full conviction...We were gentle
> among you, like a nurse tenderly caring for her own children...As you
> know, we dealt with each one of you like a father with his children, urging
> and encouraging you and pleading that you lead a life worthy of God,
> who calls you into his own kingdom and glory (1 Thess. 1.5; 2.7, 11).

Paul is not satisfied with proclamation of the gospel of forgiveness
alone. He knows that forgiveness has already been accomplished from
God's side, and that God 'does not count trespasses' against persons
who are sinners. But forgiveness has not yet been accomplished until
there is reconciliation from the human side toward God and toward one
another. This is why Paul found such encouragement in remembering
the transformation of the lives of those in Thessalonica who had received
the gospel of Christ. 'Our coming to you was not in vain', Paul writes to
them, because 'when you received the word of God that you heard from
us, you accepted it not as a human word but as what it really is, God's
word, *which is also at work in you believers*' (1 Thess. 2.1, 13, emphasis
added). This is a gospel of forgiveness which empowers ministry to those
crushed, broken and burdened, and empowers persons to move toward
wholeness.

The pronouncement of absolution from sin is not only a kerygmatic
pronouncement: it is a paracletic process! To give assurance of pardon
and forgiveness to persons based on God's reconciliation to the world
through Christ is not wrong. But it is incomplete without the assurance
which arises from within the lives of those who hear this word. The
word of absolution from sin based on the work of Christ in salvation-
history is premature apart from the praxis of forgiveness as the work of
Christ in the hearts and lives of people through the presence and power
of the Holy Spirit.

Let me say it as clearly as I can: a vision of forgiveness and freedom
comes from the burning light of Pentecost before it can be seen in the

sunless shadows of the cross. This has enormous theological significance, both for the proclamation of the gospel of Christ and for the spiritual formation of Christ in the lives of people. A theology which is not continually enlightened by the praxis of Christ at work in the transformation of human lives can become a toxic theology. A theology which does not begin and end with grace from God's side as well as from the human side is a theology which 'binds heavy burdens' (Mt. 23.4) and sets a 'yoke of slavery' (Gal. 5.1) on those who look for freedom and forgiveness. A spiritual piety which is produced by such a theology poisons rather than purifies.

All too often people become less whole and less human under the influence of a theology which does not understand that 'take up your cross' must be preceded by 'the Spirit of life in Christ Jesus has set you free from the law of sin and death' (Rom. 8.2). The litmus test of theology is not only what it says of God but what it does to persons when it is preached, taught and practiced. The theology of Pentecost humanizes and heals, for it is a theology of resurrection and life, not of death and despair.

Christopraxis in the mode of paraclesis is a summons and invitation for humanity to become truly human; it is an exhortation to move out of the place of sorrow and humiliation into a community of reconciliation, peace and dignity. Christopraxis as a form of the real presence of Christ is a pledge of comfort and consolation to the oppressed and the broken. It may have to take the 'worldly' form of the presence of Christ in many cases, or the 'non-religious' form of Christ's presence in the world, as Bonhoeffer came to see it.[22] The praxis of forgiveness must first of all be a praxis of reconciliation and restoration of humanity in the world, before it can have authenticity in the liturgy of the church.

Christopraxis means that this paracletic ministry of Jesus is a pledge of his humanity to and for all human persons in the concrete historical, social and moral dilemma of their existence. As the advocate for humanity, the criterion for what is authentically human is his own humanity, not a general principle of humanity. In his paracletic ministry, Jesus pledges his own humanity which has already passed through judgment and the penalty of death for the humanity of all persons. Jesus' advocacy is not only for the best of humanity, leaving the rest to their own fate. Rather, he is the advocate for all of humanity, bringing every human

22. D. Bonhoeffer, *Letters and Papers from Prison* (trans. R. Fuller *et al.*; London: SCM Press, enlarged edn, 1971 [1953]), pp. 300, 344, 362.

person into the place where no human distinctive, whether racial, sexual, or social, can serve as a criterion for relation with God or with one another.

For the church, Christopraxis means that actions which involve advocacy for the full humanity of persons have a priority and authority grounded in the humanity and ministry of Christ himself. The strategy of paracletic ministry is non-negotiable in terms of advocacy for persons who suffer from discrimination, oppression and human torment of any kind. This strategy is not derived from ideological concerns nor from moral law alone. The strategy of advocacy as a form of Christopraxis is God's own strategy, enacted in Jesus Christ, and through Jesus Christ for the sake of the world.

To separate evangelism and social justice as two issues to be debated and then prioritized is to split humanity down the middle. Theologically, it is a denial of the incarnation of God. In assuming humanity in its condition of estrangement and brokenness, Jesus produced reconciliation in 'his own body', so that we can no longer see humanity apart from its unity in Jesus Christ. To approach persons in the context of their social, physical and spiritual existence, and only offer healing and reconciliation for the spiritual, is already a betrayal of the gospel as well as of humanity.[23]

Christopraxis as a form of the ministry of the church *expects* the eschatological presence of Christ to be released as a 'charismatic' experience. In this is the peril of succumbing to the temptations of

23. The issue of the relation of an evangelism which is directed toward individual salvation, as contrasted with a gospel of the kingdom which seeks social justice and transformation of society, has been a continuing debate within the Lausanne Conference movement, with John Stott as a primary spokesperson. See his *Evangelism and Social Responsibility: An Evangelical Commitment* (London: Paternoster Press, 1982). A more recent discussion between John Stott and David Edwards can be found in *Evangelical Essentials: A Liberal–Evangelical Dialogue* (Downers Grove, IL: IVP, 1988), pp. 273-331. The prevailing theology of the church growth movement tends to divide social responsibility from evangelism, giving priority to evangelism, but also attempting to include social responsibility as indispensable to the mission of the church, though not a primary form of that mission: see, for example, G.W. Peters, *A Theology of Church Growth* (Grand Rapids, MI: Zondervan, 1981). The apostles, Peters writes, 'put spiritual ministries before social and material services...combined prayer with preaching without allowing either to usurp the place of the other...[and] put evangelism before all other ministries' (p. 125).

pietism, individualism and corporate inwardness, as alternatives to genuine Christian experience. To the extent that this happens, there is no longer 'danger' in the manifestation of the kingdom of God in the real presence of Christ. The authentic charism which empowers is Christ's power, which redeems humanity from the dehumanizing social, political and institutional forms of power.

The goal of Christopraxis is not merely deliverance from evil nor emancipation from structures which bind, but empowerment to be truly human under circumstances and situations which are not yet redeemed. Pentecost occurs wherever and whenever the kingdom of God appears with the power of the Spirit manifesting the eschatological signs of healing, forgiveness of sins, and restoration to emotional and spiritual wholeness in community. Pentecost promises a paraclete to everyone who stumbles and falls, to everyone who is weak and powerless, to everyone who is tormented and torn by the demons of doubt, discouragement and despair. Jesus himself is the first paraclete. The Holy Spirit continues this paracletic ministry as 'another paraclete' (Jn 14.16), sent by the Father as the very presence of Jesus.

The presence and ministry of the Spirit are the presence and praxis of Christ. This is Christopraxis—not a doctrine for which life is sacrificed, but the very being and life of God given for the sake of preserving and upholding human life; not an ideology or strategy which fights inhumanity for the sake of becoming human, but the very humanity of God which seeks the transformation of all that is inhuman in humanity. This life of Christ is vicarious in the sense that he offered his own humanity as a pledge for ours by offering up his own obedience to the Father as the faithful Son. The bond between our humanity and his is not a metaphysical or mystical connection, but is a filial bond—we are bound to him by the 'spirit of adoption' by which we have received his very own Spirit so that we too can cry, 'Abba, Father' (Rom. 8.15-17).

BISHOPS AND DEACONS:
RENEWING THE OFFICES

Ian Breward

The consecration of The Rev. Dr Jamieson in 1990 opens up important opportunities for 'co-creation' in patterns of ministry to complement what has already begun with women as presbyters and deacons. The slow emergence of a permanent diaconate in the Anglican communion and the Roman Catholic Church is itself another factor in the re-assessment of the ministry of oversight.[1] If renewed diaconates are able to embody Christ's servanthood authoritatively, and by virtue of long experience become the eyes and ears of the bishops, that will be very important for the exercise of episcopal authority in the church today.

1.   G. Hearn, 'The diaconate and the Bishop!', *Distinctive Diaconate* 26 (May 1990); G. Ogilvie (ed.), *Deliberate Oversight?* (Bramcote Grove, 1991) says little about episcopal learning from other ministries. Nor does A. Cadwallader and D. Richardson (eds.), *Episcopacy* (Adelaide: Anglican Board of Christian Education, 1994). There is a growing literature on the permanent diaconate and its implications: see J.E. Booty, *The Servant Church* (New York: Morehouse Barlow, 1982); *Concilium* 198 (1988); P. McCaslin and M.G. Lawler, *Sacrament of Service* (Mahwah, NJ: Paulist Press, 1986); D.W. McMonigle, 'The Diaconate' (MTh thesis, Melbourne College of Divinity, 1988); R. Nowell, *The Ministry of Service* (London: Burns & Oates, 1986); O. Plater, *Many Servants* (Cambridge, MA: Cowley, 1991); S. Platten, *A Diaconal Church* (Birmingham: Additional Curates Society, n.d.); Brother Victor, *The Servant Leader* (London: Advisory Council for the Church's Ministry occasional papers, 1987); see also various official Catholic reports such as *Permanent Deacons in the United States* (1985); *Service Ministry of the Deacon* (Washington, DC: US Catholic Conference, 1988); and *Deacons in the Ministry of the Church* (London: General Synod, 1988); *Deacons for Scotland* (Edinburgh: St Andrews Press, 1990); G. Hall, *The Deacon's Ministry* (Leominster: Gracewing, 1991).

1. *The Historical Struggle of the Diaconate*

Paul would be surprised by the varied conclusions which have been drawn from his greeting to the leaders of the church in Philippi. He would be even more surprised by the variety of roles performed by modern bishops and deacons, not to mention the strict liturgical and canonical boundaries between these functions and offices. Exegetes do not agree on what Paul meant precisely, and it has so far also been impossible for Christians to agree on a hermeneutic which trims the luxuriant foliage of claim and counter-claim over the ministries of over-sight and service. Even where the ambiguities of early Christian usage of the *diakonos* words are recognized, and some justice is done to the remarkable expansion of meaning and practice which has occurred over the centuries, the practice of episcopal and diaconal ministry is shaped by a variety of other considerations. In particular, cultural contexts shape the hearing of Scripture, tradition and the Spirit very powerfully.

Escaping from the weight of history so that ministry can be reshaped by the contexts of mission and service is a difficult task. Where changes have occurred, that has often been because of new religious movements and schism. Historians cannot avoid noting the irony of reformers and their successors discovering how slender can be the legacy of those bright hopes for reform of ministry and the exercise of leadership. Paul's charismatic approach has rarely been understood by later users of the titles of bishop and deacon. Nor have the collegiality and mutual sympathy sketched in the rest of the letter been noticeably present in relationships between bishops and deacons in later centuries. By the fourth century, the ministries of deacons and deaconesses in the Imperial Church appear to have been diminishing in significance as hierarchical understandings of office and authority became increasingly important.[2] There were still signs of earlier partnership between bishops and deacons,

---

2. J. Barnett, *The Diaconate* (New York: Seabury, 1981), pp. 95-122 (new edn Valley Forge: Trinity, 1995); an interesting sketch of diaconal ministry is found in J.M. Harden (ed.), *The Ethiopic Didascalia* (London: SPCK, 1920), pp. 48-53, 95-98; there is valuable historical material in J. Pokusa, *A Canonical Historical Study of the Diaconate* (Washington, DC: Catholic University of America Press, 1979); J. Grierson, *The Deaconess* (London: Church Information Office, 1987); A.J. Martimort, *Deaconesses* (San Francisco: Ignatius, 1986); see also T. Halton and J. Williams (eds.), *Diakonia* (Washington, DC: Catholic University of America Press, 1986).

but the rapid expansion of the church in the fourth and fifth centuries enhanced the authority of bishops and presbyters.

Attempts to restore significance to the ministry occurred in many of the Reformation churches, and again in the nineteenth century, but these changes did not significantly affect the practice of episcopal and presbyteral or priestly ministry. Indeed, diaconal ministry became linked with the roles of women and the development of impressive institutions for relief and social service.[3] In turn, those changes often further divorced *diakonia* from the life of the local congregation, unless there was financial and voluntary involvement.

Since the two world wars, there have been important changes which have deeply affected the assumptions about ministerial authority. The death of many monarchies, the end of the powers of aristocratic élites, and the speedy growth of democratic ideas, have weakened aspects of episcopal absolutism and clerical authority. Once-powerful churches have been marginalized and persecuted, and colonial churches have had to learn to live without privileges after the departure of the colonizing powers. Fresh attention has also been paid to the relationship between christology and ecclesiology. In a wide variety of contexts, official documents and monographs have underlined the links between mission and servanthood.[4] Thus, it has almost become a truism to speak of *diakonia* as one of the dominant motifs in all Christian discipleship within the exercise of authority and understanding of ministry.

The theologies of Barth and Bonhoeffer have been exceptionally important in bringing out the importance of servanthood for the self-understanding of the church, along with the vision of the church as a communion of the baptized, committed to ministry and mission, because they are gifted by the Spirit.[5] Within that context of the ministry of the

3. E. McKee, *Diakonia in the Classical Reformed Tradition and Today* (Grand Rapids: Eerdmans, 1989); G. Swensson, *Kyrkorma och diakonien* (Uppsala: Proveritate, 1989), deals with more recent times; J.E. Olsen, *One Ministry, Many Roles* (St Louis: Concordia, 1992) and R. Turre, *Diakonik* (Neukirchen–Vluyn: Neukirchener Verlag, 1991) both deal helpfully with diaconal history.

4. *The Role of the Diakonia of the Church* (Geneva: WCC, 1966); C. Ceccom and K. Paludan, *My Neighbour–Myself* (Geneva: WCC, 1988); P. Gregorius, *The Meaning and Nature of Diakonia* (Geneva: WCC, 1988); K. Poser, *Called to be Neighbours* (Geneva: WCC, 1987); J. van Klinken, *Diakonia* (Grand Rapids: Eerdmans, 1989); and C. Williams, *The Service of the Church in the 20th Century* (Canberra: Australian Frontier, n.d.).

5. J.I. McCord and T.H.L. Parker (eds.), *Service in Christ* (London: Epworth,

whole people of God, the meaning of ordination has undergone a sea-change in many churches—though the reasons are complex and are in part related to the shortage of priestly vocations among Roman Catholics and the growing significance of a permanent diaconate. The impact of Vatican II decrees has been momentous, as has the use of themes of *diakonia* and servanthood in the World Council of Churches, associated councils, and member churches.

The influence of these theological insights on the actual practice of ministry has been slow. Faculties and seminaries concentrate on the education of presbyters (or priests), and there are few deacons on faculty as yet, able to challenge traditional models of ministerial education and practice from the perspective of an equal but independent ministry with its own distinctive foundations and ethos. The Anglican Roman Catholic International Commission documents and *Baptism, Eucharist and Ministry* focus on the historically difficult issue of the recognition of presbyteral/priestly ministry, since diaconal ministry has been marginal to the vexed issues of authority and sacrament for centuries.

Yet the ecumenical significance of *diakonia* should not be underestimated. It provides an important seedbed for ecumenical partnership, which challenges the priorities of bishops and presbyters. A variety of churches are discovering that taking the diaconate seriously raises issues about ordination, authority, mission and discipleship. Even if some of the conclusions of John Collins's magisterial *Diakonia* are challenged by other exegetes and theologians, the political and social context of the late twentieth century makes a return to authoritarian styles of hierarchical ministry difficult—except in a sectarian religious community that abandons any concern to be comprehensive.[6] There are, however, other theological themes which underline the importance of an incarnational ministry with and for the marginal and the oppressed, even if the diaconal words in the New Testament have a more restricted meaning than many exegetes suggest.[7] The experience of base communities in Latin America provides some valuable perspectives on the relation between theology and involvement in the search for justice. They have

1966) is a fine collection of historical and theological articles on *diakonia*, written to honour Karl Barth.

6.   P. Collins, *No Set Agenda* (Melbourne: Lovell, 1991) looks at these issues in Australian Catholicism.

7.   J.N. Collins, *Diakonia* (New York: Oxford University Press, 1990); this extensive study calls into question many of the conclusions of earlier scholars.

raised sharp questions about the exercise of episcopal authority and the absence of an authentic diaconal ministry that is more than a mere apprenticeship to priesthood.

T.F. Torrance has argued eloquently for a double focus for ministry: service of the Word, and service of response to the Word. They are mutually dependent and each requires the other for its proper fulfilment:

> *The service of response to the Word* is the ministry of the divine mercy to the people in which Christ Himself is pleased to be present, acting as their Representative in lifting them up to the Face of the Father in thanksgiving and worship and in making them His fellow labourers in the pouring out of the divine mercy to all mankind. But it is a *service*, a *diakonia*, in which deacons only *prompt* the people in their responses of prayer and praise and do not act on their behalf, and in which they guide them in their service to mankind and do not undertake it for them.[8]

Torrance regards it as tragic that the church has historically so often lacked a diaconate to guide and to prompt it in the ministry of divine mercy. That has left the presbyteral ministry to fulfil its commission by usurping control over the Lord's inheritance.

Without the service which it is the office of the deacon to set out and to embody, the church has taken over worldly power to fulfil its works of love. The result has been disorder, for 'the ministry of Christ clothed with His Gospel has been kept apart from the ministry of Christ clothed with the need and plight of men, with the result that the ministry of the Gospel has so often lost its relevance to men in the concrete actualities of their existence'.[9] Torrance therefore pleads for *diakonia* based on intercession through the great High Priest, and witness which deals uncompromisingly with separation and estrangement from God, even if that means affliction. Without this service that is based on a reconciled life, the church will be broken by the divisive forces of evil, instead of overcoming them. That powerful vision of service of the gospel, however, is still hard to live. A Church of England report published in 1974, *Deacons in the Church*, explored the abolition of the diaconate but, fortunately, wiser counsels prevailed. Moreover, the British Methodist Conference decided in 1986 to restore and to widen the limited diaconal ministry, which it had abolished in 1978.

One of the great problems hindering development of a distinctive and

---

8. T.F. Torrance, 'Service in Jesus Christ', in McCord and Parker (eds.), *Service in Christ*, p. 13.

9. 'Service in Jesus Christ', p. 14.

permanent diaconate is that definition and discussion is usually dominated by bishops and presbyters, who are not able to give up control
and definition in terms of their own office. Without a strong diaconate,
with insights rooted in service of the forgotten, the other ministries too
easily assume that they know all there is to be known about diaconal
ministry—or, they can even argue that its functions are best exercised
within presbyteral ministry.

2. *A Case Study: 'The Struggle' of the Diaconate in the Australian Uniting Church*

The struggle of the Uniting Church in Australia to renew the diaconate,
and to give the existing ministry of deaconesses a clearer definition and
context, illustrates what a demanding task it can be to open out new
possibilities and to win consent from a majority in the church—especially
where very different views of *diakonia* have been inherited from parent
churches. It has proved very difficult to break free from the idea that
diaconal ministry is peripheral by comparison with the centrality of the
ministry of the Word. This tends to be reinforced by the view that
diaconal ministry is suitable for care of the poor and the disadvantaged.

An order of deaconesses was set up in 1942 by the Methodist General
Conference, and the first members were dedicated in 1945. The Conference had discussed and rejected the possibility of admitting women to
circuit ministry, and did not change that judgment until 1966.[10] By
comparison, the Presbyterian Church of Victoria had begun a deaconess
ministry in the 1890s, giving deaconesses a theological education which
by the 1950s was substantially the same as that of ministers of Word and
sacrament, even though their ministerial function was subordinate. Many
deaconesses chose not to take up the opportunity for ordination to
presbyteral ministry when that began in 1974. Furthermore, it was
deaconesses from Victoria who envisioned a renewed diaconate, while
reserving the right to remain in their ministry, if proposals did not meet
their hopes. Deaconess ministry was never so important for Congregationalists, nor confused with gender issues, for women were eligible for
ordination to the presbyterate from 1927.

The Basis of Union (1971), in article 14, set out issues of ministry,
including the recognition that many sought a renewal of the diaconate:

---

10. B. Feith, *Women in Ministry* (Melbourne: Kyarra, 1990), pp. 9-24.

[I]n which men and women offer their time and talents, representatively
and on behalf of God's people, in the service of mankind in the face of
changing needs. She [The Uniting Church] will so order her life that she
remains open to the possibility that God may call men and women into
such a renewed diaconate: in these circumstances, she may decide to call
them Deacons and Deaconesses whether this service is within or beyond
the life of the congregation (14c).

This concern reflected the theological interests of some members of the
Joint Commission, and the influential studies of deacons and deaconesses
produced by the World Council of Churches in 1965 and 1966. An
important report was produced for the Conference on the church and
society in 1966: *The Role of the Diakonia of the Church in Contemporary
Society*. Collins has argued that some of the exegetical foundations of
these studies make claims for the meaning of *diakonia* which are not
borne out by a careful study of the texts and their context in New
Testament writings. He maintains that *diakonia* refers to God in the
delivery of revelation, and that it is *not* focused on service to one's
neighbour.[11]

Collins makes some valuable points about the way in which exegesis
of diaconal passages has been influenced by German models of diaconal
service.[12] Ministry likewise shaped the way in which the negotiators for
the Uniting Church heard the diaconal texts and the summons to bring
forth justice. The work of the Latin American base communities was just
becoming known; Colin Williams was writing eloquently about the
mission of the church in his *Where in the World?* (1963) and *What in
the World?* (1964); and John Brown was pioneering witness to justice in
South Korea, when the *Basis of Union* was completed. When the first
proposals for diaconal ministry were discussed by the 1979 Assembly of
the Uniting Church, the professional social work model was also
becoming influential, and the report of the Commission on Doctrine
spoke of 'the widespread contemporary conviction that the Church
ought to provide a technically qualified ministry of caring service, and
that this is beyond the scope of the ministry of Word and sacrament'.[13]

While taking the context for ministry seriously, the report grounded
diaconal ministry in the being of Jesus Christ, in whom the church's
being and task coincide. 'The Church cannot seek his word without his

11. Collins, *Diakonia*, p. 251.
12. Collins, *Diakonia*, pp. 8-11.
13. Unpublished report of the Commission on Doctrine, 1979.

deed nor his deed without his word.' Understanding ministry as speaking and proclamation on the one hand, and as acting and healing on the other, had to be distinguished from the common gift and service involving all Christians baptized into Christ. On such grounds the Commission believed that the Uniting Church should 'articulate her diaconal service by a special ministry'. Moreover, recognizing that the early function of deacons was to help the local bishop, the Commission saw no incongruity in developing the diaconate as the serving arm in all parts of the Uniting Church's structure. Churches in the Reformed tradition recognize the importance of taking local context into account when shaping ministry. Hence, they are not prisoners of history, but argue for the freedom of God to call into being new ways of embodying the one ministry of Jesus Christ.

The report therefore proposed a diaconate which gave full attention to the caring task of the church locally in institutions of social welfare. In both the states and the Commonwealth it should stand for just structures, ensuring a fair deal for the less privileged members of our society. Both presbyteral and diaconal ministries have an 'over against' character as well as an 'in and for' nature. Duties of both ministries will overlap, but diaconal ministry must be given freedom to concentrate on its specific tasks. Working closely with local congregations also implies a diaconate with strong liturgical roots, and the responsibility of educating members to fulfil their ministry more adequately.

The referral of the Report to synods and presbyteries for comment by the end of 1980 showed that there was considerable divergence. Many replies rejected the theological distinction between Word and act, and requested clarification of the nature of the church and its ministry. Others were concerned about the danger of institutionalizing the ministry and adding regulations which constricted, rather than liberated. Others felt that ministers of the Word were excluded from protest and action against injustice, and that more scope should be given for church members working locally on social issues to be included in diaconal ministry. Many working in Uniting Church agencies also saw no need to be part of an ordained ministry in order to do the tasks they were already undertaking as employed church members.

These concerns were to take over a decade to work through. Matters were complicated by the varied perspectives of synods, and the absence of a significant number of deaconesses from states other than Victoria. Many members simply had no experience of a designated diaconal ministry. Some felt that a ministry they did not have and did not need was being imposed on them. Others felt strongly that the ministry of deaconesses was a legacy of times when the partnership of women and men in ministry of the Word was impossible. Former Methodists, deeply influenced by their heritage of one ministry, argued that it was better to keep diaconal functions within one ministry. Others felt that the Commission on Doctrine, based in Victoria, was too Barthian in its approach and unsympathetic to more pragmatic and contextual approaches to theological enquiry in other states.

At the 1982 Assembly, the Commission produced a concise summary of responses, and suggested that there were four options for a renewed diaconate:

1. to work in social justice and social welfare;
2. to complement ministry of the Word;
3. to assist ministry of the Word; and
4. to keep the status quo.[14]

The Commission was asked to produce a further report, but the Assembly made an important clarification of the situation of deaconesses by agreeing that they should be ordained, thereby recognizing their position as a distinctive ministry, and closing the debate on whether the ministry was lay or ordained.

At the 1985 Assembly there was significant opposition to the Commission's report, which set out in detail a theological rationale for a renewed diaconate. That was in part shaped by the submission of the Deaconess Association of Victoria, which argued that there was a fifth option: basing a diaconate on a special charism for service, inter-related with the ministry of the Word and the mission of the whole people of God. Diaconal ministry, they argued, had its own integrity and was not simply a bag in which to keep remainders from other ministries. The Commission, however, sought to clarify the nature of representative ministry and how a diaconate could bear witness to the kingdom inside and outside the church, 'freeing the powerless, so that they see how such freedom is grounded in Christ and the salvation he offers'. The call to service demanded 'the same kind of focus in the ordering of the church as does the summons to hear the Word of God'.[15] To the chagrin of some who were saving their salvos for the end of the debate,

14. *Assembly Minutes* (1982), pp. 28-31.
15. *Assembly Minutes* (1985), p. 77.

the President ruled that the key motions should be put so that the business of the report was completed before lunch (!). Thus, the Assembly agreed to establish a renewed diaconate, and asked another committee to draw up detailed proposals for its implementation by the 1988 Assembly, after the Standing Committee had given its approval to the submissions.

Under the leadership of Charles Lavender, the committee undertook a wide range of consultations, and carefully studied the shape of diaconates in other churches. One of the potential areas of difficulty was the relation between presbyteral and diaconal ministry, for some ministers of the Word clearly felt unhappy about working with deacons who would be constitutionally equal, and who could gather significant parish support for an emphasis on mission and justice. There were also concerns about the definition of ordination and whether there should be some way of ordering the significant numbers of youth workers.

The result was that the Standing Committee refused to recommend the implementation of the report.[16] Reservations about the model of diaconate proposed, its overlaps with responsibilities of ministers of the Word, and the failure of the report to deal adequately with the diaconal responsibilities of members, were all involved. What was needed, it was argued, was a wider study of ministry. The debates were spirited, but the Standing Committee carried the Assembly. Deaconesses and candidates for the diaconate were hurt and angered by what seemed a calculated rebuff to over a decade of attempts to give their ministry some definition. Even the proposed service of ordination for deaconesses was put on hold. Though the resolutions of the Standing Committee affirmed the ministry of deaconesses (which now included some men, one of whom was a former presbyter), the deaconesses felt that they had in fact been rejected and marginalized. In the closing sessions of the Assembly of 1988, Principal Graeme Ferguson of United Theological College, Sydney, and Dr Jill Tabart of Launceston, moved a comprensive motion which offered a way through the divisions which had been exposed.

They asked the Standing Committee to appoint a group to study issues of ministry and whatever was required to equip the whole people of God for their ministry and mission in a changing world.[17] An influential group both in the Assembly and outside it wanted a theological framework that would help the Uniting Church weigh the competing

16. *Assembly Minutes* (1988), p. 24.
17. *Assembly Minutes* (1988), pp. 24-25.

claims of revelation, history, context, and the work of the Spirit, as new forms of witness were being called into being. As a result of this, a task force was set up, based in Sydney, but with three Victorians who had served on the Lavender Committee. It was co-chaired by Graeme Ferguson and Shirley Maddox. Ferguson studied issues of ministry in Australia and elsewhere, producing a 60-page document for discussion. Other material on new ministries, non-stipendiary ministry and socio-logical trends came from other members of the task force. Reading, drafting and consultation took a heavy toll on the time of the group, but by the end of 1990 they had produced a draft report, *Vision for Ministry*, which, after comments from the Standing Committee, was widely circulated to receive comments and suggestions. A small heap of paper arrived, including some very substantial contributions, which led to some important changes to the text.

The final version of the document, *Ministry in the Uniting Church in Australia*, ran to over 60 pages, and was circulated to members of the 1991 Assembly. There was some protest that there was insufficient time to consider the significance of the changes, and that there was no proposal to send the material down to Synods and Presbyteries for report to the 1994 Assembly, despite the claim that there were issues of constitutional, theological and ecumenical importance to justify such reference. The report's recommendations were all accepted, however, with the result that a renewed diaconate has finally been established, along with recommendations for the ordering of lay preachers, lay pastors, youth workers, non-stipendiary ministers of the Word, and deacons, who are to be known as community ministers. An attempt to have the Assembly's decision on the latter rescinded and referred for report to the next Assembly failed to gain the required two-thirds majority. It is worth noting the score of Victorian candidates who have now applied for acceptance for the ministry of deacon, following this establishment of the renewed diaconate.

Though the task force was criticized for following context rather than revelation, and for imposing a corporate model of ministry that owed little to the gospel, in fact, it followed a missiological and theological method. The three key sections that expounded that theme dealt with mission and ministry; the context of ministry; and the ministry of the whole people of God. In this last section, four strands of ministry were identified:

1. commissioned ministries, like eldership, based on the gifts of the Spirit given to every member to share in Christ's ministry;
2. the part played by employed persons in the Uniting Church and its agencies;
3. specified ministries, like lay preachers, lay pastors and youth workers; and
4. ordained ministries.[18]

There were several innovations in the Uniting Church's renewal of the diaconate. Deacons are authorized to celebrate the sacraments; they have the same ordination as presbyters, but a different accreditation; and they are committed to living on the frontiers of human need. Most important of all, they are committed to witness to the presence of God among the unlovely, the forgotten and the oppressed: they 'hold before the church the model of service among those who suffer, and call the members to engage in such service. In their ministry they model Christ the servant.'[19] Their sharing in the struggle for human dignity and justice 'is motivated by a vision of the justice of God which defends and protects the disadvantaged'. Thus, deacons will be points of reference for those who wish to take up the ministry of service in a more focused way. 'The renewal of the ministry of deacon will allow the serving ministries of the church to take their proper place in the Uniting Church's life',[20] challenging and empowering the baptized for service.

Pushing out the traditional boundaries of ministry will not be achieved overnight, but this version of the diaconate will help to break down internal barriers to service by bringing the forgotten into the centre of the believing community's life. Similarly, it will contribute to moving through external barriers as it works with others who search for justice, embody compassion, and create new networks of concern, wherever community and state are forgetful of human needs. Keeping the windows of the church open so that human need is clearly seen and attended to in the name of Christ also picks up the ancient symbolism of deacons as the eyes and ears of the bishop. Their task to travel round the city and

18. Task Group on Ministry of the Church, *Ministry in the Uniting Church in Australia* (Sydney: Uniting Church, 1991), pp. 20-22.

19. *Ministry in the Uniting Church in Australia*, p. 40. Following a comprehensive report, *Ordination and Ministry in the Uniting Church*, the 1994 Assembly returned to two ordinations, but the proposal to abolish the sacramental role of deacons was rejected in later discussions.

20. *Ministry in the Uniting Church in Australia*, pp. 40-43.

see if there were dead to bury or strangers to be cared for and welcomed to worship may not have an exact modern counterpart, but it was an indication of how this ancient ministry impinged on the community, picking up responsibilities which no one else cared to undertake.

The potential strengths of the Uniting Church's diaconate will also challenge presbyters to rediscover the foci of their ministry without assuming that their office is the normative ministry. The New Testament and the Church Fathers expressed the presence of Christ within leadership in varied ways. This renewal of diaconal ministry is a reminder that new kinds of collegiality will need to grow again, especially in the corporate oversight which is such an important part of the Uniting Church's heritage. The 1991 Assembly rejected a proposal for personal 'episcopal' oversight, so that, for the foreseeable future, Paul's 'bishops and deacons' will be equal partners before God, working together in the councils of the church. That may make a modest contribution to the functioning of councils in a way which serves rather than dominates from above. The notion that the councils of the church might exist to serve the local congregation in mission and service is a novel one, but nevertheless congruent with the language of *diakonia* and its practice.

It would be romantic in the extreme to suggest that this model for the ministry of deacons is the wave of the future for all Australian churches, but it does suggest that others should be bold to draw new boundaries for the ordering of their ministries, so that deacons have the freedom to follow where service in Christ leads, without being imprisoned by ancient subordination which has nothing to do with the gospel.[21] The collegiality of oversight and service which Paul appears to imply could then offer creative possibilities for renewal of every ministry of God's people in the twenty-first century. If the office of bishop was thereby changed, that would be progress indeed.

21. C. Treasure, in *Walking on Glass* (London: SPCK, 1991), explores the experience of some deacons in the Church of England. V.K. Ratigan and A.A. Swidler (eds.), *The New Phoebe* (Kansas City: Sheed & Ward, 1990) discuss the experience of permanent deacons in the US Roman Catholic Church.

THE LIVING SPIRIT:
QUAKER CONCEPTS OF UNIVERSAL MINISTRY

Elizabeth Duke

Quakers' understanding of their own beliefs and practice is built on two main foundations; the words and experiences of the early Quakers in the English Civil War, Commonwealth and Restoration periods, and continuing Quaker experience.[1] Both practice, and the language in which it is described and justified, have undergone changes which reflect different societies and different times, but modern Quakers perceive an essential unity between their core beliefs and those of the early Friends. One such belief is the Quaker insistence on a universal call to, and practice of, ministry; I shall discuss this as a feature of both seventeenth- and twentieth-century Quakerism.

In one respect I am happy to disagree with my spiritual ancestors. While much early Quaker theology was pastoral, formulated in letters of mutual guidance and support (Quaker bodies still send epistles to one another), much was polemical, hammered out on the anvil of controversy in churches and churchyards and streets, in law-courts and prisons, and in pamphlets. Early Quakers believed that they were called by God to restore the pure apostolic church, and that other contemporary forms of church organization and practice resulted from apostate human ingenuity. Quakers today are less intolerant. Since our theology puts no limits on the gracious action of God, how can we deny that the Spirit can work through an ordained ministry? In particular, I recognize with

---

1. The formal name for Quakers is 'The Religious Society of Friends', and internally Quakers usually refer to themselves as 'Friends'. The two terms are used as synonymous in this discussion. Another technical term used is 'yearly meeting', which is an autonomous body of Quakers: there may be one or several yearly meetings within a national boundary.

loving gratitude the pastoral gifts and vocation of the minister of God whose call to service these essays commemorate.

Quakers, though given to talking and writing about themselves, are short of large-scale expositions of their theology. Robert Barclay produced his *Apology* in Latin in 1676, and in English in 1678, and there has been no real equivalent since.[2] There are theological grounds for this. Early Quakers believed that speculative theology, 'notions', intruded human ingenuity into the direct relationship between the believer and God, and that knowledge of God was based on experience. This remains a Quaker tenet. Much Quaker theology is therefore implicit rather than explicit. Hence the present discussion will often need to illustrate theology by describing practice. The dangers of individualistic interpretation are inevitable. However, Quaker theology must always, according to Quaker theology, be provisional, and these words are no exception.

Churches which root themselves in the New Testament (whether by historical succession, or in the spirit in which they were founded) cannot deny the calling of all their members to be one body, to which they contribute a variety of gifts and offices. But this has been variously interpreted, and it was a theological landmark when theologians from a great breadth of traditions gathered at Lima in 1982 were able to produce so strong a statement on ministry as 'the calling of the whole people of God'. This calling is to ministry understood as service:

> The Holy Spirit bestows on the community diverse and complementary gifts. These are for the common good of the whole people and are manifested in acts of service within the community and to the world. They may be gifts of communicating the Gospel in word and deed, gifts of healing, gifts of praying, gifts of teaching and learning, gifts of serving, gifts of guidance and following, gifts of inspiration and vision. All members are called to discover, with the help of the community, the gifts they have received and to use them for the building up of the Church and for the service of the world to which the Church is sent.[3]

2.　R. Barclay, *An Apology for the True Christian Divinity, As the Same is Held Forth and Preached by the People, Called, in Scorn, Quakers* (London [?], 1678). Spelling, capitalization and punctuation of quotations from this text have been modernized. A valuable adaptation into modern English, with an introduction and notes, is D. Freiday (ed.), *Barclay's Apology in Modern English* (Newberg, OR: Barclay Press, 1967).

3.　*Baptism, Eucharist and Ministry* (Faith and Order Paper, no. 111; Geneva: World Council of Churches, 1982), p. 20, 'Ministry', §5.

In *Baptism, Eucharist and Ministry*, the declaration of 'the calling of the whole people of God' leads on to the major discussion on ministry, in the form of ordained ministry. Historically, almost all churches have come to feel the need of a special form of ministry, consisting of a group of people specifically set aside, or ordained. There is much disagreement as to how far particular patterns of special ministry reflect the intention of Jesus, or the structures of the New Testament, or churches of the so-called apostolic age: discussion of this does not, however, belong to my argument here. More directly relevant is the function of such a special ministry. A variety of claims are made for it, some of which I shall consider shortly. I suggest, as a general definition, that the ordained or 'set-aside' ministry be seen as enabling and assisting the ministry of the whole people of God.

There are many ways of describing this function of an ordained ministry. I propose six headings: (1) serving and caring for those in need; (2) ministry of the Word and sacraments, and other liturgical acts; (3) proclaiming the gospel; (4) teaching and exemplifying; (5) leading, guiding and shepherding; and (6) representing Christ.[4] (Many of these terms are not ones which would naturely be used by many Quakers.) Though some of these roles are more easily linked with Quaker concepts of the church than others, it can be argued that Quakers see them all as elements of a universal ministry.

Some description of practice is necessary before the various roles of ministry are examined. The majority of Quakers in the world worship on a broadly Protestant pattern, with a service of prayer, hymns, Bible readings and preaching—there may or may not be a time for spontaneous contributions out of silence. Many of these groups, which tend to use the term 'Church' rather than 'Meeting', have full-time pastors, and a considerable body of them identify themselves as evangelical Christians. In a convenient but ugly Quaker jargon, those who worship in this way are known as 'programmed', while Quakers whose worship is based on silence are 'unprogrammed'. Quaker concepts of the role of pastors will

4. Materials I have found particularly useful here include the Anglican ordination services of the Church of the Province of New Zealand (*A New Zealand Prayer Book/He Karakia Mihinare o Aotearoa* [Auckland: Collins, 1989], pp. 886-921), and the Vatican II decrees on the apostolate of the laity and on the ministry and life of priests (*The Documents of Vatican II* [ed. W.M. Abbott, SJ; London: Geoffrey Chapman, 1966], pp. 486-579), together with the whole section on ministry in *Baptism, Eucharist and Ministry*, pp. 19-32.

be considered briefly later. This discussion focuses mainly on the unprogrammed tradition, which offers a more distinctive contribution to the general Christian understanding of worship and ministry.

Unprogrammed worship is based on the gathering of the group in silence, characterized as an expectant waiting on God. As the silence reaches greater depths, and the meeting becomes 'gathered', an individual may feel a call to speak, to pray, to read, or, less commonly, to sing. If the call becomes a strong conviction that it is of God, it is obeyed. Quakers have recognized from the start that such 'vocal ministry' may be, and is, the right and duty of any individual, but that over time some people will display a particular gift for, and a more regular practice of, such ministry. The term 'minister' was often applied specifically to members of this group, whose gift was recognized by their local meeting, and a practice of 'recording' those who were recognized in this way developed in Britain in the 1720s. While some unprogrammed groups in the USA still record ministers, this is not normal among unprogrammed Quakers elsewhere. Where pastors or recorded ministers exist, no specific role or type of ministry is reserved to them, and thus they do not form an exception to the concept of universal ministry.

I will now consider the various roles of an ordained ministry that were identified earlier.

1. *Serving and Caring for Those in Need*

The diaconal or serving ministry of meeting human need belongs to everyone who tries to follow the teaching of Jesus. When a religious group seeks to practise this ministry as a corporate body it needs people to organize the work, to inspire others to it, and in some circumstances to engage full-time in personal service. Quakers recognize this ministry as part of their religious commitment, having begun, like the early church (Acts 6.1-6), by meeting needs within their own group, particularly of those suffering imprisonment or financial ruin as a result of their testimony. Quaker practice sees service as a responsibility of the whole body, achieved as necessary by appointing committees, administrative staff, and field workers. All these are part of a continuum which includes local correspondents and fund-raisers, and individuals who give money or engage in service, and no part of this continuum is recognized as a separate ministry. It is for the meeting at the local or broader level to decide on its commitment to service.

2. *Ministry of the Word and Sacraments*

Quakers may be described as a non-sacramental church. It would be better to speak of a universal sacramentality, in which all experience has the potential to be a sign of God's action, and in which any person or act or moment can become a burning-glass through which the holiness of God is made clear. The response of the London Yearly Meeting (i.e. Quakers in Britain) to the World Council of Churches' text *Baptism, Eucharist and Ministry* illustrates this:

> Our understanding of baptism is that it is not a single act of initiation but a continuing growth in the Holy Spirit and a commitment which must continually be renewed. It is this process which draws us into a fellowship with those who acknowledge the same power at work in their lives, those whom Christ is calling to be his body on earth...We welcome the interpretation of the eucharist as the gift of God, granting communion between the human and the divine, renewing the members of the worshipping body and binding them together. We too see our worship as a thanksgiving and celebration of the work of God in all creation and for all people, and a recognition of the cost of love and commitment. Particularly also, we welcome the forthright statement of the implications of worship, its implicit call to reconciliation and service in our daily lives and its challenge to us to work for justice in all areas of life; our worship focuses our hope for the fulfilment of God's purpose.[5]

Growth in the Holy Spirit is a direct, gracious gift from God, though it may be implemented through many human instruments. God is also the initiator and actor in worship, while those present collaborate by silent or vocal ministry. So the Quaker understanding of sacramentality does not require—indeed it precludes—the setting aside of a group of people as particular channels for grace.

Ministry of the Word (as distinct from proclamation or teaching) can be seen as a particular liturgical activity, often symbolized in ordination services by the use of the Bible, and exemplified in worship by Scripture readings and their exposition in preaching. Early Quakers, who were

---

5. London Yearly Meeting of the Religious Society of Friends, *To Lima with Love: Baptism, Eucharist and Ministry: A Quaker Response* (London: Quaker Home Service, 1987), pp. 8-9, §§28, 33. In 1994 the name 'London Yearly Meeting' was changed to 'Britain Yearly Meeting'.

soaked in the Bible and as ready to argue from it as any of their contemporaries, considered it one of the many manifestations of the Spirit, and
not uniquely privileged. Margaret Fell reports the preaching of George
Fox in 1652:

> And then he went on, and opened the Scriptures, and said, 'The Scriptures
> were the prophets' words and Christ's and the apostles' words, and what
> as they spoke they enjoyed and possessed and had it from the Lord'. And
> said, 'Then what had any to do with the Scriptures, but as they came to
> the Spirit that gave them forth. You will say, Christ saith this, and the
> apostles say this; but what canst thou say? Art thou a child of Light and
> hast walked in the Light, and what thou speakest is it inwardly from
> God?'[6]

Friends who were charged with being unscriptural argued that all
teachings of the Spirit would be found to be consistent; thus Robert
Barclay says that one should speak during worship,

> either in the interpreting of some part of Scripture, in case the Spirit,
> which is the good Remembrancer, lead him so to do, or otherwise words
> of exhortation, advice, reproof and instruction, or the sense of some
> spiritual experiences, all which will still be agreeable to the Scripture,
> though perhaps not relative to, nor founded upon any particular chapter or
> verse, as a text.[7]

Between the seventeenth and the twentieth centuries lie the
Enlightenment, the development of biblical criticism and much more,
and Quaker views on the Bible are now highly divergent. Nevertheless,
the core concept remains that God has many ways of speaking. This is
expressed with particular clarity by the World Gathering of Young
Friends in 1985. Coming together with all shades of belief, from evangelical to universalist, they found that they were 'separated by language,
race, culture, ways we worship God, and beliefs about Christ and God'.
After sometimes painful struggle, however, they were able to declare:

> Our priority is to be receptive and responsive to the life-giving Word of
> God, whether it comes through the written Word—the Scriptures; the
> Incarnate Word—Jesus Christ; the Corporate Word—as discerned by the

---

6.   Quoted from G. Fox, *Journal*, 1694, ii (in *Christian Faith and Practice in
the Experience of the Society of Friends* [London: London Yearly Meeting of the
Religious Society of Friends, 1960], §20).

7.   Barclay, *Apology*, p. 273.

gathered meeting; or the Inward Word of God in our hearts which is available to each of us who seek the truth.[8]

Quakers who engage in biblical study and scholarship have a particular gift to contribute, but it follows from the definition of the Word just quoted that neither they nor any other group are called to a privileged ministry of the Word.

3. *Proclamation of the Gospel*

Proclamation was not just one task of early Friends; it was *the* task. As the agents of God's renewal, they had to make it known to the world, and they called themselves 'Publishers of Truth'. The call came to the individual by divine initiative. James Nayler declared in 1652: 'I was at the plow, meditating on the things of God, and suddenly I heard a voice saying to me, "Get thee out from thy kindred, and from thy father's house".'[9] George Fox wrote in 1656 to those engaged in this ministry:

> Let all nations hear the word by sound or writing...And this is the word of the Lord God to you all, and a charge to you all in the presence of the living God, be patterns, be examples in all countries, places, islands, nations, wherever you come; that your carriage and life may preach among all sorts of people, and to them. Then you will come to walk cheerfully over the world, answering that of God in every one; whereby in them ye may be a blessing, and make the witness of God in them to bless you.[10]

In this there are two elements: of explicit proclamation, and of witness by the example of one's life. These have diverged in later Quakerism, with some groups emphasizing mission and others service. Substantial attempts at dialogue between, and reconciliation of, these two callings began only in the late 1960s, and are still incomplete.[11] At a more homely level, one end of the spectrum follows the evangelical call to

8. *The World Gathering of Young Friends: Epistle to All Friends Everywhere*, which took place at Greensboro, NC, in 1985 (quoted from *The Friend* [9 August, 1985]).

9. Quoted from J. Nayler, *A Collection of Sundry Books, Epistles and Papers* (1716), pp. 12-13 in *Christian Faith and Practice*, §22.

10. *Journal of George Fox* (ed. J.L. Nickalls; London: Religious Society of Friends, 1975), p. 263.

11. H.M. Hadley, *Quakers World Wide: A History of the Friends World Committee for Consultation* (London: Friends World Committee for Consultation; York: William Sessions, 1991), p. 150.

give personal testimony in words, while the other prefers the injunction, 'Let your lives speak'. Yet in both aspects there is a continuum, in which the degree of involvement of the individual is to be determined by divine calling as experienced by the individual and, if any form of collective support is needed, as tested and recognized by the group. An individual is understood to be called to a particular task of mission or service for whatever period is necessary, rather than commissioned to a permanent role.

4. *Teaching and Exemplifying*

Teaching and exemplification within the body are parallel to proclamation to those outside. At one end of the continuum are some engaged in full-time teaching, whether in the training of pastors or by offering long- or short-term study to individuals or groups. This co-exists with more informal study on a national, regional or local basis, and with the week-by-week mutual learning within the local worshipping community. In Quaker understanding, anyone may be a vehicle of teaching ministry, because it is God who is the teacher. This was a key tenet of early Friends; so George Fox describes his preaching at Sedbergh in June 1652:

> There I declared the everlasting Truth of the Lord and the word of life for several hours, and that the Lord Christ Jesus was come to teach his people himself and bring them off all the world's ways and teachers to Christ, their way to God.[12]

In Quaker groups where pastors are appointed, they have a general role of teaching and pastoral oversight. Preaching is a particular duty, but it may or may not be the pastor who prepares and guides the programmed worship. The pastoral tradition sees full-time ministry as part of the continuum of gifts:

> Friends have no 'ordained' clergy. Humans do not ordain, only *God* can. What we can do is to recognize that God uses some people in obvious ways, and then we *record* that God has given them certain gifts or abilities for ministering. This does not mean that 'recorded' ministers have special access to God. It does mean their gifts for serving others are recognized and recorded by members in the community of faith. The recording policy varies between yearly meetings, and some groups hold to the testimony that ministry must never be confused with a service done

12. *Journal of George Fox*, p. 107.

for hire. Although ministers from unprogrammed meetings are recorded, their subsistence comes from secular employment (as did the apostles'). Other Friends feel that ones who are gifted and prepared for ministry should be *released* from having to be gainfully employed so that they can devote themselves entirely to serving human needs, unencumbered by lack of finances. This is very different from the idea of receiving payment for ministry, and the critical factor is whether or not it is done in the power and inspiration of the Spirit. Ministerial training may enhance inspired ministry, but it can never replace it.[13]

Such ministry is not a substitute for the divine teacher.

5. *Leading, Guiding and Shepherding*

The one who teaches is also the leader, the guide and the shepherd. Any church which recognizes the headship of Christ (in whatever language it is expressed) has to find forms in which it can be perceived and followed. Leadership is not necessarily restricted to a few; one may cite the recognition by the Second Vatican Council of a partnership between ordained and lay in this role:

> In the Church, there is diversity of service but unity of purpose. Christ conferred on the apostles and their successors the duty of teaching, sanctifying, and ruling in His name and power. But the laity, too, share in the priestly, prophetic and royal office of Christ and therefore have their own role to play in the mission of the whole People of God in the Church and in the world.[14]

A tempting conclusion from Quaker theology would be that leadership and authority rest in the individual, guided directly by God. But this does not allow for self-delusion, and it gives no guidance to the corporate body; which individual's 'leadings' is it to follow? So Quakers very early evolved the practice of putting decision-making in a framework of worship, of waiting on God, where the leadings of the individual are tested against the search of the group to find God's will. This might seem to be a simple matter of democracy, a yielding of the individual or the minority to the majority. But Quaker practice is not to rely on majorities, indeed, not to use voting at all; the group wrestles with all the

---

13. P. Anderson, *Friends and Ministry* (*Meet the Friends*, 4; Newberg, Oregon: Department of Christian Testimonies, Northwest Yearly Meeting of Friends Church, 1982 [?]).

14. *The Documents of Vatican II*, p. 491.

insights offered in an attempt to discern where God is leading. It is recognized (however fallible Quakers are in practice) that the true leading may eventually be found in the contribution of an individual who seemed at first to be at odds with the rest of the group. There is, at best, a continuous reciprocal interchange between individual and group which enables both to be the means of understanding and serving God.[15]

A particular example of this interplay is the role of the clerk, who arranges the presentation of business to the meeting, and then listens to what is said, and what is not said, before drafting a minute to express the unity which has been reached. This minute is read to the meeting, and if it is not felt to be satisfactory the group works to revise it. Hence, the clerk and the meeting collaborate in the search for a true expression.

> The Clerk serves for a limited time and is the servant of the meeting. 'The power of God is the authority of all your men's and women's meetings' wrote George Fox. This authority becomes a real one, and commands allegiance, as the power of God in individual disciples recognises and answers to the power of God in the gathered meeting.[16]

A similar interplay is found in the appointment, for a limited term, of Friends traditionally, but not universally, known as Elders and Overseers; the former to promote the spiritual life of the meeting, the latter to look to personal needs. The meeting does not, by this appointment, discharge its collective responsibility, and that of each individual, for these ministries.

6. *Representing Christ*

Since Quakers insist on the direct guidance of God, they are unlikely to see a need for a ministry of representing Christ. If the concept has any role in Quaker theology, it would have to be in terms of Mt. 25.31-46: 'As you did it to one of the least of these...you did it to me'. Certainly the receiving of service is itself a ministry.

The compilers of *Baptism, Eucharist and Ministry* sought for a new general definition of the ordained ministry:

---

15. For an outsider's analysis of Quaker decision-making see M.J. Sheeran, *Beyond Majority Rule: Voteless Decisions in the Society of Friends* (Philadelphia: Philadelphia Yearly Meeting of the Religious Society of Friends, 1983).

16. *To Lima with Love*, p. 4, §10.

In order to fulfil its mission, the Church needs persons who are publicly and continually responsible for pointing to its fundamental dependence on Jesus Christ, and thereby provide, within a multiplicity of gifts, a focus of its unity. The ministry of such persons, who since very early times have been ordained, is constitutive for the life and witness of the Church.[17]

The theology implicit in Quaker practice leads to the response that the whole body holds the public and continuing responsibility, and that the focus of unity (very imperfectly recognized among Quakers as they are) is precisely dependence on God. The Quaker claim is that 'it works'. The London Yearly Meeting replied: 'Our own experience leads us to affirm that the church can be so ordered that the guidance of the Holy Spirit can be known and followed without the need for a separated clergy'.[18]

A theology of ministry is rooted in a theology of the church. Early Quaker theology, as well as recognizing the use of the term 'church' for contemporary 'apostate' structures, saw the church as 'Gospel order' restored,[19] but also as 'Creation order' restored. Their understanding of redemption was that it restored humanity to God's original intention, to the state before the Fall. George Fox records it in visionary terms in his Journal relating to 1648:

Now was I come up in spirit through the flaming sword into the paradise of God. All things were new, and all the creation gave another smell unto me than before, beyond what words can utter. I knew nothing but pureness, and innocency, and righteousness, being renewed up into the image of God by Christ Jesus, so that I say I was come up to the state of Adam which he was in before he fell...But I was immediately taken up in spirit, to see into another or more steadfast state than Adam's in innocency, even into a state in Christ Jesus, that should never fall. And the Lord showed me that such as were faithful to him in the power and light of Christ, should come up into that state in which Adam was before he fell, in which the admirable works of the creation, and the virtues thereof, may be known, through the openings of that divine Word of wisdom and power by which they were made.[20]

17. *Baptism, Eucharist and Ministry*, p. 21, 'Ministry', §8.

18. *To Lima with Love*, p. 11, §42. For a fuller working out of some implications of direct guidance by God, see *Friends: An Historically Normed Introduction*, prepared and presented by Dean Freiday for the Conference of Secretaries of Christian World Communions, Geneva, 22–24 October, 1991 (London: Friends World Committee for Consultation, 1991), pp. 5-15.

19. *To Lima with Love*, pp. 11-12, §43; Freiday, *Friends*, pp. 9-10.

20. *Journal of George Fox*, p. 27: see also Fox's Epistle 222 = Letter 86 (in

Fox and others relied on Paul's concepts of the first and second Adam (1 Cor. 15.45), and the new creation (Gal. 6.15), in which the barriers established in a fallen society are dissolved: 'There is no longer Jew or Greek, there is no longer slave or free, there is no longer male and female; for all of you are one in Christ Jesus' (Gal. 3.28). Much early Quaker theology of the church could be described as a commentary on this verse. Robert Barclay depicts the universal church in a grand sweep which eliminates distinctions of race and religious profession:

> ...the Church being no other thing, but the society, gathering or company of such as God hath called out of the world, and worldly spirit, to walk in his LIGHT and LIFE. The Church then so designed is to be considered, as it comprehends all, that are thus called and gathered truly by God, both such as are yet in this inferior world, and such as, having already laid down the earthly tabernacle, are passed into their heavenly mansions, which together do make up the one catholic Church (concerning which there is so much controversy) out of which Church we freely acknowledge there can be no salvation, because under this Church and its denomination are comprehended all, and as many of whatsoever nation, kindred, tongue, or people, they be (though outwardly strangers and remote from those who profess Christ and Christianity in words, and have the benefit of the Scriptures) as become obedient to the Holy Light and testimony of God in their hearts, so as to become sanctified by it, and cleansed from the evils of their ways.[21]

More directly relevant to a theology of ministry is the parallel concept of the visible church:

> Secondly the Church is to be considered, as it signifies a certain number of persons gathered by God's Spirit, and by the testimony of some of his servants, raised up for that end, unto the belief of the true principles and doctrines of the Christian faith, who, through their hearts being united by the same love, and their understanding informed in the same truths, gather, meet and assemble together, to wait upon God, to worship him, and to bear a joint testimony for the Truth against error, suffering for the same, and so becoming, through this fellowship, as one family and household in certain respects, do each of them watch over, teach, instruct and care for one another, according to their several measures and attainments.[22]

C.W. Sharman [ed.], *No More But My Love: Letters of George Fox, Quaker* [London: Quaker Home Service, 1980], p. 25).

21. Barclay, *Apology*, pp. 191-92.
22. Barclay, *Apology*, pp. 192-93.

'No longer slave or free' was reinterpreted in a society where Quakers, with other sects of the English Radical Reformation, were reminded by preachers that Adam could be a symbol for egalitarian revolution, as he had been in the peasants' revolt of 1381:

> When Adam delved and Eve span,
> who was then the gentleman?[23]

In this respect early Friends believed that the restoration of the order of creation restored the true apostolic nature of the church:

> And if in any age, since the Apostles' days, God hath purposed to show his power by weak instruments, for the battering down of that carnal and heathenish wisdom, and restoring again the ancient simplicity of Truth, this is it; for in our day God hath raised up witnesses to himself, as he did fisher men of old, many, yea most of whom are labouring and mechanic men.[24]

Barclay, with other Quaker thinkers, draws upon Paul's depiction of the church at Corinth: 'not many of you were wise by human standards, not many were powerful, not many were of noble birth; but God chose what is foolish in the world to shame the wise' (1 Cor. 1.6-7). The 'mechanic men' were set against the professional or 'hireling' priests, 'bred at Oxford or Cambridge'.[25] The key to being part of this visible church, and so, in Quaker thought, a minister, is the divine initiative; Paul's 'God chose' is echoed by Barclay's 'God hath purposed' and 'God hath raised up'.

God's initiative is also the basis of the early and continuing Quaker partnership of women and men ('no longer male and female') in religious service and preaching. Margaret Fell prefaces her *Women's Speaking Justified, Proved and Allowed of by the Scriptures*[26] with four scriptural quotations, each of which focuses on the dependence of the believer on

---

23. J. Huizinga, *The Waning of the Middle Ages* (Harmondsworth: Peregrine Books, 1976), p. 61; and C. Hill, *The World Turned Upside Down* (Harmondsworth: Penguin Books, 1975), p. 35—on the political radicalism of the early Quakers, see in particular ch. 10.

24. Barclay, *Apology*, p. 223.

25. *Journal of George Fox*, pp. 7-8.

26. The Augustan Reprint Society Publication, no. 194 (Los Angeles: University of California, 1979; reproduced from a copy of the second [1667] edition). The writings of Quaker women of the early period have been less widely published than those of men. Much is now being done to redress this imbalance caused by social and cultural influences: see the report cited in n. 38.

the active Spirit: Acts 2.17 = Joel 2.28 ('I will pour out of my Spirit upon all flesh; your sons and daughters shall prophesy'); Jn 6.45 ('They shall all be taught of God'); Isa. 54.13 ('All thy children shall be taught of the Lord'); Jer. 31.34 ('They shall all know me'). Early in her argument she turns to Paul's assertion (1 Cor. 1.27) that God has chosen the weak and despised.[27] To the argument from Scripture Robert Barclay adds that from experience:

> Seeing male and female are one in Christ Jesus, and that he gives his Spirit no less to the one than to the other, when God moveth by his Spirit in a woman, we judge it no ways unlawful for her to preach in the assembly of God's people...And lastly it hath been observed, that God hath effectually in this day converted many souls by the ministry of women, and by them also frequently comforted the souls of his children, which manifest experience puts the thing beyond all controversy.[28]

George Fox defends the establishment of Women's Meetings, with their own sphere of authority, on the basis of the restored created order: 'And if there were no Scripture for our Men and Women's Meetings, Christ is sufficient, who restores men and women up to the image of God'.[29]

The early Quakers' concept of themselves as the church was Pauline in scope; the whole body was 'loved by God, called, saints' (Rom. 1.7).[30] Differing gifts were recognized, but did not confer a different status, and pre-existing distinctions in status were washed over by the tide of the Spirit. Modern Quaker theology of the church has moved away from the exclusive position of holding other visible church bodies to be apostate. Quakers of evangelical and pastoral traditions emphasize their unity with other Christians, while strongly conscious of a distinctive Quaker heritage. Quakers of the more liberal unprogrammed tradition recognize the validity of other churches, but perhaps lay more stress on their own distinctiveness, and see their relations with other churches in terms of dialogue, in which Quakers have a specific contribution to make: 'We believe we have been entrusted with these insights as our offering to the common life of the whole church'.[31]

27. Fell, *Women's Speaking*, p. 3.

28. Barclay, *Apology*, p. 231.

29. Epistle 320 = Letter 109 (*No More But My Love*, p. 103).

30. I have translated literally here: other New Testament quotations are from the NRSV.

31. *To Lima with Love*, pp. 14-16, §§55, 59. It is noticeable that of the three

All traditions of Quakers continue to see the church as a body in which God interacts directly with each individual and calls them to whatever ministry is required. Of the three claims in Gal. 3.28, 'no longer Jew or Greek' is reflected in the movement of one stream of liberal Quakerism towards universalism in a more radical form than that of seventeenth-century Quakers, and 'no longer slave or free' is perhaps embodied more in Quaker social action than in the composition of the group; but Quakers still feel the need to proclaim to many other churches the equality of male and female. A modern expression of this from the programmed tradition roots equality in Christ's call to ministry and, like its seventeenth-century predecessors, argues from experience:

> To say that ministry is *universal* is to say that everyone is included in Christ's calling to serve. Friends believe that the distinction between laity and clergy is a false one, and that because Christ Himself is our High Priest we have no need of an earthly intermediary. All are equal before God, and if we are indwelt by Christ we become priests to one another. The universal ministry involves the priesthood of all believers. For this reason Friends perceive women as ministers as well as men. History leaves no doubt that God has used women in some powerful ways.[32]

A statement from the unprogrammed tradition, while recognizing seventeenth-century foundations, looks to the role of the Spirit in the church:

> The Spirit has led us from our foundation to recognise the equality of women and men in the people of God. Early Friends taught that the redemptive activity of Christ restored men and women to their position before the fall, as equal help-meets both made in the image of God. Though we have not been immune from influences in our surrounding culture, we have sought to practise this equality in our structures. We know that the Spirit gives as wide and diverse gifts to women as to men and acts as effectively through women as through men.[33]

Whether it uses Christ-language or Spirit-language, a Quaker theology of the church is rooted in a theology of the continuing activity of the

---

Quaker bodies who have responded to date to *Baptism, Eucharist and Ministry*, two (the Dutch Yearly Meeting and the London Yearly Meeting) are in the unprogrammed tradition, and one (the Canadian Yearly Meeting) combines programmed and unprogrammed groups: see *Churches Respond to BEM* (ed. M. Thurian; Geneva: World Council of Churches, 1987), III, pp. 297-302.

32. Anderson, *Friends and Ministry*.
33. *To Lima with Love*, p. 12, §44.

Spirit. The account of ministry last quoted is immediately preceded by the statement:

> This Spirit, which was poured out at Pentecost on all the church, young and old, women and men, continues in our experience to call and empower all members of the church in a variety of ministries.[34]

Dean Freiday sees a reliance on the Spirit as fundamental to early Quaker Christology, which expressed itself via the titles used of Christ. Many apply to his divinity, sovereignty and mission:

> But neither metaphysics nor mission overshadows the immanent functions through the Holy Spirit implied by Counsellor, Life, Light, Sanctifier, Teacher, True Prophet, Truth, Way, Wisdom, Word, and Water of Life. Of these, Christ the Great Prophet and Teacher, and Christ the Light are undoubtedly of central significance. This salvific effect of personal and corporate attention to the Light of Christ and his guiding and directive effect together constitute a *vast theology of Grace*, in which the terms are often fluid and interchangeable. It creates an indissoluble link between belief and practice and is the major preoccupation of early Quaker theology.[35]

The 'link between belief and practice', with both as the locus of grace, remains fundamental in modern Quaker theology. The Spirit is experienced not only in continuing revelation but in continuing guidance:

> We know the power of God's Spirit at work in the lives of people within the community of our meetings. These people may have been drawn into the community by a sudden convincement, a long period of seeking, or have grown up within it from childhood. We also know that we are engaged in a life-long growth into faith, and experience a continuing irruption of grace into our lives which demands and sustains a commitment to a life of discipleship.[36]

In Quaker belief the Spirit is free and sovereign, not bounded by human institutions or human understanding (Jn 3.8). This is the basis for Quakers' abstention from specific sacramental acts and from ordaining ministers. Because the Spirit may lead us in unpredictable ways there can be no definitive statements of Quaker theology (a favourite Quaker 'query' reads: 'Are you open to new light from whatever source it may

---

34. *To Lima with Love*, p. 12, §43.
35. Freiday, *Friends*, p. 7.
36. *To Lima with Love*, p. 8, §27.

come?'[37]). Trust in the continuing guidance of the Spirit is strengthened by experience, and today's Quakers, from their lives and their reflection, find themselves in unity with their seventeenth-century friends:

> Friends, we are all called into wholeness and into community, women and men alike, sharing the responsibilities God has given us, and assuming the leadership we are called to. We begin where we are, in our homes and meetings or churches, our work and communities, celebrating the realization of the New Creation.[38]

---

37. *Questions and Counsel: Version of September 1991* (Yearly Meeting of Aotearoa / New Zealand, 1991), A8.

38. *Epistle of the First International Theological Conference of Quaker Women* (Woodbrooke, July 24–31, 1990), quoted from *Report of the First International Theological Conference of Quaker Women* (ed. D. Meredith; Earlham School of Religion/Friends World Committee for Consultation/ Woodbrooke College, 1991), p. 4.

'IN SPIRIT AND IN TRUTH'—ROOM FOR THE OTHER: SOME REMARKS ON THE ORDINATION OF WOMEN FROM AN ECUMENICAL PERSPECTIVE

Irmgard Kindt-Siegwalt

1. *Introduction*

The ordination of women to the pastoral or priestly ministry continues to be a burning issue in ecumenical dialogue, both between member churches of the World Council of Churches (hereafter WCC) and with those outside it. The matter has been present on the agenda of the WCC for almost forty years. Numerous consultations, both interconfessional and international, have been organized, and corresponding studies and documents have been published. Nearly every argument that could possibly be thought of in relation to the subject seems to have been dealt with. Yet all these efforts have not led to a consensus acceptable to all. A number of churches have, after a long period of opposition, re-examined their earlier negative decision.[1] However, the Orthodox and Roman Catholic churches—as well as some churches of Protestant descent, as well as certain Free Churches—have reiterated their fundamental

---

1.   The Evangelical Lutheran Church of Finland announced at the end of 1987 that it was to have its first women ordained in the following year (*Bulletin d'Information Protestant* 1076 [1987], p. 6); see also P. Luumi, 'The Ordination of Women—Churches at the Breaking-Point' (unpublished paper presented at the conference of Lutheran Women Theologians, 1990, Loccum, Germany). The Synod of the Old Catholic Church in Germany voted in favour of women's ordination in May 1989. The Uniting Church in Australia published a critical document in 1990, on the basis of which it decided to ordain women ('Why Does the Uniting Church in Australia Ordain Women to the Ministry of the Word?'). The Lutheran churches of India ordained their first two women in September 1991 (see *Lutheran World Information* 27 [1991], pp. 5-6).

disapproval of the ordination of women. Churches within the Anglican communion are deeply divided on the issue. At the 7th Assembly in Canberra, Orthodox churches designated the question of women's ordination as one of the factors that actualized 'the experience of the cross of Christian division'.[2] In view of this estimation, one wonders how the institutional churches will ever reach 'a visible unity', if a solution to a problem of this order cannot be achieved.

However, the bilateral and multilateral dialogues have not only revealed the profound divergences that exist between churches concerning ordination, but also the continuing interest in dialogue, and even the need for it. In addition to this, more attention is being paid not only to what is said, but to what is meant in the context of a particular experience or statement. For a number of years now the question of ordination has been studied in all its complexity—in its theological, historical, cultural and, especially, in its spiritual dimensions.

The reflections presented here attempt to continue this more diversified approach. They will not discuss once again the well-known arguments *pro* and *contra*, that is, deal with the respective passages of the Scriptures that are considered to be normative for churches within the Protestant tradition. They will not pose the so-called order of creation against the new order of faith revealed in Christ. Nor will they explicitly discuss the 'Catholic' position, that is, deal with our theological understanding of the image of God (*eikon theou*) and the representation of Christ in relation to questions of gender. Instead, after a brief summary of the development of the question of female ordination in its ecumenical context, some characteristic opinions of the churches that have responded to the Lima document *Baptism, Eucharist and Ministry*[3] will be surveyed. What is said here is not intended to cover the ecumenical scene globally—we still lack a general study that contains adequate statistical information on the actual practice of ordination in the different churches (probably a regrettable thing but, then again, any statistics may well prove to be dated as soon as they are produced, since the situation in the many relevant countries is changing so quickly[4]). Then, on the

2. See 'Reflections of Orthodox Participants at the 7th Assembly in Canberra', in M. Kinnamon (ed.), *Signs of the Spirit: Official Report 7th Assembly, Canberra, Australia, 7–20 February, 1991* (Geneva: WCC, 1991), p. 282.

3. *Faith and Order Paper* 111 (Geneva: WCC, 1982).

4. The Conference of European Churches (CEC) published a document in 1980 on the practice within European Protestant Churches (*The Ordination of Women*

basis of this brief overview, I shall consider the implications for the future for those churches that remain faithfully committed to the ecumenical movement.

2. *A Brief History of the Issue in its Ecumenical Setting*

The ordination of women, although addressed very early within ecumenical circles as one of the issues that demanded just and adequate treatment,[5] does not figure in the work of the WCC as a distinct topic until after 1954 and the Assembly at Evanston. Since then, the women's department, 'Cooperation of Men and Women in Church, Family and Society', has made it a regular study project and, since 1961, 'Faith and Order' has also participated. As a result of this interest and involvement, in 1968 the study 'The Meaning of Ordination—a Study Paper of the Faith and Order Commission' was published.[6] This document describes two classic positions on the issue: on one hand, the tradition of the church, 1900 years old, which must not be changed and, on the other, the positive experience of those churches that have ordained women to the pastoral ministry. The study also mentions some practical pastoral concerns which need to be taken into account.

In the follow-up to this document a new methodological approach was proposed, and the churches were asked to engage directly in the process of research. Consequently, after the meeting in Accra in 1974, the questionnaires were sent out world-wide. Scholars representing the different theological traditions were also invited to study 'the evidence of Scripture and Tradition as it relates to the role and participation of women and men in the church'.[7] Two perspectives were therefore pursued by the commission: while theological questions concerning ordination were dealt with within the ongoing *Baptism, Eucharist and Ministry* (or *BEM*) process, the new project 'The Unity of the Church and the Unity of Humankind' looked at the relationship between women

[Geneva: WCC, 1980]). At present the World Alliance of Reformed Churches is also preparing a publication on the practice of their member churches—I am grateful to Ms U. Rosenhäger from the Geneva secretariat for sending me the results that have been collected so far.

5. See C. Parvey (ed.), 'Ordination of Women in Ecumenical Perspective', *Faith and Order Paper* 105 (Geneva: WCC, 1980), p. 80.

6. *Study Encounter* 4.4 (Geneva, WCC: 1968).

7. Commission on Faith and Order, 'Sharing in One Hope', *Faith and Order Paper* 92 (Bangalore: WCC, 1969), pp. 269-70.

and men from a more general point of view.[8] The resulting booklet, 'Ordination of Women in Ecumenical Perspective', covered, in a representative manner, the different opinions collected so far within this process. Different voices concerning other ministries carried out by women—religious and lay—were also echoed in it, and other dimensions related to the issue of female ordination were analysed, for example, language patterns and their influence on theological thought.

Two years later, in 1982, the churches were asked to respond 'on the highest level of authority' to the convergence document *Baptism, Eucharist and Ministry*.[9] Many churches did not express themselves, whether generally or in some detail, on the question of the ordination of women, possibly for a variety of different reasons. For the majority of churches which had been practising ordination for some time, this issue may no longer have posed a problem, particularly as compared with other issues raised in *BEM*. Conversely, other churches less favourably disposed may deliberately have chosen not to discuss, or to re-discuss, the subject, to prevent further conflict. Moreover, the *BEM* text was admittedly not very explicit, only describing two main positions.[10] The churches that did respond, however, referred to their own practice and generally made use of arguments that confirmed the well-known positions, and it was once again interesting to note that churches of the same confessional tradition in different countries and contexts could easily hold different views.

In my more detailed survey of the responses of various churches to the Lima document *BEM* (noting in addition a few opinions expressed elsewhere) I will speak in terms of eight broad positions.

1. The decision to ordain women to the pastoral ministry was first undertaken by churches in the USA in a liberal Methodist and Congregationalist tradition.[11] Thus, it is not surprising that churches coming from the same background continue to take a position in favour of

8. Parvey (ed.), 'Ordination of Women', p. 27.

9. Preface to *Baptism, Eucharist and Ministry*, p. x.

10. This was criticized by the Church of Christ in Thailand: see M. Thurian (ed.), *Churches Respond to BEM: Official Responses to the 'Baptism, Eucharist and Ministry' Text* (vols. I-VI; Geneva: WCC, 1986–88), V, p. 174; see also the response of the Burma Baptist Convention (in *Churches Respond*, IV, p. 189). Thurian's edition contains the significant *Faith and Order Papers* 129, 132, 135, 137, 143 and 144.

11. R. Radford Ruether, 'The Preacher and the Priest: Two Typologies and the Ordination of Women', in Parvey (ed.), 'Ordination of Women', pp. 69-73 (p. 70).

ordination as they responded to *BEM*. Among them we find Methodists
from the USA, the UK, the Federal Republic of Germany, New Zealand,
and Disciples from Thailand, Canada and the United States.[12]

The United Methodist Church (USA) summarized its point of view as
follows:

> So strongly are we convinced that God is calling both women and men to
> ministry, and that willingness to ordain women is required, if we are to
> remain faithful to our understanding of the gospel, that we cannot allow
> any prospect that ordination of women could be given up for the sake of
> church unity.[13]

2.   In Western countries, the majority of the mainline Protestant
churches (i.e. Presbyterian, United and Lutheran) had opened the ordained ministry to women for many years, and therefore also welcomed
the significant paragraphs in *BEM*,[14] and I shall give some representative statements of this position here. The Evangelical Lutheran Church
of Iceland declared:

> [W]e call for a more thorough consideration of the ordained ministry of
> women in the church. In our church women are ordained into the ministry
> and the number of women studying theology is increasing gradually. The
> ministry of women has proved to be of great value, and we maintain that
> we are by duty bound to make real, what has been testified, that in Christ
> there is neither male nor female, with him distinction between people is
> made 'void'.[15]

The Presbyterian Church (USA) said:

---

12. For the response of the United Methodist Church (USA), see Thurian (ed.),
Churches Respond, II, p. 195; for that of the Methodist Church (UK), see II, p. 216;
for the United Methodist Church of Central and Southern Europe, II, p. 207; for the
Methodist Church of New Zealand, I, p. 80; for the Christian Church (Disciples of
Christ) in Canada, III, p. 266; for the Christian Church (Disciples of Christ) in the
USA, I, p. 120; for the Church of Christ in Thailand, I, p. 174; and for the Church of
the Brethren (USA), VI, p. 111.

13. See Thurian (ed.), *Churches Respond*, I, p. 120.

14. For the Lutheran Church in America see Thurian (ed.), *Churches Respond*, I,
p. 35; for the Church of Sweden, II, p. 135; for the Evangelical Lutheran Church of
France, III, p. 162; for the United Protestant Church of Belgium, III, p. 180; for the
Evangelical Presbyterian Church in Ghana, VI, p. 102; and for the United Church of
Christ in Japan, II, p. 290.

15. See Thurian (ed.), *Churches Respond*, IV, p. 69.

We affirm that the Spirit has led churches, among them our own, to perceive the ordination of women as consistent with the gospel and, in the belief that God can do a new thing, to accept the ordination of women as a part of the tradition which is ongoing and developing.[16]

The Evangelical Church of Westphalia, a United church, underlines this with the following statement:

We know of no biblical or theological reasons for excluding women from ordination. For us the mutual recognition of ministries thus includes the recognition of the ordination of women and we hope that churches which do not allow the ordination of women themselves will recognize it in other churches.[17]

Several churches of the same tradition have also urged their synods to prepare for far-reaching discussion on ordination since the publication of the *BEM* text. Among these, while rather reluctant in its initial response to *BEM*, the Evangelical Lutheran Church of Finland passed a motion through its synod in 1987, and now has more than 400 ordained women.[18] In many other countries *BEM* has also stimulated the debate on ordination. In Africa, Presbyterian churches in Angola, Liberia, South Africa and Togo, and Lutheran churches in Namibia and South West Africa, are ordaining women.[19] The United churches of South and North India have had a small number of women pastors for six years, while the Lutheran churches of that country took a positive vote at the end of 1990, and in 1991 ordained their first two women to the ministry.[20] By way of comparison, all the Protestant churches of Indonesia have been ordaining women for some time—some of them for as long as thirty years—probably because of the influence of their Dutch mother churches.[21] There are 155 ordained women in the United Church of Christ in Japan.[22] And in Latin America the Presbyterian churches of

16. See Thurian (ed.), *Churches Respond*, III, pp. 200-201.

17. See Thurian (ed.), *Churches Respond*, IV, p. 148.

18. M. Kanyoro, 'The Ordination of Women in Africa' (unpublished lecture presented at the meeting of the Kirchenrechtliche Arbeitsgemeinschaft der Forschungsstätte der Evangelischen Studiengemeinschaft, Heidelberg, 1991).

19. According to statistical material collected by WARC: see n. 4; see also Kanyoro, 'Ordination of Women in Africa'.

20. *Lutheran World Information* 27 (1991), pp. 5-6.

21. A. Lumentut, 'Towards Greater Participation and Contribution of Women in Asian Churches', *Asia Journal of Theology* 1 (1987), pp. 206-11.

22. See *Christianity in Japan 1971–1990* (Tokyo: Christian Literature Society of Japan, 1990).

Argentina and Venezuela, and the Lutheran churches in Brazil and El Salvador, have opened the ministry to women.[23]

3. Free Churches, other than those that have already been mentioned, hold very different views on ordination and towards *BEM*. Baptists have divided on the issue. An outspokenly positive position may be found in the churches of Sweden and Denmark, and in the Burma Baptist Convention,[24] but Baptists in the USA and Scotland have reservations.[25] The Mennonite tradition is more favourably disposed,[26] while the question for Moravians remains open.[27] Quakers and The Salvation Army, however, have expressed themselves very positively on the ministry exercised by women and men alike—but of course they do not practise ordination in the traditional sense of the term.[28]

4. A number of churches within the Protestant tradition remain opposed to the ordination of women. Two broad reasons for this can be identified.

a. In the majority of cases it is the socio-cultural context of a church, together with its corresponding ethical values, which seems to have influenced the general attitude towards women. In a predominantly non-Christian society, with women in a very restricted position, churches find it difficult to allow for women to be ordained. The Mar Thoma Syrian Church of Malabar is a typical example: 'Barriers due to custom,

---

23. According to the WARC (see n. 4); see also N. Ritchie, 'Women's Participation in the Church', in P. Fabella and M.A. Oduyoye (eds.), *With Passion and Compassion: Third World Women Doing Theology* (Maryknoll, NY: Orbis Books, 1988), pp. 151-58; and A. de Rocchietty, 'Women and the People of God', in E. Tamez (ed.), *Through Her Eyes: Women's Theology from Latin America* (Maryknoll, NY: Orbis Books, 1989), pp. 96-117.

24. For the Church of Sweden, see Thurian (ed.), *Churches Respond*, II, p. 135; for the Church of Denmark, see III, pp. 251-52; for the Burma Baptist Convention, see IV, p. 189.

25. For the American Baptist Church, see Thurian (ed.), *Churches Respond*, IV, p. 262; for the Baptist Union of Scotland, see III, p. 245.

26. For the General Mennonite Society (Netherlands), see Thurian (ed.), *Churches Respond*, III, p. 294; for the United German Mennonite Congregations, see VI, p. 128.

27. For the Moravian Church in Jamaica, see Thurian (ed.), *Churches Respond*, V, pp. 171-72; for the Moravian Churches in America Southern Province, see II, p. 258.

28. For the Religious Society of Friends (Quakers) in Great Britain, see Thurian (ed.), *Churches Respond*, IV, p. 222; for The Salvation Army, see IV, pp. 248-49.

culture and tradition' have so far rendered it impossible to open the ministry to women.[29]

A similar thing can be said of a number of churches in the Asian, African and Pacific regions—although it would be wrong to assume that such societies are necessarily opposed to the leadership of women: there are quite a few examples of indigenous matriarchal societies in, for example, African countries. In Korea, however, a country in which 22 per cent of the population is Christian, of more than 50 existing Presbyterian churches, only seven are ready to ordain women—and this only as long as they stay unmarried. Among the other Korean churches, some even refuse to admit women to the ministry of eldership.[30]

The Protestant churches of Greece (Lutheran), and Poland (Lutheran and Reformed), also abstain from the ordination of women—and one may ask whether this conformity is generated, at least in part, by the overwhelmingly non-Protestant Catholic and Orthodox contexts of these churches.

b. Related in some way to what has been said under group (a) is the so-called 'fundamentalist' or 'evangelical' position, held by a number of churches within the Protestant and Free Church traditions. Normally these churches argue their position on the basis of the respective passages in the Pauline and Pastoral letters, as they refuse to change the existing practice of the church.[31] One suspects that in Western societies, which grant equal rights to all their members, this seems in part generated by a need to define one's identity in opposition to democratic values.

A special case of fundamentalist opposition occurs in some daughter churches of European and American mission churches in Africa, Latin America and Asia. For example, the leadership of the Evangelical Lutheran Church in Namibia (ELCIN), a Finnish foundation, firmly resisted the wish of several of its members to comply with a positive vote on female ordination, which had passed the general synod of its mother church in Finland.[32] A conservative attitude is maintained by

29. See Thurian (ed.), *Churches Respond*, IV, p. 12.

30. This information is from a member of the National Council of Churches in Korea; see also *Lutheran World Information* 31 (1991), p. 10.

31. For the Lutheran Church, Missouri Synod, see Thurian (ed.), *Churches Respond*, III, pp. 140-41. Recently a pastor of this church had to leave, after openly expressing his view in favour of women being ordained (see *Lutheran World Information* 44 [1990], p. 15). For the views of the Independent Evangelical Lutheran Church (then FRG), see Thurian (ed.), *Churches Respond*, VI, p. 56.

32. Kanyoro, 'Ordination of Women in Africa'.

some Latin American churches too. On this continent the majority of
Protestant churches come from a Free Church background, often
Pentecostal. Quite a few seem to attract people because of their
opposition to any engagement in political liberation or emancipation.[33]

Finally, the Lutheran churches should be mentioned that grant to the
opponents of women's ordination the possibility to abstain on the basis
of a so-called 'conscience clause'. This possibility, however, creates the
further, dangerous prospect of new divisions.[34]

5.   Churches of the Anglican communion have been seriously affected
by the different views on ordination held and practised within the
communion. Since the first provinces—Hong Kong, the USA, Canada
and New Zealand—decided to ordain women to the ministry, and
especially now with the first two women bishops being consecrated, full
participation in the threefold ministry has been opened to women.
However, serious repercussions have arisen around these decisions. Not
only is it feared that relations with the Roman Catholic and Orthodox
churches might suffer. The interchangeability of ministries within the
Anglican communion is also no longer permitted, since ordained women
ministers are not recognized in all the provinces.[35] Thus, the Church of
England in its response to *BEM* says: 'we must face the question of
whether reconciliation to full communion is possible, while we hold
different views on this subject'.[36] Participants at the Lambeth Conference
in 1988 were at least agreed on maintaining 'the highest degree of
communion possible'.[37] And the Roman Catholic Church to date 'has

33.   So Ritchie, 'Women's Participation', and Rocchietty, 'Women and the People
of God'; also O. Ortega, 'Women and Theology: A Latin-American Viewpoint',
Ministerial Formation 48 (1990), pp. 4-13; and R. Panizo, 'An Interview with N.
Ritchie', *Latinamerica Press* 5 (January 1989), p. 5.

34.   See, for instance, the Church of Sweden, where this clause has existed since
it was decided to ordain women in 1958 (see *Christianisme au XXe siecle*, 11
[1989], p. 3; and K. Boberg, 'Doing Feminist Theology in Sweden' [unpublished
paper presented at the conference of Lutheran Women Theologians, Loccum, 1990]).
For the Church of Denmark, see *Lutheran World Information* 11 (1991), p. 9. A
similar clause will safeguard the rights of opponents to ordination within the Church
of England, but the danger of creating two separated classes of clergy has been
described by B. Prideaux in 'The Eames Report—A Way Ahead for Anglicans?',
Ecumenical Trends 19.8 (1990), pp. 113-16.

35.   M. Tanner, 'Ordination of Women', in N. Lossky *et al.* (eds.), *Dictionary of
the Ecumenical Movement* (Geneva: WCC, 1991), pp. 752-55.

36.   See Thurian (ed.), *Churches Respond*, III, p. 72.

37.   See Tanner, 'Ordination of Women', p. 755.

not in fact broken off theological discussions with the Anglican Communion for this reason'.[38] Moreover, the Church of England, in 1990 and 1992, passed, by the slimmest of margins, several documents through its general synod in favour of ordination,[39] although even here, care has also been taken to balance the different arguments and to safeguard the rights of those who remain opposed.

6.   In the Old Catholic churches things are not yet decided. In 1989 the Old Catholic Church in Germany suggested a positive vote on the Union of Utrecht. A study document tries to do justice to the different arguments *pro* and *contra*; however, so far the Union has not followed the proposal.[40]

7.   Among the documents which express the position of the Roman Catholic Church, the declaration *Inter Insignores* remains determinative. The text, published by the Congregation for the Doctrine of the Faith in 1976, is referred to in the famous document of Pope John Paul II, 'The Dignity and Vocation of Women'.[41] In accordance with these texts the Roman Catholic Church in its response to *BEM* refers to the tradition of the church, and consequently states 'that we have no authority to change it'.[42] Since tradition is considered to follow the practice of Christ and the apostles, the priesthood of women seems excluded. It is, however, worth mentioning that some scholars point to the special status of the document *Inter Insignores*, which has not received the final doctrinal approval of the pope, and therefore leaves the way open for a later decision which might be more favourable.[43]

38.   'The Ordination of Women to the Priesthood: A Digest of the Second Report by the House of Bishops' (1990 General Assembly, 829; London, 1990), p. 29; see also J. Röser, 'Wechselbäder: Ist eine Kircheneinheit zwischen Anglikanern und Katholiken noch möglich?', *Christ in der Gegenwart* 34 (1991), pp. 275-76.

39.   'The Ordination of Women to the Priesthood'; see also 'Reference of Draft Legislation to the Diocesan Synods', 1990 General Assembly, Misc. 336; and the vote of the General Synod on 11 November 1992.

40.   See n. 1.

41.   Apostolic letter *'Mulieris Dignitatem* of the Supreme Pontiff John Paul II on the Dignity and Vocation of Women on the Occasion of the Marian Year, Rome 1988' (see esp. pp. 96-98); which refers to the 'Declaration concerning the Question of the Admission of Women to the Ministerial Priesthood *Inter Insignores*, 15 October, 1976' (*Acta Apostolicae Sedis* 69 [1977], pp. 98-117).

42.   See Thurian (ed.), *Churches Respond*, VI, p.30.

43.   See H. Legrand and J. Vikstroem, 'L'admission des femmes à l'ordination', in *Face à l'unité* (Commission Internationale Catholique Luthérienne; Paris: Cerf, 1986), pp. 268-70.

8.   Orthodox churches have expressed their deep dissatisfaction with the way in which the *BEM* text has addressed the ordination of women. In the main, they find a solid ecclesiological basis lacking.[44] An inter-Orthodox consultation, which was organized on the subject and met in Rhodes, has again affirmed the 'the unbroken Tradition of the church'.[45] Thus, however open Orthodox churches have become with regard to a fuller participation of women in the life of the church and the restoration of the female diaconate, 'the *Non posse* of the entry of women to the ranks of the ordained priesthood is categorical for the Orthodox Tradition'.[46] In any case, Orthodox women themselves do not seem to feel a special vocation to the priesthood.[47]

3. *An Evaluation of the Present Situation—and Future Prospects*

Although the majority of churches in the Protestant tradition are committed to the openness of the pastoral ministry to women, and an increasing number of churches are prepared to ordain women, an equal share of the ministry is still far from being realized in many churches. In a number of countries ordained women pastors may only undertake special tasks, often in the social or in the diaconal sectors. Others are called to do administrative work. Sometimes, those who are allowed to minister in a parish are sent to a place where men have refused to go, or would not accept work.[48] And in some countries, parishes are simply not ready to welcome a woman in leadership.

The concept and structure of the pastoral ministry is still primarily androcentric, and hardly applicable to a female mode of exercise. A

44. For the Ecumenical Patriarchate of Constantinople, see Thurian (ed.), *Churches Respond*, IV, pp. 4-5; for the Russian Orthodox Church, see II, pp. 9-10; and for the Romanian Orthodox Church, see III, p. 13.

45. 'The Place of Women in the Orthodox Church and the Question of the Ordination of Women: Inter-Orthodox Consultation, Rhodos, October 30th–November 7th 1988, Ecumenical Patriarchate' (Katerini: Tertios, 1988), p. 6.

46. Metropolitan Chrysostomos of Myra; in a paper presented at the Rhodes consultation (see n. 45).

47. D. Koukoura, 'The Spiritual Experience of Orthodox Women and the Challenge of a United Europe' (unpublished paper presented at the conference of Lutheran Women Theologians, 1990, Loccum, Germany).

48. Kanyoro, 'Ordination of Women in Africa'; I.O. Kaori and A. Eiko, 'Church Women's Movement in Japan' (unpublished paper given at the eighth workshop of the Programme for Theology and Culture in Asia, Korea, 1990).

woman pastor has to overcome many obstacles, not least psychological ones: in order to prove that she is as good at leading a parish as a man, she usually needs to be better; to work harder, and to be more committed in terms of time. Her personal life is accordingly often more affected. Recently, some female students have even expressed their unwillingness to be ordained as long as the traditional concept of the ministry is not revised.[49]

It is therefore imperative to develop structures which apply to actual needs and to the conditions of modern life. Theological and practical training have to be reoriented, in many cases from the beginning, and in view of women and men living and working together and sharing their gifts.[50] Much can be learned here from the experience of other churches. Base Ecclesial Communities in Latin America, and Minjung communities, have been practising inclusive leadership for quite some time. Moreover, Quakers feel the Spirit calling them to the temporary exercise of ministries.[51]

Looking at ordination from the larger ecumenical perspective, it seems that the same basic difficulties have to be faced as are encountered on a small scale. Nevertheless, the various responses to *BEM* show that ecumenical dialogue has helped in part to meet such difficulties, often expressed in other churches' positions, and that it has also deepened awareness of the problems involved. Non-theological factors continue to be tackled: the socio-cultural situation, and psychological and linguistic problems. These are not, however, the focus of the difficulties. Solving them, it would seem, will not help to bridge the fundamental theological divergences, which—it is only realistic to expect—will continue to exist.

In the final analysis, an answer to the question of women's ordination cannot be given outside of each church's hermeneutics. Any normative presupposition, however different in practice these may be, is at the same time recognized as being a witness of the Holy Spirit itself. Churches are legitimized by reference to the Spirit, whether or not they ordain women. It is the Spirit who obliges us to safeguard with all

49. Information about female students of theology in a seminary in Brazil given informally at the meeting of the Kirchenrechtliche Arbeitsgemeinschaft der Forschungsstätte der Evangelischen Studiengemeinschaft, Heidelberg, 1991.

50. See Lumentut, 'Towards Greater Participation and Contribution of Women in Asian Churches', p. 211; and Kanyoro, 'Ordination of Women in Africa'.

51. See Thurian (ed.), *Churches Respond*, IV, p. 224.

strictness the same understanding of the Scriptures and the practice of the church's tradition throughout history.[52] And it is, once again, the Spirit who has led others to re-read the same Scriptures and to re-interpret the tradition in a new way, without becoming disobedient. On both sides of the issue, there is confidence in the Spirit's continuous guidance of the church on its pilgrimage—in fact, it is because of this very obedience to the Spirit that some churches feel that they cannot reverse their decision for the sake of unity, whereas others, for the same reason, consider a positive response inappropriate.

How then do we understand the suggestion of the *BEM* text that 'obstacles...must not be regarded as substantive hindrance for further efforts towards mutual recognition'?[53] Does this statement not plaster over the ecclesiological cracks too easily? Can one really recognize another ministry, when it is rooted in a different ecclesiology, and based on a different theology and hermeneutic? Can ecclesiologies expected to remain different co-exist? Is an overarching ecclesiology that safeguards the otherness of the various ecclesial understandings, and yet embodies the fundamental unity of the church, a realistic hope at all?

Any such overarching understanding would of course have to give up the idea of a univocal concept and practice of ordination that is definite and final. Accordingly, the concept of unity would have to comprehend the possibility of opposite expressions of truth that co-exist, but do not coincide. This in turn would pose problems for traditional logics and their realization in practice, but it may, nevertheless, have to be implemented, since only this sort of approach leaves room for 'the other' church and its own spiritual discernment. Thus, 'the Spirit may well speak to one church through the insights of another'; a phrase in the *BEM* text that has been welcomed by more than a few.[54]

A touching illustration of the attitude needed is portrayed in the last conversation between the risen Lord and Peter, as depicted by the Gospel of John. Peter, who has just been presented with the leadership

---

52. For the Malankara Orthodox Syrian Church, see Thurian (ed.), *Churches Respond*, V, p. 7; for the Bulgarian Orthodox Church, see II, pp. 21-22; for the United Protestant Church of Belgium, see III, p. 180; for the Presbyterian Church (USA), see III, p. 200; for the Episcopal Church (USA), see II, p. 60; for the Christian Church (Disciples of Christ) (USA), see I, p. 120.

53. *Baptism, Eucharist, and Ministry*, p. 32.

54. See, for instance, the Church of England in Thurian (ed.), *Churches Respond*, III, p. 72; and the Roman Catholic Church, in VI, p. 30.

of the church, asks the Lord about the Beloved Disciple: 'What about this man?' Peter here is immediately forced to respect the possibility that Jesus have the disciple 'remain until I come...' And he is simply exhorted not to judge Jesus' relationship with this other person (Jn 21.21-23). With regard to our topic, the ordination of women, I would conclude in like manner: may there be room for the other; may there be room for the Spirit; and may the churches—inside and outside their realm—create the openness for the sovereign Spirit to guide them into all truth (Jn 4.24; 16.13).

ECUMENISM AND THE ORDINATION OF WOMEN:
ROMAN CATHOLIC FEMINIST REFLECTIONS

Rosemary Radford Ruether

In September 1976, as the 65th General Convention of the Episcopal Church in the United States gathered in Minneapolis to confirm finally the ordination of women after a long struggle—which included fifteen illegal ordinations of women—Roman Catholic women stood in vigil, praying for a positive vote. Roman Catholic women came both to show their solidarity with their Episcopal sisters, but also to counteract the leadership of their own church.

These women also wanted to counteract 'the ecumenical argument' among conservative Episcopalians that the ordination of women would derail Roman Catholic–Episcopal relations. They wanted to remind such Episcopalians that Roman Catholics are not just the hierarchy. There is also the Roman Catholic people, the majority of whom are women, and there was much support for the ordination of women among these people.

When the Episcopal Church in the United States took the next step and ordained a woman, Barbara Harris, to the episcopacy in 1989, there were similar lamentations from conservative Anglicans, particularly in England, where many Anglicans seem to have had the impression that the ordination of women was invalid, since they themselves had not yet done it. Again it was said that any such step would jeopardize ecumenical relations with Rome. The Pope also encouraged this concern with a note to the Archbishop of Canterbury to that effect. This warning was echoed by an occasional Roman Catholic bishop, such as Raymond Lessard, one of the 24-strong panel of the international Anglican–Roman Catholic unity talks. Finally, in 1994, the Church of England accepted the priesthood of women.

As far as I know, there was been no general outcry from most Roman Catholic bishops, nor from Roman Catholic theologians, nor from laity, against these Anglican developments. One suspects that if conservative Roman Catholics could not be found to oppose the ordination of women, some Anglicans would invent them. Needless to say, Roman Catholic women applaud these developments, and hope that each new step toward the full acceptance of women in all ordained ministries in the churches of the Anglican communion will make such opposition among Roman Catholic hierarchs increasingly incredible to all people.

The ordination of Penelope Jamieson as bishop in the Anglican Church in New Zealand advanced that process another step, and I welcome the opportunity to send my greetings to her in this article within a commemorative volume in her honor.

There are several startling assumptions that lie behind the right-wing ecumenical argument. First of all, one assumption seems to have been that church unity lies in relations between the Pope and the Archbishop of Canterbury—a kind of mutual appreciation club between patriarchs. Church unity is seen as an alliance, or even a merger, arranged between heads of two ecclesiastical multi-national corporations. Thus, it does not seem startling to these 'ecumenists' to imagine a Rome–Canterbury agreement that was predicated on insulting and disregarding the full humanness and Christian status of the majority of both churches— namely, some 500 million women. It is hardly imaginable that these same right-wing ecumenists in the Anglican churches would allow principles that affect their own status and beliefs, such as the right of the clergy to marry, and the right of national churches to govern their own affairs, to be forfeited for the cause of unity with Rome. Yet, with a reactionary papacy upholding celibacy for Roman Catholic priests, and intervening throughout the world in episcopal appointments to shore up its centralized control, it is unlikely that there will be much give on these points in negotiations with Anglicans. In the face of the acceptance of the priesthood of women by the Church of England, the Pope could only warn and scold and finally reiterate his own negation in successive documents.

The occasional acceptance of an Anglican priest who is already married into communion with Rome does not fundamentally change the Vatican's principle of priestly celibacy as normative. But the issues of universal jurisdiction, together with infallibility—the cornerstones of the Vatican I papacy—are the key ones. The present papacy has been adamant in re-establishing these principles in conflict with a populist

Catholicism and potential national church government under bishops' councils. One wonders why Anglican ecumenism expends all its efforts on Rome and does not make more effort to support these liberalizing Catholic movements?

Perhaps it is time for those concerned with ecumenical unity to ask in new ways what church unity is all about. Is church unity primarily a matter of church corporation mergers? Is its goal one vast, centralized world church? Or is church unity not primarily a question of churches in communion with each other—a spiritual rather than an institutional relation? Such an understanding of churches in communion existed in the early centuries of the church, when there were virtually no organizational forms above the local church level.

Unity in the Spirit also needs to be able to respect cultural differences, a diversity of liturgical traditions, and even some theological pluralism. Communion, as the Anglican communion itself proclaims, does not contradict the existence of a plurality of self-governing churches. The historical plurality of the churches needs to be viewed not only as a scandal, but also as a gift. It is a scandal when plurality is translated into enmity. But once brought into dialogue, historical plurality should be seen as a multi-faceted richness of the understanding and cultural expression of the Christian message, which cannot be found in one tradition alone. It is through this dialogue in historical plurality that we gain a true understanding of the church's catholicity.

Morever, I am inclined to believe that the maintenance of some plurality of churches may be important to preserve genuine Christian freedom. Does anyone really want one universal papal empire? Would it not be more helpful for the welfare of the Roman Catholic church if Anglicans spent more time making an attractive presentation of their own tradition of communion between autocephalous churches, rather than muting a critique of the papal model of church unity based on world monarchical centralization?

Another assumption within the right-wing Anglican ecumenical argument against the ordination of women puzzles me. It seems to ignore or to relegate to second place ecumenical relations between Anglicans and the rest of world Protestantism. For these Anglicans only ecumenism between Rome and Canterbury (or, now, the Orthodox) counts. They seem to want to confirm their membership in an 'Old Boys' club' of ancient patriarchs. The fact that 400 million Christians, a fourth of world Christianity, are Protestants, and that Anglicans are closer to these other

Christians as part of a growing body of churches that do ordain women, is discounted.

The patriarchal ecumenists among the British particularly, such as the archetypal William Oddie,[1] have a strange habit of speaking as if the experience of many Christian churches with ordained women did not exist, an experience which goes back more than 100 years among Congregationalists, and now fifteen years among American Episcopalians. Even among priestly churches that claim an unbroken apostolic succession of bishops through the Latin Middle Ages, such as the Swedish Lutheran church, women have been ordained since 1958. Instead, Oddie spoke of women's ordination as if it were an untried, impending disaster, and promptly departed to the Roman church once the Church of England finally 'took the plunge'.

Another typical assumption, and one which patriarchal thinkers, such as Oddie, share with the Pope on the matter of the ordination of women, is that Christian practices which have gone on through much of the historical memory of the church must be infallible and unchangeable by virtue of the very fact that they have gone on for a long time. The church as a historical institution is not recognized to be an expression of sinful and fallible human beings that are capable of significant wrongdoing even in long-established practices.

This assumption of infallibility in long-established practices is hardly in accord with what we would have to acknowledge in many other areas. For example, in the Bible, both Old and New Testaments, one finds a qualified acceptance of the institution of slavery. The major line of Christian theologians, as well as canon law and church practice, accepted the arguments (formulated especially by St Augustine) that slavery was an acceptable social institution. This argument continued among both Catholics and mainline Protestants into the mid-nineteenth century. In the 1850s, Presbyterian theologians at Princeton were publishing books with titles like *Slavery Ordained of God*.[2] Can anyone doubt today that this long-established tradition was sinfully erroneous?

Religious and racial animosity toward Jews has also been accepted by

---

1. W. Oddie, *After the Deluge: Essays Toward the Desecularization of the Church* (London: SPCK, 1987); see also his *What Will Happen to God? Feminism and the Reconstruction of Christian Belief* (London: SPCK, 1984).

2. See E. McKitrech, *Slavery Defended* (Englewood Cliffs, NJ: Prentice–Hall, 1963); also J. Maxwell, *Slavery and the Catholic Church* (London: Anti-Slavery Society for the Protection of Human Rights, 1975).

Christians until very recently. This tragic conflict arose with the separation of church and synagogue in the apostolic period, and is reflected in
hostile diatribes against Jews in the New Testament. Theology and canon
law taught through the Middle Ages and early modern period that Jews
were under a divine curse, and that their religion had been superseded
and no longer carried any salvific efficacy. Significant questioning of
these views in the Christian churches began only in the 1960s after the
Nazi Holocaust.[3] Yet can anyone today argue that this long-established
tradition of anti-Semitism was not also sinfully erroneous?

The history of sexism in the church parallels these forms of racial,
ethnic and class discrimination. It is part of a history of patriarchal
society in which women were regarded as less than fully human, lacking
the capacity for independent thought and life, and therefore incapable of
social leadership. These views of women were taken over by Christianity
from Greek philosophy and Roman law, as well as from Hebrew
patriarchy.

In Aristotle we find the argument that women are inherently defective
biologically.[4] Aristotle based his argument on the (false) biological claim
that the male alone contributes the formative power of procreation,
while the mother is a mere incubator for the male seed. The relation of
male to female in procreation is that of formative power to passive
matter. However, on a regular basis it happens that the male formative
power fails to form fully the female matter and an incompletely formed
or defective human is born, which is female. Thus, femaleness is defined
as a lack of full humanness, and a defective capacity for mental, moral
and physical prowess.

This false Aristotelian biology underlay the claims of the medieval
scholastics, such as Thomas Aquinas, that Christ had to be a male in
order to represent the normatively human. Only males in turn can represent Christ, therefore, only males can be ordained.[5] This conception, that
women cannot be ordained because women by their very nature cannot
'image Christ', continues to be the centerpiece of the Roman Catholic
hierarchy's argument against the ordination of women. It appeared in
the 1976 Vatican Declaration against the Ordination of Women, and was

---

    3.   R. Ruether, *Faith and Fratricide: The Theological Roots of Anti-Semitism*
(New York: Seabury Press, 1974).

    4.   Aristotle, *Generation of Animals* 729b, 737-38.

    5.   Thomas Aquinas, *Summa Theologica*, Part. 1, q. 92, article 1.

repeated in the pastoral epistle of Pope John Paul II 'On the Dignity and Vocation of Women'.[6]

To this Greek argument for women's defective nature, the New Testament and subsequent Christian theology added the myth of Eve, joined to the doctrine of Original Sin (which was not a part of Old Testament thought). According to this reading of the stories of Genesis 1 and 2, women are secondary in the very order of creation, created out of, and to be an adjunct to, the male. Moreover, women sinned and caused Paradise to be lost, thereby incurring a fault that is passed on to all women collectively. Women are to pay for this collective sin of being female by subjugation to the male as their 'head', and by painful childbearing.

The New Testament epistle of 1 Timothy uses this argument for the purpose of silencing women in the early church who were teaching and preaching. Such women, and the men who supported them, understood the Pauline teaching that 'in Christ there is neither male nor female' to mean that in Christ there was a new redemptive relation between men and women in which women too were given the gifts of prophecy and teaching.[7]

It would be no exaggeration to say that, for the 2000 year history of the Christian churches, there have never ceased to be women (and men) who have understood the good news of Christ as opening up equality for women. At the same time, the adversarial use of these biblical texts to silence such women has had an equally long history.

A consistent development of the Christian teaching of women's inclusion in both the image of God in creation, and in redemption in Christ, was blocked for most of Christian history by dualistic splits between creation and redemption, and between soul and society. Women's sharing in the image of God and women's redemption in Christ were read as applying only spiritually, to women's souls, and hence to be expressed in personal holiness and life after death. Creation was read as a patriarchal order, and women were to express their obedience to God by submission to this patriarchal order of society. The

---

6.   *Vatican Declaration of the Question of the Admission of Women to the Ministerial Priesthood* (1976), §27; see also the pastoral letter by Pope John Paul II, 'The Dignity and Vocation of Women', 31 September 1988, §26.

7.   E. Schüssler Fiorenza, *In Memory of Her: A Feminist Theological Reconstruction of Christian Origins* (New York: Crossroad, 1983), *passim*.

church in history was also to mirror this patriarchal order in its institutional structure.

Only in the late eighteenth and the nineteenth centuries did the notion that patriarchal hierarchy, along with class hierarchy, was the 'order of creation' begin to be questioned as a foundational social myth. Modern democratic societies took their theological anthropology from the foundational concept of the equality of all human persons in 'original nature'. Social hierarchy thus became, not 'nature', but an unjust distortion of nature, creating privileged and non-privileged classes, races and genders. It was the task of social reform to create new legal institutions which gave equal citizenship to all adult persons. Gradually, through the nineteenth and twentieth centuries, this foundational assumption was extended to conquered and enslaved racial groups, and to women.

The movement for the ordination of women began in the mid-nineteenth century in the United States, as part of the movement for the abolition of slavery and the extension of civil rights to all adults. Already, in 1848, the Declaration of the First Women's Rights Convention in Seneca Falls, New York, concluded with the ringing demand:

> *Resolved*: that the speedy success of our cause depends upon the zealous and untiring efforts of both men and women for the overthrow of the monopoly of the pulpit, and for the securing to women of equal participation with men in various trades, profession and commerce.[8]

The first woman to be ordained in the United States was Congregationalist Antoinette Brown. In her ordination service in 1853, preacher Luther Lee used as his key texts Gal. 3.28 ('in Christ there is no male and female') and Acts 2.17 ('Your sons and your daughters shall prophesy'). He argued that Christ reopened the prophetic office to women, affirming women's equality as an image of God redeemed in Christ. Since, for Lee, the preaching office was the prophetic office, the church had sinned against its Lord throughout its history in denying this office to women.[9]

---

8. 'Declaration of Sentiments and Resolutions: Seneca Falls, July 19, 1848', in M. Schneir (ed.), *Feminism: The Essential Historical Writings* (New York: Vintage Books, 1972), pp. 76-82.

9. L. Lee, 'Women's Right to Preach the Gospel, A Sermon Preached at the Ordination of the Rev. Miss Antoinette Brown, at South Butler, Wayne County, New York, September 15, 1953' (Syracuse, NY: n.p., 1853).

In the second half of the nineteenth century various small denominations, such as Congregationalists, Unitarians, Universalists and Methodist Protestants, opened the ministry to women. Mainline Protestants—Presbyterians, Lutherans, Methodist Episcopals and Episcopalians—rejected the ordination of women, but attempted to divert women's new energies for ministry into missionary work. Unordained orders of deaconesses were invented to provide vocational organizations for single women in professional church work.

Significant change in this stance among Protestants did not take place until after the Second World War. Women had entered higher theological education in the first half of the twentieth century, side by side with the opening of university education to women. In Europe during the Second World War, many of these theologically-educated women were allowed to take over the ministry of churches in the absence of men who were at war. After the war was over there was an effort to send these women back to the home, but the women protested the injustice of this.

Thus the debate began which led to the ordination of women in the Lutheran and Reformed Churches in Scandinavia and Germany in the late 1950s and 1960s. At the same time (1958), Northern Presbyterians and mainline Methodists accepted women's ordination in the United States. The 1970s saw a continual expansion of Protestant churches that ordained women, both in the West and around the world, and also increasing numbers of women in theological education. This expansion of theologically-educated women as students, and then as professors, in theological schools, made possible the systematic examination and critique of the arguments that had kept women out of ordained ministry for so long.

For example, it is common among conservative Christians to claim that ordination is not a 'right', and hence that one cannot apply the arguments for civil rights to this question. But this begs the question. Holding political office is also not a 'right', but the possibility of all citizens running for office *is* a right. If women are excluded from presenting themselves for office, we understand that they lack full membership in the body politic. The same is true of the church.

Moreover, the arguments that have kept women marginalized in the body politic and in the church are not divided along secular–theological lines. Historically, they are the same arguments. They are arguments that define women as defective persons, lacking full humanity, and hence lacking the capacity 'to image God' and 'to represent Christ'. The theological arguments are, at base, anthropological arguments. These anthropological arguments have been discredited scientifically and socially, and have lost their political basis in women's legal subjugation. Hence, the effort to continue to maintain them on a purely 'theological' basis in the church is untenable.

However, I think that it is not enough for Christians merely to say that 'times have changed' and so now women can be ordained. What is more difficult—and perhaps this is the real stumbling block for infallibilist Christians—is accepting this change as *metanoia* for the churches. Like racism, slavery and homophobia (which most churches also have not acknowledged as sinful faults), sexism must be recognized as a sin. The exclusion of women from ordained ministry represents a failure of the church to accept the full vision of the gospel, and a capitulation to unjust social structures, which were then rationalized theologically. Such reforms require not merely legal change, but repentance; the spiritual acknowl-edgment of having sinned against our sisters in Christ for most of the church's history.

Turning back to questions of ecumenism: authentic intercommunion between divided churches must be based on truth and justice, and not just on a flattering sense of belonging to one of the world's oldest male clubs. Decisions to enter into communion should spring from prophetic renewal among these churches, a renewal of the vision of the church as a discipleship of equals in the community of redemption.

Anglicans can serve this cause of prophetic renewal by affirming that repentance from sexism is an integral expression of this Christian vision of redemptive community. It is not simply an expendable accommo-dation to contemporary society. Anglicans should make clear that the recent shift to women's ordination among growing numbers of churches reflects this rediscovery of the original vision of the church as a disciple-ship of equals, rather than lamenting that the inclusion of women in ordained ministry might disqualify them from membership of a partic-ular ecclesial, patriarchal club.

A large number of Roman Catholics see the ordination of women as a necessary development that must take place in their church in order to move forward the Vatican II vision of the church as the People of God. A significant share of the pastoral ministry in the Roman Catholic Church is, in fact, being done by women, precisely because of the unten-ability of the all-male, celibate clergy. With the failure of sufficient numbers of men to come forward to accept this type of clerical life,

Catholic bishops all over the world are having to turn to theologically-educated lay people, mainly women, to do parochial ministry. This means that more and more Catholic parishes are actually experiencing much of the day-to-day work of ministry as done, and done well, by women. It is not these lay people who are the stumbling block to women's ordination in this church!

Roman Catholic theologians and scholars of Scripture have made clear that the Vatican declarations against the ordination of women cannot be sustained biblically or theologically. Karl Rahner, the leading twentieth-century Catholic theologian, even called the 1976 Vatican Declaration against the Ordination of Women 'heretical'. He characterized statements like the infamous claim that women cannot 'image Christ' as theologically scandalous.

These reform movements in Roman Catholicism deserve support from authentic ecumenical reformers in the Protestant and Anglican churches. On the other hand, right-wing 'ecumenical' alliances of Anglicans and Roman Catholics which aim at subverting these reform movements can certainly not be regarded by progressive Catholics as helpful to their church. They are reactionary movements that retard the renewal efforts in both churches.

Today it is not enough to assume that official conversations between hierarchical representatives constitute 'ecumenism'. One has to recognize the internal divisions of the churches along reactionary and progressive lines. These divisions similarly divide ecumenical relations. Two quite different kinds of ecumenism have emerged that one might call 'institutional' and 'movement' ecumenisms.

Institutional ecumenism is expressed in 'Faith and Order' dialogues. The goal is agreements on doctrine and polity that might lead to intercommunion or even to church merger. The means to this goal are essentially conservative. The very process of such dialogues calls each church to return to the 'classic' stances of its 'tradition'. This means that recent developments in the interpretation of theology and democratic reforms of polity are ignored. It is this pattern of ecumenism that regards women's ordination as an expendable 'barrier' to ecumenical 'understanding'.

'Movement' ecumenism, by contrast, takes place in the progressive sectors of the churches which are committed to the struggle for a more participatory church and a more just society. These Christians are in solidarity with each other in a common struggle. I have experienced very dynamic examples of such movement ecumenism in countries like El Salvador. The Lutherans, Baptists, Roman Catholics and Anglicans experience themselves there as part of one community in a common struggle for a just society, and for a renewed church that understands its mission as one of holistic liberation.

Such Christians often find themselves experiencing the same repression from the government. For example, on 5 April 1989, Baptist leader Maria Christina Gomez was kidnapped on the steps of the school where she taught, tortured and then shot. Her body was dumped in a cemetery. During the same period the major Lutheran church in San Salvador was bombed and its leading bishop had temporarily to flee the country to escape assassination. At the end of the year, six Jesuits were murdered in their residence. These events were not isolated, but were part of a concerted effort by the government to target the progressive Christian leadership of the country.

Today one must speak of 'the politics of ecumenism'. In the choice of ecumenical alliances church leaderships reveal their political preferences and ethical stances. By ordaining women to the priesthood and now, in the United States and in New Zealand, to the episcopacy, Anglicans have the possibility of representing a prophetic avant-garde in the promotion of women's equality in the church, not simply for the church itself, but as a witness to society. We Roman Catholic women applaud them, and we also encourage them to have the courage of their convictions.

THE *EKKLESIA* OF WOMEN:
RE-VISIONING THE PAST IN CREATING A DEMOCRATIC FUTURE

Elisabeth Schüssler Fiorenza

The *Great Nobel Debate*, held in Stockholm in 1991 and broadcast in the US by PBS,[1] brought together recipients of the Nobel prize to debate the future of the world. One part of the panel contended that humanity has the knowledge and the will to make the world's future possible. The other group of Nobel laureates argued to the contrary that modern knowledge and technology have brought our planet to the brink of destruction. Nadine Gordimer, the South African novelist, summed up the deadlock of the debate. In this debate 'knowledge' and 'spiritual vision', she argued, are blindfolded and turned away from each other. Only when knowledge and spiritual vision embrace each other will we be able to create a humane future. However, Gordimer did not point to another impairment of knowledge and vision. The audience gathered in the Swedish academy of Arts and Sciences consisted primarily of white, élite men.

One hundred years earlier, Anna Julia Cooper, an African-American feminist, made a similar appeal to restore the wholeness of vision and imagination. But in distinction to Gordimer, she insisted that those who until now have been excluded must participate in such a re-visioning:

> It is not the intelligent woman vs. the ignorant woman; nor the white woman vs. the black, the brown, and the red—it is not even the cause of woman vs. man. Nay, it is woman's strongest vindication for speaking that the world needs to hear her voice. It would be subversive of every human interest that the cry of one half of the human family be stifled. Woman ...daring to think and move and speak—to undertake to help shape, mold and direct the thought of her age, is merely completing the circle of the

---

1. See PBS broadcast of the debate on 2 January 1991, at 12 am.

world's vision. Hers is every interest that has lacked an interpreter and a defender. Her cause is linked with that of every agony that has been dumb—every wrong that needs a voice…The world has had to limp along with the wobbling gait and one-sided hesitancy of a man with one eye. Suddenly the bandage is removed from the other eye and the whole body is filled with light. It sees a circle where before it saw a segment. The darkened eye restored, every member rejoices with it.[2]

Following the vision of Anna Julia Cooper, feminist theory asks: how can we complete the full circle of the world's vision so that our planet can have a future? Utilizing a critical analysis of patriarchy, it seeks to remove the bandage from our mind's eye in order to restore full vision. Feminist theology in turn explores what kind of role religious vision and imagination play in the limited imagination of the West. At the same time, it searches for religious visions that can help repair the full circle of the world's vision. Feminist biblical interpretation in turn seeks to restore those segments of the biblical vision that have been marginalized, submerged or erased from our political and religious consciousness.[3]

Positioned on the threshold not only of 'the global village', but also of the 500th anniversary of the European 'discovery' of the Americas, of Abia Yala (to use an indigenous American expression), feminist biblical interpretation searches for a biblical imagination that can serve the present and the future. It not only embraces knowledge and vision, but also seeks to rectify our knowledge and vision of the world which is still one-sided and one-eyed to the extent that it continues to be articulated by élite white men. If vision and knowledge are limited by their sociopolitical location and function, then a biblical imagination for liberation that strives to be multifocal and multilocal must be situated within the diverse feminist struggles which seek to overcome patriarchal oppression. It must articulate a critical theory of patriarchy[4] that can understand

2.   A.J. Cooper, *A Voice From the South* (originally published in 1892; republished in the Schomburg Library of Nineteenth-Century Black Women Writers; New York: Oxford University Press, 1990).

3.   For such a hermeneutical perspective see my book *Bread Not Stone: The Challenge of Feminist Biblical Interpretation* (Boston: Beacon Press, 1985).

4.   I do not understand 'patriarchy' in the sense of sexism and gender dualism, or use it as an undefined label. Rather, I construe the term in the 'narrow sense' as 'father-right and father-might'. I understand it as a heuristic concept that seeks to name the complex systemic interstructuring of sexism, racism, classism and cultural-religious imperialism that has produced the Western 'politics of Otherness'. Although patriarchy has changed throughout history, its Aristotelian articulation is

women's oppression not just in terms of gender but in terms of the multiplicative interstructurings of racism, class exploitation, heterosexism, and colonialist militarism.[5] Whether and how much biblical religion and theology are able to engender a liberating imagination for the future, will depend on how much we are able to create a multifocal analysis of patriarchy and a multivocal discourse of liberation.

Feminism, when understood as social movement to transform patriarchy,[6] seeks to engender a different historical 'imagination'. It constructs history as 'a conceptual vision', a perspectival optic, or 'a vantage point',[7] in order to enable us to understand and to change patriarchal reality. Since a critical biblical interpretation for liberation is committed to emancipatory struggles around the globe, it seeks to articulate a biblical imagination that can shape a more just future for the global village. Such a biblical imagination must be a *historical* imagination that can retrieve Christian history and theology, not just as the memory of the suffering and victimization of all non-persons.[8] It must also seek to repossess this heritage as the memory of those women and men who have shaped Christian history as religious interlocutors, agents of change, and survivors[9] in the struggles against patriarchal domination.

Women have always transmitted history, told stories and kept their memories alive. However, history has by and large been written by élite

still powerful in Western cultures today. For a review of the terminology see V. Beechey, 'On Patriarchy', *Feminist Review* 3 (1979), pp. 66-82; and G. Lerner, *The Creation of Patriarchy* (New York: Oxford University Press, 1986), pp. 231-41.

5. K.L. Cannon and E. Schüssler Fiorenza (eds.), *Interpretation for Liberation* (*Semeia*; Atlanta: Scholars Press, 1989); D.K. King, 'Multiple Jeopardy, Multiple Consciousness: The Context of Black Feminist Ideology', *Signs* 14 (1988), pp. 42-72; and especially P. Hill Collins, *Black Feminist Thought: Knowledge, Consciousness and the Politics of Empowerment* (Boston: Unwin Hyman, 1990).

6. For such an understanding of feminist movement see b. hooks, *Feminist Theory: From Margin to Center* (Boston: South End Press, 1984).

7. J. Kelly, 'The Doubled Vision of Feminist Theory', in *Women, History, and Theory* (Chicago: University of Chicago Press, 1974), pp. 51-64.

8. See G. Gutiérrez, *The Power of the Poor in History* (Maryknoll, NY: Orbis Books, 1984) for this expression.

9. In distinction to liberation and political theologies a critical feminist theology insists that women cannot be understood just as victims of, or collaborators in, their oppression. 'Solidarity with victims' does not suffice. The self-understanding of women as historical and theological subjects is crucial for a feminist theological reconstruction.

men as their own story and in their own interests. The apostle Peter, who according to some traditions was the first witness to the resurrection, has been hailed throughout centuries as having primacy among the apostles.[10] In contrast, Mary of Magdala, who according to other traditions was the primary witness to the resurrection, has lived in Christian memory as a repentant whore and sinner.[11] Christian historical imagination has been deprived of its fullness of vision.

Like historians of other oppressed groups, feminist historians, therefore, seek to break through the silences and biases of historical records in order to reappropriate the past of women who have participated as historical agents in social, cultural and religious transformation. Such a task of a historical re-imagination and reconstruction that seeks to recover early Christian history as 'a dangerous memory',[12] and an inspiring heritage for all non-persons, encounters great methodological difficulties which are aptly characterized by the Caribbean writer Michelle Cliff:

> To write as a complete Caribbean woman, or man for that matter, demands of us retracing the African past of ourselves, reclaiming as our own, and as our subject a history sunk under the sea, or scattered as potash in the canefields, or gone to bush, or trapped in a class system notable for its rigidity and dependence on class stratification. On a past bleached from our minds...It means realizing our knowledge will always be wanting. It means also, I think, mixing in the forms taught us by the oppressor, undermining his language and co-opting his style and turning it to our purpose.[13]

In other words, the point of a feminist historical reconstruction cannot

10. See R.E. Brown, K.P. Donfried and J. Reumann (eds.), *Peter in the New Testament* (Minneapolis: Augsburg, 1973); and G. O'Collins, 'Peter as Easter Witness', *HeyJ* 22 (1981), pp. 243-56.

11. See L. Schottroff, 'Maria Magdalena und die Frauen am Grabe', *EvT* 42 (1982), pp. 3-25; G. O'Collins and D. Kendall, 'Mary Magdalene as Major Witness to Jesus' Resurrection', *TS* 48 (1987), pp. 631-46: J.K. Coyle, 'Mary Magdalene in Manicheism', *Le Muséon* 104 (1991), pp. 39-55: H.M. Grath, *Saint Mary Magdalene in Mediaeval Literature* (Baltimore: Johns Hopkins University Press, 1950); M.M. Malvern, *Venus in Sackcloth: The Magdalen's Origins and Metamorphoses* (Carbondale, IL: University of Illinois Press, 1975).

12. For this expression see the work of J.B. Metz, esp. his *Faith in History and Society: Toward a Practical Fundamental Theology* (trans. D. Smith; New York: Seabury [Crossroad], 1980).

13. M. Cliff, 'A Journey into Speech', in R. Simonson and S. Walker (eds.), *The Graywolf Annual Five: Multicultural Literacy* (Saint Paul, MN: Graywolf Press, 1988), p. 59.

be to distil, for instance, the factual 'truth' of Mary of Magdala, one of Jesus' disciples, from its discursive representations. Nor can such a reconstruction attempt to recover the 'real' Mary of Magdala. And neither should it try to establish 'the actual event' of her first encounter with Jesus. Rather, a critical emancipatory historiography seeks to open up to historical memory all that has been suppressed in traditional historiography in order to explore the reasons for the exclusions and choices which constitute our historical knowledge of early Christian beginnings.

In order to re-imagine and to reconstruct early Christian history as the history of the discipleship of equals, feminist biblical studies must do more than question the prevailing accounts of the past. It must also situate its historical reconstructions within a critical democratic imagination that can conceptualize the writing of history not as an antiquarian science but as a rhetorical practice which shapes our vision of the present and the future. For instance, in her 1989 Harvard Commencement address the former Prime Minister of Pakistan, Benazir Bhutto, singled out 'democracy' as 'the most powerful political idea in the world today', and called for the creation of an Association of Democratic Nations that could promote democracy which appears today as a universal value and global vision.

Acknowledging the influence of Western democratic institutions, Benazir Bhutto also underscored the influence of religion in shaping democratic vision. In her country, she asserted, the love of freedom and human rights 'arises fundamentally from the strong egalitarian spirit that pervades Islamic traditions'. She pointed to herself, a Muslim woman and Prime Minister of some hundreds of millions of Muslims, as the living refutation of the argument that a country cannot be democratic because it is Muslim. Islamic religion and its strong democratic ethos, she insisted, have inspired and provided sustenance to democratic struggles, and confidence in the righteousness of just causes, as well as sustained faith in the Islamic teaching 'that tyranny cannot long endure'. Therefore, the maxim that the progress of a society can be judged by the progress of its women must be applied also to the sphere of religion. The criterion for measuring whether a religion is democratic and liberating consists in the practical test of whether it allows for the full participation and leadership of women.

If one accepts as a pragmatic criterion for judging whether a religion can sustain and nurture a democratic imagination and society the extent to which that religion allows for women to exercise full leadership, then biblical interpretation must seriously attend to feminist questions and analyses. Since Western society has realized democracy only in its patriarchal form,[14] feminist theory and theology seek to re-vision democracy as *the ekklesia of women*. As long as the practice of democracy remains patriarchal, it is necessary, I have argued, to qualify *ekklesia* with 'women' in order to lift into consciousness that a radical democratic imagination and politics must include women as full democratic citizens, who equally participate in deciding the future of our 'global village'.

The radical democratic imagination of *the ekklesia of women* is at once a historically accomplished, and a future, imagined, reality, already partially realized but still to be struggled for. This democratic vision is already present in reality in society and church and yet it is not fully accomplished: it is both real and in the process of realization. Historically and politically the image of *the ekklesia of women*, in the sense of the Western democratic assembly or of the congress of women, is an oxymoron, a combination of contradictory terms for the purpose of articulating a feminist political vision which identifies Christian community and biblical interpretation as important sites of feminist political-intellectual struggles to transform Western patriarchy.

As the intersection of a multiplicity of public feminist discourses, and as a site of contested socio-political contradictions, feminist alternatives, and unrealized possibilities, *the ekklesia of women* requires a rhetorical rather than a scientistic-positivistic conceptualization of biblical interpretation.[15] Theological discourses, then, are best understood in the classical sense of deliberative rhetoric that seeks to persuade the democratic assembly, and to adjudicate arguments, in order to make decisions for the sake of the welfare of everyone. Such a critical imagination of radical democracy provides an 'emancipatory vantage point' *within* Western society and biblical religions. This location within political and cultural struggles is 'acquired by acknowledging one's commitment to projects for political and cultural transformation'.[16] Its democratic re-visioning of

14. For a review of the classic debates on democracy and their feminist re-visioning, see A. Phillips, *Engendering Democracy* (University Park: Pennsylvania State University, 1991).

15. For a fuller development of my argument see my *But She Said: Feminist Practices of Biblical Interpretation* (Boston: Beacon Press, 1992).

16. Compare, for example, N.M. Hartsock, 'The Feminist Standpoint: Developing the Ground for a Specifically Feminist Historical Materialism', and S.M. Harding, 'Why Has the Sex/Gender System Become Visible Only Now?', in S. Harding and M.B. Hintikka (eds.), *Discovering Reality* (Dordrecht: D. Reidel, 1983), pp. 283-310

the past seeks to construct and reconstruct a *different* socio-historical imagination.

Since women and all other non-persons participate not only in the androcentric cultural discourses of marginalization and subordination, but also in the democratic 'humanistic' discourses of freedom, self-determination, justice and equality, feminist scholars can create out of the tension between these discourses a different historical imagination for reconstructing the past. Such 'imagination' is not fictive fantasy. It is rather *historical* imagination because the reality to which it refers has been at least partially realized in the historical lives and struggles of 'the subordinated others' who have refused to be defined by the patriarchal politics of inequality, subordination and dehumanization.

A different historical imagination that re-visions early Christian roots in terms of radical democracy must articulate critical models[17] of historical reconstruction that can break the ideological hold of andro-centric biblical texts on the historical representation and imagination of early Christian life and history.[18] Since lack of a written history is a crucial sign of oppression, such a feminist reconstruction is not just an academic affair; for it also seeks to empower *the ekklesia of women* in the liberation struggle.

The reconstructive historical model seeks to reshape our historical and theological self-understanding by displacing hegemonic androcentric reconstructions of early Christian origins which marginalize or eliminate women and other non-persons from the historical record. It does so by questioning the rhetorical strategies of androcentric biblical texts in order to subvert them. For it is in and through such a critical analysis that the 'reality' which the text marginalizes and silences is brought to the fore. Indeed, androcentric language and male-authored texts presuppose women's historical presence and agency; for the most part, however,

and 310-24; more recently, see T. Winant, 'The Feminist Standpoint: A Matter of Language', *Hypatia* 2 (1987), p. 142.

17. See especially the first three chapters in my *In Memory of Her: A Feminist Theological Reconstruction of Christian Origins* (New York: Crossroad, 1983); Judith Plaskow has adapted this model for a feminist reconstruction of Jewish history ('Standing Again at Sinai: Jewish Memory from a Feminist Perspective', *Tikkun* 1 [1987], pp. 28-34); and Carol P. Christ for reclaiming Goddess history (*Laughter of Aphrodite: Reflections on a Journey to the Goddess* [San Francisco: Harper & Row, 1987]).

18. See my article 'Text and Reality—Reality as Text: The Problem of a Feminist Historical Reconstruction Based on Texts', *ST* 43 (1989), pp. 19-34.

they do not articulate it. Consequently, the relationship between andro-centric text and historical reality cannot be construed as one of mirror-images. Rather, it must be decoded as a complex ideological construction. The androcentric text's rhetorical silences, contradictions, arguments, prescriptions and projections; its discourses on gender, race, class, culture or religion, must be exposed as the ideological inscriptions of the Western politics of patriarchy.

Furthermore, a reconstructive historical model that is able to examine the rhetorical strategies of the androcentric text and its symbolic universes provides means not only for exploring what the text excludes, but also for investigating *how* the text constructs what it includes.[19] Androcentric biblical texts tell stories and construct social worlds and symbolic universes which mythologize, reverse, absolutize and idealize patriarchal differences. In so doing, such texts obliterate or marginalize the historical presence of the devalued 'others'.[20]

As rhetorical texts they create a world in which those whose arguments they oppose either become the 'deviant others', the opponents and heretics, or are no longer heard at all. Yet freeborn women and slave women and men were present in the early Christian movements—not only as victims, but also as historical subjects and agents. A critical feminist reconstruction of early Christian beginnings such as I have elaborated in *In Memory of Her* seeks to re-read early Christian androcentric texts in their Greco-Roman and Jewish contexts in order to re-imagine early Christian history in terms of social-ecclesial struggles and rhetorical arguments through which the 'politics' of exclusion and submission unfold.[21] The so-called household code texts, or injunctions to patriarchal submission, of the Christian Testament can only be understood when they are seen as rhetorical statements seeking to adapt the egalitarian and therefore subversive Christian movement to

19. A. Munich, 'Notorious Signs, Feminist Criticism, and Literary Tradition', in G. Green and C. Kahn (eds.), *Making a Difference* (New York: Methuen, 1985), p. 256.

20. See my article 'The Politics of Otherness: Biblical Interpretation as a Critical Praxis for Liberation', in M.H. Ellis and O. Maduro (eds.), *The Future of Liberation Theology: Essays in Honor of Gustavo Gutiérrez* (Maryknoll, NY: Orbis Books, 1989), pp. 311-25; T.T. Minh-ha, *Woman, Native, Other: Writing Postcoloniality and Feminism* (Bloomington: Indiana University Press, 1989).

21. See also my article 'Die Anfänge von Kirche, Amt, und Priestertum in feministisch-theologischer Sicht', in P. Hoffman (ed.), *Priesterkirche* (Düsseldorf: Patmos, 1987), pp. 62-95.

its Greco-Roman patriarchal society and culture.[22] They would not have been necessary if from its inception Christian community and faith existed as a patriarchal formation.

Rather the patriarchal rhetorics of the early Christian writings still allow us to glimpse 'the dangerous memory' of a movement and community of radical equality in the power of the Spirit. The early Christian missionary movements proclaimed that all religious and social status distinctions and privileges between Jews and Greeks, slave and free, both women and men, were abolished in the *ekklesia*.[23] They understood themselves to be called to freedom. The *ekklesia*'s equality in the Spirit is expressed in alternating leadership and partnership; in equal access for everyone, Greeks, Jews, Barbarians, slaves, free, rich, poor, both women and men. Therefore its proper name is *ekklesia*: the full decision-making assembly of free citizens who are resident aliens in their societies and constitute a different 'third race'.

This rhetorical model of historical reconstruction can relate diverse texts to each other—texts about women's leadership, clues as to the inclusive and egalitarian organization of early Christian communities, passages such as the baptismal proclamation of Gal. 3.28 and the list of names in Romans 16, the ethos of suffering discipleship rather than patriarchal adaptation, the notion of the *ekklesia* as a community of friends. This model poses these as one side of the argument. The other side of the debate emerges, for instance, through Paul's incipient patriarchal rhetoric, or in the construction of early Christian beginnings by Luke–Acts. This side is also represented by both the household code texts

22. D.L. Balch, *Let Wives Be Submissive: The Domestic Code in 1 Peter* (Chico, CA: Scholars Press, 1981); for a socio-historical reconstruction in terms of Max Weber's model see M.Y. Macdonald, *The Pauline Churches: A Socio-Historical Study of Institutionalization in the Pauline and Deutero-Pauline Writings* (Cambridge: Cambridge University Press, 1988); see also M. Gielen, *Tradition und Theologie neutestamentlicher Haustafelethik* (Frankfurt: Hain, 1990); however, her discussion does not explicitly refer to the extensive work of Balch on the Greco-Roman context of these texts, nor is it aware of feminist theory and exegesis.

23. See R. Banks, *Paul's Idea of Community: The Early House Churches in their Historical Setting* (Grand Rapids: Eerdmans, 1980); W.A. Meeks, *The First Urban Christians: The Social World of the Apostle Paul* (New Haven: Yale University Press, 1983); R.A. Atkins, *Egalitarian Community: Ethnography and Exegesis* (Tuscaloosa: University of Alabama Press, 1991); A. Clark Wire, *The Corinthian Women Prophets: A Reconstruction through Paul's Rhetoric* (Minneapolis: Augsburg–Fortress, 1990).

requiring submission from wives, slave women and men, and young people to the *paterfamilias*, as well as by the ecclesial adaptation of the patriarchal 'politics of submission', which was adopted also by the Pastoral Epistles, the letters of Ignatius, *1 Clement* and later 'patristic' and 'gnostic' writings. A feminist rhetorical model of historical reconstruction interrelates both sides of the tradition as an ongoing argument and debate rooted in socio-political and ecclesial struggles. Such a displacement of androcentric source-texts, and their reorganization in terms of the 'contradiction' which has generated the politics of submission and rhetorics of otherness, reconstructs socio-historical 'reality' not as 'a given fact' but as a plausible historical context evoked by the androcentric text.

However, this articulation of a conflictive model of historical reconstruction would be misapprehended if it were read either in terms of linear development or in terms of rapid and uncontested decline from *ekklesia* as the discipleship of equals to *ekklesia* as the patriarchal household of G-d.[24] Instead, this model seeks to conceptualize early Christian history as a struggle that is still going on.

A reconstructive model that reads androcentric biblical texts in terms of the early Christian struggles and arguments about 'the politics and rhetorics of patriarchal submission' also allows one to understand the cultural dependencies and effects generated by the early Christian debates and struggles. The reconstructive paradigm of a multicultural religious history can be likened to a Russian doll. Just like a Russian doll, within which smaller dolls nestle inside ever bigger ones, so the reconstructive model of *In Memory of Her* seeks to situate the religious history of women within early Christian history, within Jewish history, within Greco-Roman history, and within the history of Western society, rather than playing one of these off against the other. The tensions and contradictions between patriarchy and democracy in Greco-Roman society which have engendered 'the patriarchal politics of submission' did not originate with—but were mediated by—Christian Scriptures. This 'politics of submission' was not invented by Christian theology, but was first articulated in the context of the Greek city-state.[25]

---

24. I have adopted this traditional Jewish spelling of the name of G-d in order to indicate the brokenness and inadequacy of human language for naming the Divine.

25. See S. Moller Okin, *Women in Western Political Thought* (Princeton: Princeton University Press, 1979), pp. 15-98; E.V. Spelman, *Inessential Woman: Problems of Exclusion in Feminist Thought* (Boston: Beacon Press, 1988), pp. 19-56.

In ancient Greece the notion of democracy was not constructed in abstract and universal terms, but was seen as rooted in a concrete socio-political situation. Greek patriarchal democracy constituted itself by the exclusion of the 'others' who did not have a share in the land but whose labor sustained society. Freedom and citizenship were not only measured over and against slavery, but were also restricted in terms of gender. Moreover, the socio-economic realities in the Greek city-state were such that only a few select freeborn, propertied, élite, male heads of house-holds could actually exercise democratic government. The attempt to equalize the situation by paying male citizens, who did not have sufficient wealth on their own, for participating in government could not balance out the existing tension between equality and community.[26]

According to the theoretical vision but not the historical realization of democracy, all those living in the *polis* should be equal citizens, able to participate in government. In theory, all citizens of the *polis* are equal in rights, speech and power. As the assembly of free citizens the *ekklesia* came together in order to deliberate and to decide the best course of action for pursuing their own well-being and for securing the welfare of the *polis*. Democratic political practice was not to be disengaged and detached. On the contrary, by engaging in the rhetorical deliberation of the *ekklesia* citizens were to be the arbiters of their fate and to promote the well-being of all.

However, the socio-economic realities in the Greek city-state were such that only a very few actually exercised democratic government. Active participation in government was conditional not only upon citizenship, but also upon the combined privilege of property, education and freeborn male family status. As Page duBois has succinctly pointed out:

> The ancient democracy must be mapped as an absence. We have only aristocratic, hostile, representations of it... The *demos*, the people themselves, have no voice in history; they exist? only figured by others.[27]

It is this contradiction and tension between the ideal of democracy and the actual socio-political patriarchal structures that has produced the

---

26. See C. Farrer, *The Origins of Democratic Thinking: The Invention of Politics in Classical Athens* (Cambridge: Cambridge University Press, 1988); however, Farrer does not problematize the exclusion of women from Athenian democracy.

27. P. duBois, *Torture and Truth* (New York: Routledge & Kegan Paul, 1991), p. 123.

kyriocentric (master-centered)[28] ideology of 'natural differences' between élite men and women, between freeborn and slaves, between property owners and farmers or artisans, between Athenian-born citizens and other residents, between Greeks and Barbarians, and between the civilized and the uncivilized world.

Feminist theorists[29] have shown that Plato and Aristotle, who were critics of the democratic Athenian city-state, articulated their philosophy of patriarchal democracy in order to argue why certain groups of people, such as freeborn women or slave women and men, were not capable of participating in democratic government. These groups of people were not fit to rule or to govern, they argued, on grounds of their deficient natural powers of reasoning. Such an explicit ideological justification always becomes necessary at points in history when democratic notions are introduced into patriarchal society. Philosophical rationalizations for the exclusion of certain people from government were engendered by this contradiction between the democratic self-definition of the city-state and its actual patriarchal socio-economic structures.

The Roman imperial form of society exemplified the monarchical pyramid of patriarchal rule, although it also incorporated elements of democratic practices. The Roman form of imperial domination determined the world and experience of Jesus and his followers. It is eloquently depicted by the Jewish scholar Ellis Rivkin:

> The Roman emperor held the life or death of the Jewish people in the palm of his hand; the governor's sword was always at the ready; the high priest's eyes were always penetrating and his ears were always keen; the soldiery was always eager for the slaughter...The emperor sought to govern an empire; the governor sought to hold anarchy in check; the high priest sought to hold on to his office; the members of the high priest's Sanhedrin sought to spare the people the dangerous consequences of a

---

28. By the term *kyriocentric* I mean to indicate not that all men dominate and exploit all women without difference, but that élite, Western-educated, propertied, Euro-American men have articulated and benefited from women's and other 'non-persons'' exploitation: see my article, 'The Politics of Otherness', pp. 311-25.

29. P. duBois, *Centaurs and Amazons: Women and the Pre-History of the Great Chain of Being* (Ann Arbor: University of Michigan Press, 1982); M.E. Hawkesworth, *Beyond Oppression: Feminist Theory and Political Strategy* (New York: Continuum, 1990); H. Schrüder, 'Feministische Gesellschaftstheorie', in L.F. Pusch (ed.), *Feminismus: Inspektion der Herrenkultur* (Frankfurt: Suhrkamp, 1983), pp. 449-78.

charismatic's innocent visions of the Kingdom of God, which they themselves believed was not really at hand...For he had taught and preached that the Kingdom of God was near at hand, a kingdom which were it to come, would displace the kingdom of Rome. By creating the impression that he...would usher in the Kingdom of God...he had readied the people for riotous behaviour. The fact that the charismatic of charismatics had taught no violence, had preached no revolution, and lifted up no arms against Rome's authority would have been utterly irrelevent. The High Priest Caiphas and the Prefector Pontius Pilate cared not a whit how or by whom the Kingdom of God would be ushered in, but only that the Roman Emperor and his instruments would not reign over it.[30]

Jesus and his first followers, women and men, stood in a long line of Sophia's prophets and witnesses. They sought the renewal and well-being of Israel as the people of God, a 'kingdom of priests and a holy nation' (Exod. 19.6). They announced the *basileia*, the empire of God, as an alternative vision to the imperial utopia of Rome. The *basileia* of God was not only a tensive religious symbol alluding to a range of ancestral religious traditions which proclaimed God's power of creation and salvation. It was also a political symbol that appealed to the oppositional imagination of people victimized by the Roman imperial system. It envisioned an alternative world free of hunger, poverty and domination.

This 'envisioned' world was already present in the inclusive table-community, in the healing and liberating practices, as well as in the domination-free kinship community of the Jesus movement, which found many followers among the poor, the despised, the ill and possessed, the outcast, the prostitutes, and sinners—both women and men. In distinction to patriarchal democracy, the *basileia-ekklesia* did not secure its identity by drawing exclusive boundaries, but by welcoming all the people of God, even tax collectors and sinners.

This conflict and contradiction between socio-political structures of domination and the democratic vision of God's inclusive world of salvation engendered the need for apologetic legitimization. Colonial patriarchal domination was legitimated especially by neo-Platonic and Aristotelian political philosophy. Such patriarchal legitimizations found their way into Christian Scriptures in the form of the patriarchal injunctions to submission. Whereas 1 Cor. 11.2-16, for example, argues on Scriptural grounds for women's subordination in terms of the neo-Platonic chain of the

30. E. Rivkin, 'What Crucified Jesus', in J.H. Charlesworth (ed.), *Jesus' Jewishness: Exploring the Place of Jesus within Early Judaism* (New York: Crossroad, 1991), pp. 247-52.

hierarchy of beings, the First Epistle of Peter, for instance, utilizes the neo-Aristotelian pattern of patriarchal submission. 1 Peter admonishes Christians who are servants to be submissive even to brutal masters (2.18-25), and instructs wives to subordinate themselves to their husbands, even to those who are not Christians (3.1-6). Simultaneously, it entreats Christians also to be subject and to give honor to the emperor as well as to his governors (2.13-17). The paradigm of patriarchal submission that most closely resembles the Roman imperial pyramid in Christian terms developed institutional structures in the second and third centuries and determined the post-Constantinian Roman church. Although the Greek aristocratic/oligarchic and the Roman imperial/colonialist forms of patriarchy have been modified under changing socio-economic and political conditions, they seem to have been the two prevailing forms of patriarchy in Western history.

A similar theoretical legitimization process becomes evident again with the emergence of the modern Western democracy that has articulated itself as *fraternal* capitalist patriarchy.[31] Since patriarchal democracy is modeled after the classical ideal, it has inherited some of the same ideological contradictions insofar as it claims that its citizens 'are created equal' and are entitled to 'liberty and the pursuit of happiness', yet it still retains 'natural' patriarchal, socio-political stratifications. It is 'property' and the élite male status of birth and education, not simply biological-cultural masculinity, that entitles one to participate in the government of the few over the many.

The ideological justification of the domination of men over nature, male over female, free over slave, and Greek over Barbarian, which was articulated as 'natural superiority' in classical philosophy, is also inscribed in the discourses of modern Eurocentric political philosophy and theology. This classical patriarchal discourse has been mediated not only through Christian Scriptures but also through Christian theology. Pablo Richard, for instance, has pointed to the intrinsic correlation between colonial domination and racist, sexist, Eurocentric domination in the writings of the colonial theologian Sepulveda:

> It is just and natural that prudent, honest, and humane men should rule
> over those who are not so...[and therefore] the Spaniards rule with perfect
> right over these barbarians of the New World and the adjacent islands
> who in prudence, intellect, virtue and humanity are as much inferior to the

---

31. See J.B. Landes, *Women and the Public Sphere in the Age of the French Revolution* (Ithaca, NY: Cornell University Press, 1988).

Spaniards as childen to adults and women to men, since there exists between them as great a difference as that between wild and cruel races and races of the greatest clemency, and between the most intemperate and the continent and temperate, and I would say between apes and men.[32]

This patriarchal Eurocentric discourse is also reproduced in Western political science. It is apparent in the construction of 'the Man of Reason' by Enlightenment philosophy,[33] and of 'the White Lady' in Euro-American racist discourses,[34] as well as in the Western colonialist depiction of 'inferior races' and of 'uncivilized savages'. Like 'the White Lady', Christian religion was considered to be a civilizing force among the savages. This political, philosophical and religious rhetoric of domination and 'natural' differences serves not only to exclude the 'others' of white, élite, propertied, Eurocentric Man from democratic government, citizenship and individual rights, but also to exploit their labor and natural resources.

In sum, the Western symbolic order not only defines woman as 'the other' of the Western 'Man of Reason' but also maps the systems of oppression which stand in opposition to the democratic logic of radical equality for *everyone*. It must not be overlooked, however, that this institutionalized contradiction between the ideals of radical democracy and their patriarchal actualizations has also produced movements for emancipation seeking full, self-determining citizenship.

In the last centuries the emancipatory struggles for equal rights as citizens have gained national independence, voting and civil rights for all adult citizens. Yet these movements have not been able to overcome the patriarchal stratifications that continue to determine modern constitutional democracies. They were only able to create liberal democratic formations that simply made the democratic circle coextensive with the patriarchal pyramid, thereby reinscribing the contradiction between democratic vision and patriarchal political practice. In turn, liberal

32. Quoted from P. Richard, '1492: The Violence of God and the Future of Christianity', in L. Boff and V. Elizondo (eds.), *1492–1992: The Voices of the Victims* (*Concilium*; Philadelphia: Trinity Press, 1990), pp. 59-67 (p. 62).

33. See G. Lloyd, *The Man of Reason: 'Male' and 'Female' in Western Philosophy* (Minneapolis: University of Minnesota Press, 1984); C. Di Stefano, *Configurations of Masculinity: A Feminist Perspective on Modern Political Theory* (Ithaca, NY: Cornell University Press, 1992).

34. See K. Pui Lan, 'The Image of the "White Lady": Gender and Race in Christian Mission', in A. Carr and E. Schüssler Fiorenza (eds.), *The Special Nature of Women?* (*Concilium*; London: SCM Press, 1991), pp. 19-27.

theorists of democracy have sought to reconcile this contradiction through procedures such as periodic voting, majority rule, representation and procedural resolution of conflicts. In the process, democratic liberty is construed merely as the absence of coercion, and democratic process is reduced to the spectacle of election campaigns.

In an article on 'the Red Roots of White Feminism' Paula Gunn Allen, one of the foremost Native American literary critics in the USA, has argued that the roots for such a feminist vision cannot be found in the democratic traditions of ancient Greece, which did not know a pluralistic concept of democracy nor allowed women to participate in decision-making and government. Rather, the feminist vision of radical democracy must be derived from tribal governments in the Americas, such as the Iroquois Confederacy, in which the Council of Matrons was the ceremonial, executive and judicial center.

> The root of oppression is loss of memory. An odd thing occurs in the minds of Americans when Indian civilization is mentioned: little or nothing...How odd then must my contention seem that the gynocratic tribes of the American continent provided the basis for all the dreams of liberation that characterize the modern world...The vision that impels feminists to action was the vision of the Grandmothers' society, the society that was captured in the words of the sixteenth-century explorer Peter Martyr nearly five hundred years ago. It is the same vision repeated over and over by radical thinkers of Europe and America...That vision as Martyr told it, is of a country where there are 'no soldiers, no gendarmes or police, no nobles, kings, regents, prefects, or judges, no prisons, no lawsuits...All are equal and free...'[35]

To European eyes, Native Americans seemed gloriously free. Their willingness to share their goods, their respect for the earth and all living beings, their preference for scant clothing, their derision of authoritarian structures, their permissive childrearing practices, their frequent bathing, their living in a classless and propertyless society, all these attitudes led to the impression of 'a humanity unrestrained'. Iroquois observers who traveled to France in the colonial period in turn expressed shock at the great gap between the lifestyles of the wealthy and the poor, and marveled that the poor endured such injustice without rebellion. In addition, Paula Gunn Allen argues that Columbus's and other Europeans' contact with the indigenous populations of the Americas, and their reports about

---

35. P. Gunn Allen, 'Who Is Your Mother? Red Roots of White Feminism', in Simonson and Walker (eds.), *Multicultural Literacy*, pp. 18-19.

the free and easy egalitarianism of indigenous Americans, were in circulation by the time the Reformation took hold. Gunn Allen's view is corroborated by Gary Nash, a historian of colonial America:

> Many of the early colonists had envisioned a virtuous society organized around concepts of reciprocity, spirituality and community. [With the passage of time] the only people in North America who were upholding these values, and organizing their society around them, were the people who were being driven from the land.[36]

Although the system of modern democracy resembles in many ways the non-feudal Iroquois Confederacy, it is also quite different from it. According to Gunn Allen, two of the major differences consist in the fact that the Iroquois system is Spirit-based, and that the clan matrons performed the executive function which was directly tied to the ritual nature of the Iroquois democracy. 'Because the matrons were the ceremonial center of the system, they were also the prime policy makers.'[37] In short, only the 'Indianization' of classical notions of democracy, a merging of 'the Grandmothers' society' with Western visions of individual freedoms and equal rights, will result in a feminist vision and practice of radical egalitarianism. A feminist theological re-visioning of the Christian past for creating a future of 'the global village' must consequently locate itself in such a radical, oppositional, democratic imagination. The radical democratic imagination of the Grandmothers' society challenges liberation theologies of all colours to re-vision Christian community and faith in such a way that they can help create a Spirit-center for a radical democratic Confederacy of global dimensions.

36. G.B. Nash, *Red, White and Black* (Englewood Cliffs, NJ: Prentice–Hall, 1974), p. xiv.
37. Gunn Allen, 'Who Is Your Mother?', p. 219.

TOWARD INCLUSIVE MINISTRY:
THE LOGICAL IMPOSSIBILITY OF RELIGIOUS AND THEOLOGICAL INCLUSIVISM, PLURALISM AND RELATIVISM

Alan J. Torrance

It has become a truism to say that in the modern world of fast travel, telecommunications and the internet, we are increasingly obliged to regard ourselves as world citizens, or even global villagers. At the same time, one cannot but be aware of the religious and cultural diversity of our 'global village', of the ethnic and religious polarization to which this can sometimes lead and, consequently, the tragic outcome (for example, in the form of 'cleansings') which can result from reactionary isolationism and religious alienation. In Aotearoa–New Zealand the question of inclusiveness is raised from a variety of different quarters reflecting (1) the differing status and histories of the indigenous and migrant populations of the land, (2) the diversity of 'spiritualities' identified with these and, finally, (3) recent critiques of the sexism inherent in these cultures and their various religions. Thus the socio-political challenges of conflicting religious loyalties, not to mention the intellectual challenges of the diversity of religious claims, present the ministry of the church and its leadership with a burning question—one which relates to the very integrity of its mission, its message and its 'catholicity'. How far can the Christian church be 'inclusive' with respect to the plurality of religious affiliations and diverse cultural self-understandings constitutive of the modern world? And what form might such 'inclusive' engagement take? In short, the Christian church is presented with a challenge from various sides to practise and to exhibit 'inclusive' forms of ministry vis-à-vis the diverse groupings and divergent affiliations represented within contemporary society. It is the concern of this paper to explore how far and in what ways Christian theology is, and may be, 'inclusive' with respect to such diverse affirmations and allegiances. I shall begin by addressing the issue of differing religious affiliations and the conflicting truth claims involved in these. The hope is that by this means the fundamental question at issue will be expressed in its most extreme form to facilitate our focusing on precisely what an inclusive approach to ministry *may* and *may not* mean and involve.

1. A Threefold Typology

During this last decade, the case for inclusivism has been associated with a threefold typology that has become particularly influential in characterizing the different attitudes which may be adopted with respect to religious diversity. This typology was first expounded by Alan Race in 1983,[1] receiving further endorsement and extensive popularization by Gavin D'Costa in a book published three years later.[2] The typology distinguishes three different kinds of approach, namely, exclusivism, inclusivism and pluralism. As D'Costa emphasizes, these distinctions are not reserved for Christian approaches to other religious views but apply to those of all religions—they may apply as much to Hindu views of Christianity as to Christian views of Hinduism. What is particularly pertinent to the concerns of this paper is the extent to which this kind of typology is widely believed to apply not only to inter-religious debates but to *intra*-religious theological debate. It is often assumed that approaches *within* the Christian faith to those of other Christian theological viewpoints can be categorized in similar terms, that is, as being either exclusivist, inclusivist or pluralist.

Recently, however, Gavin D'Costa announced that he had changed his mind and now regarded the very notion of religious pluralism as incoherent. The consequence of this he makes quite clear: 'the logical impossibility of a pluralist view of religions means that the typology of exclusivism, inclusivism and pluralism is untenable'.[3] The underlying reason for this change of attitude is the perception that 'pluralism must

---

1. *Christians and Religious Pluralism: Patterns in the Christian Theology of Religions* (Maryknoll, NY: Orbis Books, 1983).

2. *Theology and Religious Pluralism: The Challenge of Other Religions* (Oxford: Basil Blackwell, 1986).

3. 'The Impossibility of a Pluralist View of Religions', unpublished paper presented to the Conference on Religious Pluralism, sponsored by the Centre for Philosophical Studies, King's College London, London, 25 February 1995.

always logically be a form of exclusivism and that nothing called pluralism really exists'.[4] The obvious conclusion is that all so-called pluralists
are, as a matter of fact, 'anonymous exclusivists'.[5]

The essential thrust of D'Costa's paper is quite simply a 'logical point'
made at the level of second-order discourse—it relates to the *possibility*
of describing certain positions in certain terms. What it accomplishes,
however, is the disposal of a myth—and not an innocent or insignificant
one, but a myth which deceives us about the facts and blocks our understanding of them to the serious detriment of open, intra-theological and
inter-religious dialogue. Before going any further, however, I must offer
a brief summary of the typology to which I have referred and which is
now so widely accepted:[6]

1. *Exclusivism* holds that only one single revelation or religion is
   true and that all other 'revelations' and 'religions' are false. This
   position resembles that to which Jürgen Moltmann has referred
   as 'absolutism'—the claim that a particular position has an
   absolute and exclusive monopoly on the truth.[7]

2. At the other end of the spectrum, *pluralism* suggests that all
   religions contain elements of truth and true revelations but that
   no religion can claim final and definitive truth. This leads to the
   conclusion that the main religious traditions share more or less
   equal degrees of validity. The appeal of this position is that it
   appears to accord respect to diverse religious views and to
   recognize that other religions include among their adherents
   good, holy and compassionate people.

3. *Inclusivism* seeks to embody both these positions simultaneously. Its advocates believe that there is one revelation or
   religion which is true but that truth is found in various
   fragmentary and incomplete forms within the claims of other
   religions. Religious claims are, however, on this position only
   deemed true to the extent that they conform to the one
   normative revelation or religion which is deemed to be true.

---

4. 'The Impossibility of a Pluralist View of Religions', p. 3.
5. 'The Impossibility of a Pluralist View of Religions', p. 15.
6. I am following here D'Costa's summary of the three positions in the paper
just cited.
7. With respect to the Christian church, Moltmann comments, 'The church's
exclusive absolutism has made Christianity invulnerable, inalterable and aggressive'
(*The Church in the Power of the Spirit* [London: SCM Press, 1977], p. 153).

Friedrich Schleiermacher's description of the essence of Christian piety[8] or, more recently, Wolfhart Pannenberg's Nature-Supernature model may be seen as different examples of this approach.[9] The shared view is that Christian theology, as they differently define it, includes and transcends the essential claims of all other religions. It constitutes, therefore, the supreme form of religion in general.

The entire typology collapses, however, as D'Costa shows, because 'all pluralists are committed to holding some form of truth criteria and by virtue of this, anything that falls foul of such criteria are excluded from counting as truth (in doctrine and practice)'.[10] If this is the case with pluralism, then it is *a fortiori* the case with 'inclusivism'. The conclusion is quite simple: *all* approaches to the truth claims and status of religions and theologies are *exclusive* of contrary positions and are in essence, therefore, 'exclusive' positions. That is, they make truth claims —and no assumed reverence for the views of others can pretend otherwise!

2. An Alternative Twofold Typology?

At this point, one might ask whether an alternative typology of religions or theological approaches might not be required to accommodate another alternative to 'exclusivism', namely, 'anti-realist' relativism. Such a position is explicitly endorsed by Don Cupitt, for example, but is quite often tacitly assumed by people who might not formulate their relativist leanings in such an explicit way.[11] A reason that could be offered for distinguishing this from the incoherent alternatives to 'exclusivism'

8. H.R. Mackintosh and J.S. Stewart (eds.), *The Christian Faith* (Edinburgh: T. & T. Clark, 1928), see esp. ch. 1, §8, which opens: 'Those forms of piety in which all religious affections express the dependence of everything finite upon one Supreme and Infinite Being, i.e. the monotheistic forms, occupy the highest level; and all others are related to them as subordinate forms, from which men are destined to pass to those higher ones' (p. 34).

9. See W. Pannenberg, 'Towards a Theology of the History of Religions', in *Basic Questions in Theology* (London: SCM Press, 1971), II, pp. 65ff. (cited in *The Church in the Power of the Spirit*, pp. 157-58, where Moltmann criticizes the absolutism which underlies this kind of 'inclusivism').

10. 'The Impossibility of a Pluralist View of Religions', p. 5.

11. See D. Cupitt, *After All: Religion Without Alienation* (London: SCM Press, 1994), and *The Last Philosophy* (London: SCM Press, 1995).

discussed above is that the anti-realist does not pretend to be making truth-claims at all, and hence offers a genuine alternative to realist claims which must, by the nature of the case and as we have seen, be exclusive. On the anti-realist view, what we term 'truth' denotes quite simply 'the state of play' and nothing more. If everyone believes that hanging criminals or regarding women as inferior is morally virtuous, then it is *true* that such activities are virtuous. Moreover, if a particular ethnic group is hounded to extinction leaving all those who remain believing that they were morally virtuous in bringing this about, then it is *true* that they *were* morally virtuous in accomplishing this state of affairs. On this view, the business of theology is not assessing or formulating truth-claims about the way things are. Rather, it is nothing more than a form of creative therapy, making any additional concern with questions of truth-claims confused and misleading. The underlying reason given for this position is the claim that 'reality' is simply the construct of our 'language-games' and inseparable from them. Consequently, it is confused to view our 'language-games' as answerable in any sense to reality for the simple reason that no such independent 'reality' exists. The essential supposition underlying exclusivism (namely, that reality cannot simultaneously be x and not-x and, therefore, that logically incompatible truth-claims cannot simultaneously be affirmed) is thus regarded as vacuous.

On these grounds it might be argued that the new typology which emerges is twofold, distinguishing, quite simply, between the two real alternatives, exclusivism and anti-realism. But this argument is also flawed. Precisely to argue for or even to suggest an anti-realist position is to make a truth-claim. Moreover, to state that theology is simply a form of therapy and that the whole matter of truth-claims is unimportant is also to make a truth-claim. To this, the response might be offered that truth-claims may be important in other fields but not in theology. However, any such statement would be committed to making truth-claims (perhaps only negative ones) about the nature and 'object' of the theological enterprise. No such escape, therefore, is possible. Anti-realist approaches to theology cannot be made self-referentially coherent. The anti-realist is hoist on her or his own petard and left practising a therapy which cannot be defined as such let alone advocated. Any force attaching to the anti-realist's rejection of other positions is necessarily and completely dissolved by precisely those claims that lead to the rejection of the alternative position. Since a typology cannot accommodate a position which cannot be stated, our original typology is left therefore with only one member, namely, 'exclusivism'.

3. *The Confused Appeal of the Alternatives to Exclusivism*

The logical clarity of D'Costa's rejection of the threefold typology leaves one wondering how things could ever have been perceived differently. It amounts, indeed, to an emphatic statement of the obvious! Consequently, it is worth considering the mind-set of the person who wishes to conceive of himself or herself as an 'inclusivist'. In our liberal democracy the word 'inclusive' has come to be more than a merely descriptive term: it is an evaluative one. 'Inclusive' denotes a virtue. By contrast, the word 'exclusive' carries strongly pejorative connotations. Whereas 'exclusive' may mean quite simply the neutral, logical characteristic 'exclusive of claims to the contrary', when used of religious claims in a multi-religious society it is normally taken to mean 'exclusive of persons' thereby denoting an evil akin to racism. To be a *religious* exclusivist, therefore, is to be socially, politically and culturally reprehensible if not potentially subversive. Christian exclusivists establish a dangerous precedent and set a bad example to those of other religions who also tend toward 'exclusivism' in their approaches. It is, thus, to inspire religious frag-mentation and isolationism with all the risks to society which this entails. That is, the exclusivist, by virtue of the nature of the universal truth-claims she or he makes, must necessarily be committed to some kind of intellectual cleansing. The underlying supposition, of course, is that an exclusivist must be opposed to dialogue or, at best, can only approach it with a closed mind.

An underlying reason for this judgment may be the assumption that to be inclusive of persons *is* to be inclusive of their beliefs. There may, moreover, appear to be some warrant for this. Given that our personal identities are at least to some degree constituted by our language-games, our value systems, our horizons of meaning and our cultural contexts, it is easy to assume that to adopt a system which is exclusive of the religious affirmations and beliefs of others is ultimately to be exclusive in one's attitudes toward them *as persons*. Consequently, there is an ethically motivated drive, not least in academic theological contexts, toward inclusivism—an inclusivism which, however, refuses to recognize that the claims one makes, no matter how generous the spirit in which they are made, *are necessarily exclusive of contrary claims* and of the positions identified with these. Thus, unless they are so general, insipid and amorphous as to be saying nothing at all, one's inclusive claims will almost inevitably be exclusive of the (religious) beliefs of others.

4. *How Exclusive is Exclusivism?*

In the light of the above discussion, it should be clear that it is necessary to reject as incoherent an *a priori* inclusivism. The advocate of such an approach desires a foundational, Archimedean point with recourse to which positions making exclusive claims may be subsumed within a more foundational 'inclusivist' framework. As we have seen, however, to the extent that all positions are internal to a system of beliefs and truth criteria, any such position becomes internally inconsistent. This is because it must *itself* be an 'exclusive' position of the kind which it seeks to reject. What should be immediately clear, therefore, is that there is no sense in which 'inclusivism' can offer any social or political advantages. This is simply because no such position exists!

This helps to clear the way for the important debates at issue. These concern the nature of the claims internal to mutually exclusive belief systems. To this end distinctions may be drawn from within the valid 'exclusivist' perspective, namely, between approaches which are internally[12] *inclusive* with respect to people of other positions (and thus dialogically open to engage with alternative truth-claims) and those which are internally[13] *exclusive* of other people and thus also of their truth-claims.

In other words, what may now be seen to be important is the *internal* content of diverse[14] positions, and to what extent and in what ways their internal content is *inclusive* and/or *exclusive*. To this end, we are obliged to distinguish further between the acceptance and affirmation of *persons* and the endorsement of their *belief-systems* (and this despite the apparent integration of personal identities and religious or cultural apperceptions). The validity of this distinction (between the acceptance of persons and the acceptance of their beliefs) will be established if we can show that in order to be *inclusive* of persons it *may* be necessary to be *exclusive* of

12. That is, *inclusive* with respect to the internal content of their religious truth-claims.

13. That is, *exclusive* with respect to the internal content of their religious truth-claims.

14. Diverse positions are 'mutually exclusive' positions.

statements they themselves would make or even, indeed, a position with which they *subliminally* identify themselves. An example of precisely such an argument is to be found in the central thesis of Paulo Freire's *Pedagogy of the Oppressed.*[15]

The very nature of oppression, he suggests, is that it conditions its subjects into an oppressed self-understanding. Women and the poor of the two-thirds world, for example, are conditioned into self-denigratory modes of self-evaluation which compound their oppression. An 'inclusive' liberation of such people involves an exclusive attitude toward the views which they hold and which are indeed constitutive of their identities to some degree. Consequently, an inclusive attitude towards such people involves a dialogical (indeed, for Freire, pedagogical) engagement with them from the perspective of a position that is *not* theirs and which is incompatible with the belief systems to which they hold.

What this example suggests is that an inclusive attitude *may* be exclusive of belief systems in order to be 'inclusive' (i.e. non-marginalizing) in its approach to persons. This, indeed, will characterize every approach that may be described as 'dialogical', and is required by the positions most widely identified with 'political correctness'! A socially inclusive and constructive dynamic may depend therefore on belief systems which are fundamentally exclusivist. And, as I have suggested, all dialogical approaches will be of such a kind.

Now it may be objected here that the Paulo Freire example suggests an approach which, far from being dialogical, is, rather, monological to the extent that it is pedagogical. I would suggest, however, that a pedagogical concern and a concern for the kind of dialogue that respects differences are not necessarily mutually incompatible. Teaching, to the extent that it involves listening, will be dialogical if it is to be more than the impersonal dissemination of propositional 'truths'. Such a distinction, however, will clearly not be applicable where the religious believer assumes an *absolute* identification between the Truth and her or his formulations of the truth.

This brings us to our central concern. If inclusive attitudes involve exclusive affirmations, what kind of exclusive religious affirmations are likely to lead to exclusive attitudes towards persons and thereby become socially divisive? Clearly, the kinds of religious affiliation which are *least* likely to be socially constructive will be soteriologically exclusivist and/or

15. Trans. M.B. Ramos; New York: Herder & Herder, 1970.

fundamentalist approaches which risk denigrating the value of persons outside of a defined group. It is precisely these kinds of approach which give rise to that form of exclusivism which is potentially socio-politically disruptive. This is true to the extent that they are not only epistemologically exclusive logically (one can have no objection to that) but also personally exclusivist and non-dialogical by virtue of (1) making an intrinsic identification between the identities of persons and the truth-claims which they make; (2) making an absolute identification of the Truth with their own particular formulations of the truth,[16] and (3) deriving divine warrant for the conditional acceptance (and/or valuation) of other persons.

It is 'internally exclusive' positions of this kind which give genuine cause for concern in that they lead to 'civil religion' of a kind which may generate social conflict and division. Both Islamic fundamentalism and certain forms of Christian fundamentalism, be they of culture or Scripture,[17] have led to oppressive consequences when they have exhibited these features. In sum, 'Death to the blasphemer' has been advocated by Moslem and Christian alike and the features of the relevant faith systems were identical in the respects I have mentioned. It is these kinds of phenomena which create the mind-set that is concerned to advocate inclusive models for religious debates—a mind-set which has found itself opting for less than convincing suppositions, as we have seen.

5. Some Theological Reflections

I shall now consider an alternative approach which, it may be argued, emerges from within the perspective of Christian theology and in which certain central facets of the Christian faith are examined with recourse to the schema defined above. Clearly, the Christian faith is exclusive—it shares this with every other system that makes truth-claims. It also affirms, however, that there is—in Kierkegaard's phrase—a particular

---

16. This dangerous supposition must be distinguished from the innocent and necessary recognition that all truth-claims are exclusive of alternative claims. One may well recognize that truth-claims to which one holds are exclusive without confidently affirming that the claims to which one holds are indubitably true!

17. Such cases have been witnessed in extreme form in the Crusades, as also in the case of the German Christian Movement of the 1930s and, more recently, in certain forms of Calvinist support for the apartheid regime in South Africa.

historical occasion or moment which is of *decisive* significance for its truth-claims.[18] Moreover, the historical occasion associated with the person of Christ is not only of decisive significance materially but also formally. That is, it is not simply of decisive significance with recourse to (Christian) 'data' which we process with recourse to prior paradigms, but it is of decisive significance for the very nature of the paradigms with which we operate.[19] Consequently the Christian faith is exclusive to the

18. S. Kierkegaard, *Philosophical Fragments* (ed. H. and E. Hong; Princeton: Princeton University Press, 1985), pp. 13ff. For an outstanding exposition of Kierkegaard's theology, and a critical assessment of the arguments of the *Philosophical Fragments*, see M. Rae, 'By Faith Transformed: Kierkegaard's Vision of the Incarnation' (PhD dissertation; King's College London, 1995).

19. It is of decisive significance and not of relative significance because if it were of relative significance it would be ratifiable from a ground outside of itself and with recourse to prior, independent criteria. If this were the case the historical events could do no more than simply exemplify, illuminate and ratify views or suppositions held in advance. The historical would simply instantiate religious ideas which were generally and universally immanent within the human subject. The reconciling 'once and for all' presence of the Word of God to humanity, and the historical events associated with this, could ultimately therefore have neither material nor formal significance. This is necessarily the case given that the nature and content of the claims themselves are such as to include irreducibly formal implications. (It is suggested, for example, that our cognitive paradigms are in need of reconciliation, that we require to be 'reconciled in our minds', 'given the eyes to see and ears to hear', and so on.) Indeed, if the historical occasion were only of relative significance, then once the merely incidental and illuminatory function of the Word was completed, the Word would ideally fade into the background so as not to distract from the truths to which he had referred us and with respect to which he is not of decisive significance in himself. Christ would thereby become an incidental or arbitrary facilitator or 'Socratic midwife' helping to bring forth from us the perception of truths and insights which are universally immanent within us as human beings. As Kierkegaard demonstrates through Climacus in the *Philosophical Fragments*, such an approach is essentially incompatible with the whole thrust of the New Testament, since an absolute distinction must be drawn between truth-claims made from a Socratic or idealist base which suppose the truth is already within us, and truth claims which recognize an intrinsic and decisive connection between religious truth and the person of Christ, and between its historical focus and the epistemically transformative presence of the Holy Spirit. In sum, if the Occasion or the Teacher is not of decisive significance then the incarnation becomes no more than an instantiation of a religious idea. When this happens the epistemic activity of the Spirit is simply identified with the process of the 'recollection' of or expression of the agendas and suppositions immanent within us—and we can claim divine ratification for whatever our innate propensities might suggest to us. There takes place nothing less than a *metabasis eis allo genos* of

extent that it is exclusive of any foundationalist basis at all—its central and essential affirmation is that the foundations and grounds of its endorsement are integral to it. It may not and cannot be affirmed on the basis of external criteria which are independent of our being brought by the Spirit into relation with the historical person who is its focus. There is thus an essential and intrinsic relationship between the revelation which is the focus of the Christian faith, and the conditions of its recognition: between the person of Christ and the Holy Spirit. The Christian faith is, therefore, perhaps *uniquely* incompatible with all forms of pluralism which operate from a (monological) foundationalist basis.

However, the Christian faith is *inclusive* of persons. Intrinsic to it is the perception of the absolute value of other persons whatever they may believe or do. The Christian gospel affirms that God is love and that God loves all people equally and unconditionally. For precisely this reason it suggests that we also must love all people unconditionally. Indeed, we are to love and to pray for our enemies. This is *not* a supererogatory recommendation; it is of the very essence of the Christian life. It is, moreover, counter-intuitive to think that we ought to do this and counter-inclinational to do so!

This must not, however, be interpreted as some form of *a priori* inclusivism with respect to affirmations made by others. This element of non-inclusivism is integral *precisely* to its recognition, and 'exclusive' affirmation of the unconditional value of persons. The Christian faith cannot affirm fascism or sexism or racism or either cultural or religious oppression precisely *because* it affirms the unconditional value of all people. And this affirmation is grounded in the perception that in Christ there is neither Jew nor Gentile, male nor female, black nor white. Its ethical impetus is thus integrally bound up with its Christocentric focus and certainly not with any universal, foundational 'religious' common denominator.

Finally, to the extent that it recognizes and affirms that the Truth is a person and not a series of infallible propositions, it does not allow us to make absolute identifications between the Truth and human formulations of the truth.[20] There is thus an *essential a posteriori* openness to

the Christian faith, that is, a translation of it into something of an entirely different kind—what amounts ultimately, indeed, to its inversion!

20. *Ecclesia semper reformanda!* The declarations of the church (as the church itself) must continually be reformed in the light of Christ, so that they might become truer to him in the contexts in which they are made.

dialogue and, indeed, its capacity to correct our perception of the Truth.

What must be recognized is that dialogical inclusivism grounded in a non-pluralist, exclusive series of claims may be more inclusive of persons and more open to ideas than the (supposed) inclusivisms which D'Costa has shown in any case to be incoherent. In other words, pluralism is not only short on logical correctness; it must ultimately sell short the 'political' correctness which drives it!

6. *Conclusion*

In sum, the focus and indeed impetus for Christian God-talk is a historical reality that is of decisive significance. From this emerges a series of indicatives giving rise in turn to a radically inclusive series of imperatives to love and to value others unconditionally. These imperatives include dialogical imperatives. To love one's enemy or to pray for those who despitefully use one but to refuse either to listen to them or to attempt to understand them is inconceivable. As Jürgen Moltmann has long argued, discipleship of the Suffering Servant is intrinsically dialogical.[21]

Secondly, the very nature of the one to whom Kierkegaard refers as the 'Occasion', and who constitutes in his person the warrant for these indicatives, is such that we cannot identify the Truth with our formulations of it. Inter-religious dialogue—indeed, all dialogue with other persons with differing horizons—serves as a means of our having opened up for our own purview failings and inconsistencies in our own conceptualities which can only serve to obscure our perception of the Truth who stands as the focus of our faith.

What I am suggesting, then, is that the impetus for constructive dialogue with other religions, as this is grounded in the inclusive affirmation of those of other faiths, is not merely 'tradition-specific', but 'occasion-specific' in the Kierkegaardian sense—that is, grounded in a particular historical event of decisive significance for our knowledge of the Truth. Without such a historical grounding of the indicatives of the Christian faith there could be no imperatives other than those resting either on utilitarian grounds of common interest[22] or, worse, on the all

---

21. See, for example, his discussion of this in *The Church in the Power of the Spirit*, pp. 159-63.

22. Such a position cannot ultimately, of course, resolve the question as to how we might agree on how to determine any such relative common interest!

too arbitrary and thus dangerous grounds of human 'religiosity', where easy divine ratification is called upon for whatever ethical agenda an individual might choose to adopt.

For the sake of ministry in a multi-religious and multi-cultural world, and in order that we might discover the uniquely inclusive nature of our Christian resources, it is imperative that we are not misled by a logically incoherent, foundational attitude to the status of religions and thus of Christianity. Consequently, I have ended by offering an *a posteriori* argument for the incoherence of a 'foundationally pluralist' interpretation of the Christian religion. I have argued that the Christian faith should be interpreted from within an 'exclusivist' viewpoint (as are all religions and theories of religion) but that it is also internally *inclusive* vis-à-vis persons precisely because it is also internally *exclusive* of claims incompatible with the affirmation of the One who is of decisive significance. I also argued, however, that, although it is exclusive of incompatible claims, Christian faith is also intrinsically dialogical, given that the Truth at its centre denotes not a series of propositions but God as the One who addresses us concretely and specifically in the Person of the Word. The theologian cannot and must not thereby make any absolute identification between her or his formulations of the truth and the Truth itself. This is not because of some prior commitment to a liberal ideology (which can no more ultimately be 'liberal' than it can be 'inclusive'!) but because being true to *this* Truth involves the calling— and indeed inspiration—to engage openly and dialogically with others. It is precisely, therefore, an 'exclusive' and non-foundationalist interpretation of the Christian faith which provides the impetus for an 'inclusive' and dialogical engagement with those of other religions.

The ministry and leadership of the church is thus called to be dialogical in its engagement with those of other religions, views and affiliations, and never to represent the gospel in a manner that is incompatible with this calling. The refusal to recognize the otherness of a dialogue partner, to hear the distinctiveness of her or his claims, is also the refusal to speak to the other out of the discipleship of the crucified Word (without whom we have nothing to say); such refusals can only ultimately reflect as much a failure to love the other as they reflect the refusal to love and confess the One who gave his life for the other.

THE MINISTRY OF WOMEN[*]

Thomas F. Torrance

1. *Ancient Perspectives on Women in Ministry*

In one of the earliest of the catacomb paintings in Rome in the *Capella Greca*, within a century after the death and resurrection of Christ, there is a remarkable mural depicting the breaking of bread at the celebration of the Eucharist. Seven presbyters are seated in a semi-circle behind the Holy Table, assisted by several deacons. This is known as 'the Catacomb of Priscilla', for Priscilla is seated to the right of the presiding presbyter (presumably her husband, Aquila), the *proestos* or bishop, and is actively engaged with him in the Eucharistic rite. There are two points about this painting on which I would like to comment.

1. The first has to do with the number seven. In the great Temple Synagogue in Jerusalem there was a Sanhedrin of 71 elders (*zekenim*), or presbyters, together with its president or *Sagan*. What of the smaller synagogues in the communities outside Jerusalem, or in the diaspora? According to the Mishnah tractate *Sanhedrin*, it was laid down that a large Jewish community might have 23 elders, presumably plus its president, making 24 in all, but if a community were 120-strong it was allowed to have its 'seven' elders, who would normally be presided over by an *Archisynagogos*, such as Jairos or Crispos of whom we read in the New Testament. *Sanhedrin* tells us that these presbyters were to be arranged 'like the half of a round threshing floor so that they all might see one another'. It was thus in accordance with the regulations of Jewish law that at Alexandria, where there were well over a million Jews in the first century, the local Sanhedrin numbered 23 or 24, while at Rome the

[*] This article is reprinted here with the generous permission of Handsel Press (it is available separately from Send the Light Distributors, UK, under the same title).

Jewish community, which was differently distributed, was served by a number of smaller synagogues each with its Sanhedrin of seven elders. Regarded in this light, the fact that the disciples, who with Peter formed the original Christian community in Jerusalem, numbered about 120 (Acts 1.15) is significant, for it helps us to understand why shortly afterwards the twelve apostles appointed specifically 'seven' disciples (presumably as 'presbyters', not 'deacons' as is usually held) to serve the needs of the primitive church in Jerusalem, while they gave themselves over 'to prayer and the ministry of the Word' in fulfilment of their universal apostolic ministry. We also learn, however, that in due course, with the growth of its membership, the Jerusalem church came to have a Christian Sanhedrin of 70 presbyters, which is again in accordance with Jewish regulations, probably presided over by James (not the apostle, but the brother of our Lord).[1]

It is not surprising, then, that in Alexandria the church had 24 presbyters, 12 for the city and 12 for rural districts around the city, presided over by one of their number whom they elected and consecrated as bishop. Nor is it surprising that in Rome, on the other hand, as we learn from Optatus,[2] there were at least 40 small churches, which evidently had their due number of presbyters after the pattern of the Jewish communities in Rome, but with bishops rather than rulers of the synagogue as their presidents. This helps, incidentally, to explain why 'monepiscopacy' was comparatively late in developing in Rome, and why Clement acted as the chosen spokesperson for all the churches in Rome to those beyond. It is in the *Capella Greca* that we are given a glimpse into the assembly of one of these small congregations of believers meeting in the catacombs with their seven presbyters, Aquila and Priscilla and five others, arranged in a semi-circle 'like the half of a round threshing-floor'. Moreover, the Jewish as well as the Christian character of this Eucharistic celebration, together with its very early date, is accentuated by a rough Hebrew inscription in the foreground.

2.   The second point about this wall-painting to which I wish to draw attention is that a woman is presented as concelebrating with men at the breaking of bread. Priscilla (or Prisca) is a *presbytera* officiating along with *presbyteroi* in the central act of the worship of the church. At first sight this is rather startling in view of the statement of St Paul:

1.   This also correlates with the 70 disciples sent out by Jesus on the mission of the kingdom mentioned by Luke (see 10.1, 17).

2.   Libri VI, CSEL, XXI, pp. 187-204.

> As in all the churches of the saints the women should keep silence in the churches. For they are not permitted to speak, but should be subordinate, as even the law says. If there is anything they desire to know, let them ask their husbands at home. For it is shameful for a woman to speak in church (1 Cor. 14.33-35).

If our Jewish friends are right, what St Paul has in view here relates to the customary arrangement of synagogues in which women who usually occupied seats apart from, or overlooking, the main area were forbidden to chatter or otherwise to interrupt the conduct of worship. That may well be how we are to regard St Paul's injunctions here. Otherwise the passage is rather difficult to understand in view of the fact that in an earlier chapter in the same epistle it is assumed that women do pray and prophesy aloud in church, although it is made clear that when they do so they must have their heads covered, if only out of respect for their husbands' authority over them (1 Cor. 11.3-4). Thus it would appear that the apostle has no objection to women praying or prophesying in church provided that they wear a fitting cover over their heads. In the same epistle (1 Cor. 16.19) he refers to the church in the house of Aquila and Prisca, in which it is hardly likely that Prisca kept silent!

Another passage from 1 Timothy must also be considered: 'Let a woman learn in silence with all submissiveness. I permit no woman to teach or to have authority over men; she is to keep silent' (1 Tim. 2.11-12). Here women are explicitly enjoined *to be silent* and also, not to teach (*didaskein*) in public, and perhaps also not even to teach their husbands in private! This hardly accords with the interpretation given by some Jews to the passage just cited from 1 Corinthians, but whatever it means it must surely be understood in accordance with the activity of Prisca in Ephesus, as recorded by St Luke, when, along with Aquila, she expounded the way of God more accurately to Apollos (Acts 18.26). It is hardly surprising, then, that St Paul applies to her along with Aquila the term 'fellow-worker' (*synergos*), which he used to refer to people associated with him in the ministry of the gospel, such as Timothy (see Rom. 16.3, 21; see also 1 Tim. 3.2; 1 Cor. 3.9), or Clement (Phil. 4.3), or Mark and Luke (Phlm. 24).

One must also recall how St Paul mentioned in a similar way women like Nympha who, like Priscilla, had a church in her house (Col. 4.15), or Junia, his female relative, whom he refers to as a noted apostle (Rom. 16.7). Reference should be made as well to the four virgin daughters of Philip the Evangelist who were spoken of as endowed with the gift of prophecy, that is, with the gift of proclaiming the gospel, and not only of foretelling events. In his own list of those endowed by the ascended Lord with gifts for the ministry, St Paul put apostles first, prophets second, evangelists third, followed by pastors and teachers (Eph. 4.11). That order gives us some indication of the way in which the great apostle to the Gentiles regarded the ministry of women like his kins-woman Junia, and the daughters of Philip. St Paul also speaks of women as holding the office of deaconess (1 Tim. 3.11), with the explicit mention of Phoebe in the church at Cenchrea (Rom. 16.1)—with which should be associated the order of 'widows', who were evidently not ordained, but held a place of honour in the apostolic church in fulfilling a ministry of prayer and intercession (1 Tim. 5.3-16).

All this must be taken fully into account in reaching any balanced understanding of what St Paul meant in the two passages commonly adduced by those who oppose the ordination of women in the ministry of the gospel. When we consider all that is recorded in the New Testament in this regard, it is rather difficult, to say the least, to accept the idea that there is no biblical evidence for the ministry of women in the early church. It also helps us to understand why the early Christians, who were hounded to death in the catacombs of Rome for their fidelity to the gospel and the normative tradition of the apostles, should have left the church with such a definite depiction of the place of a woman pres-byter at the celebration of the Lord's Supper.

The office of deaconess was developed in the early centuries of the Catholic Church, appointed through the laying on of hands by the bishop (*Apostolic Constitutions* 3.15), but there is no canonical record of any office of woman presbyters. There were evidently no women serving with men in councils of 'elders of the people' (*seniores plebis*) in the North African Church who, although not reckoned among the clergy (*cleri*), assisted bishops, presbyters and deacons in the public life of the local community. Mention is sometimes made of elderly women who exercised a prominent role in the worship of a congregation, known as *presbytides*, but, as Epiphanius insisted, they were not to be regarded as female presbyters or priestesses (*Haereses* 79.4). Attempts were obvi-ously made by authorities in the early church to play down the New Testament evidence for women in the ministry, apparent in alterations introduced into the Greek text of St Paul's references to Junia and Nympha, which were changed to Junias and Nymphas, thereby making them out to be men! However, in spite of the rather Manichaean depreciation of the female sex widely found in the Mediterranean church, there were strange exceptions to the canonical restriction of clerical office to women. For instance, in a mosaic still extant in the Church of Sancta Praseda in Rome, built by Pascal I toward the end of the ninth century in honour of four holy women, one of whom was his mother Theodora, we can still read around her head in bold letters THEODORA EPISKOPA! And so we have papal authority for a woman bishop, and an acknowledgment by the Pope that he himself was the son of woman bishop!

It is of course the case throughout the general history of the church in East and West, and until recently in Protestant churches as well, that tradition regularly restricted the priesthood or ordained ministry to men, but this was done on grounds of ecclesiastical convention and canonical authority. Appeal has also been made to dominical authority for, as we learn in the Gospels, our Lord appointed only men to be his disciples and apostles, which was in line with traditional Jewish convention. On the other hand, as St Paul himself wrote to the Galatians, a radical change had come about with Christ, for in him 'there is neither Jew nor Greek, there is neither slave nor free, there is no male and female, for you all are one in Christ Jesus' (Gal. 3.28). This means that there is no *theological* ground for the exclusion of women from the holy ministry, for the old division between men and women in the fallen world has been overcome in Christ and in his body, the church.

2. *A Theological Perspective on the Gender of Christ*

In modern times the argument has been put forward that it is only a man who can represent Christ in the celebration of the Eucharist, for it is only a man who can be an icon of Christ at the altar. To back up this claim, reference is often made to the Pauline statement that 'man ought not to cover his head, since he is the image and glory of God, but woman is the glory of man, for man was not made from woman but woman from man' (1 Cor. 11.7-8). Appeal is also made to St Augustine's interpretation of these words, offered by way of a comment upon what is written in Genesis: 'God created man in his own image, in the image of God created he them; male and female created he them' (Gen. 1.27). This means, St Augustine once claimed, that while man and woman together are in the image of God, woman on her own, considered apart from her character as a helpmeet for man, is not in the image of God. In effect, man may be in the image of God apart from woman, but not woman apart from man (*De Trin.* 12.7.10). If that were the case, the mother of Jesus considered in herself as a virgin could not have been said to be in the image of God! This is a quite offensive notion of womankind that conflicts directly with the truth that in Christ Jesus there is neither male nor female, and even conflicts with Augustine's own statement in the same passage that 'human nature is complete only in both sexes', and it conflicts directly with our Lord's teaching that in the beginning God made humanity male and female in such a way that what he has joined together may not be put asunder (Mt. 19.4-5; Mk 10.6-7). Thus it also conflicts with the orthodox understanding of the incarnation as the saving assumption of the whole of humanity, male and female, and as the healing of our complete human nature. This must surely be understood as involving the healing of any divisive relation between male and female due to the curse imposed upon them at the fall (Gen. 3.16) while sanctifying the distinction between them, and thus also as rejecting any Manichaean denigration of the female sex. Moreover, the fact that the Son of God became man through being conceived by the Holy Spirit and being born of the Virgin Mary, that is, not of the will of the flesh nor of the will of a human father but of God, means that at this decisive point in the incarnation the distinctive place and function of man as male human being was set aside.

Thus, as Karl Barth pointed out, in the virgin birth of Jesus by grace alone, without any previous sexual union between man and woman, there is contained a judgment upon man (*Church Dogmatics* 1.2, pp. 188ff.). This certainly implies a judgment upon the sinful, not the natural, element in sexual life, but it is also to be understood as a judgment upon any claim that human nature has an innate capacity for God or any property in virtue of which a human being may act in the place of God. Moreover, the sovereign act of God in the virgin birth of Jesus carries with it not only a rejection of the sovereignty of man over his own life, but a rescinding of the domination of man over woman that resulted from the fall (Gen. 3.16). Thus, any pre-eminence of the male sex, or any vaunted superiority of man over woman, was decisively set aside at the very inauguration of the new creation brought about by the incarnation. In Jesus Christ the order of redemption has intersected the order of creation and set it upon a new basis altogether. Henceforth, the full equality of man and woman is a divine ordinance that applies to all the behaviour and activity of 'the new man' in Christ, and so to the entire life and mission of the church as the body of Christ in the world.

In thinking and speaking of the incarnation it is important for us to keep close to the biblical witness that in becoming human (i.e. *anthrōpos*, not *anēr*; *homo*, not *vir*) the Word was made flesh, not just male flesh. All human flesh was assumed in Christ, the Son of God, the Creator Word become man, so that now all men and women alike live and move and have their being in him. We must not forget that our Lord regularly identified himself as 'the Son of Man' (*ho huios tou anthrōpou*), which clearly had divine and final import, as Jesus acknowledged before the high priest (Mk 14.62). The being of Jesus, the Son of the Virgin Mary, was not just male being but divine-human Being with universal import as the saviour of all humankind. This is not, of course, to deny that he was physically a male, but to hold that the human nature of Jesus as son of Mary was taken up into, and united with, his divine Nature in one indivisible personal reality—it is as such that he was and is the incarnate Son of God. Hence, it would be a grave biblical and theological mistake to connect the incarnation with the gender of Jesus in such a way that everything in his incarnate life and work depended on his maleness, for that would seriously call into question the salvation of female human being, and detract from the incarnation as the assumption of complete human being and the redemptive recapitulation (*anakephalaiōsis*) in Christ of the whole human race of men and women. After all, the Greek term for incarnation adopted by orthodox Christian theology from the beginning, in line with the biblical witness, was *enanthrōpēsis*, i.e. 'inhomination'.

In view of the soteriological nature of the incarnation, it is understandable and highly significant that the Augustinian conception of man apart from woman was never employed, to my knowledge, in any official council of the universal church, as a theological reason for the claim that only a male human being may image or represent Christ at the altar. This strange and unorthodox idea is a modern innovation evidently put forward by certain reactionary churchmen in the nineteenth century, but has recently been revived as a convenient (although specious) argument for the exclusion of women from ordination to the Holy Ministry, and has been made to look ancient by being cast in the terms that only a man can be an *ikon* of Christ at the altar.

What has happened here is that an old ecclesiastical convention has been put forward quite wrongly as a *theological truth* or a *dogma* of the Apostolic and Catholic Church. Hence I believe that Dr George

Carey, the new Archbishop of Canterbury, was quite right in his assertion that the idea that only a male can represent the Lord Jesus Christ at the Eucharist is a serious *theological error*. He was not declaring that those churches and churchmen who reject the ordination of women, because it conflicts with a convention long sanctioned by Catholic tradition or canonical authority, are to be judged heretics, but asserting that it is a very grave mistake for anyone to convert such a convention, no matter how strongly enforced by Catholic tradition, into a dogma or an intrinsic truth of the Christian faith. I would also add that it is a serious epistemological error (often denounced by the great theologians of the early church) to confuse what may be held on conventional grounds (*thesei*) to be the case with what must be held on true or real grounds (*phusei*).

Basic to this whole discussion is the theological use of creaturely terms and images taken from God's self-revelation to humankind in the Holy Scriptures. 'Image' is surely to be understood in a strictly *relational* sense in accordance with the Old Testament teaching that God has created humanity for fellowship with himself in such a way that, in spite of the utter difference between them as Creator and creatures, human beings are made after the image and likeness of God. The Latin translation 'ad imaginem Dei' is quite right, for it does not mean that the image of God inheres in human nature, far less in specifically male or female nature, but that it is a *donum superadditum*, a gift wholly contingent upon the free grace of God—that is why St Athanasius used to refer to 'the image of God' as 'the grace of the image' (*he kat'eikona charis*; see for example *De Incarnatione* 12). Hence, we are not to think that human beings through their creaturely human nature, by virtue of some intrinsic analogy of being, reflect God's uncreated Nature, but that we are specifically destined by grace to live in faithful response to the purpose and movement of God's love toward us as his creaturely partners, and thereby to live and to act in personal conformity to what God reveals of himself to humankind through his Word.

In making himself known to human beings God certainly communicates with them in human forms of thought and speech, so that there is necessarily an anthropomorphic ingredient or coefficient in his revelation which is very evident in the Holy Scriptures. Nevertheless, God makes his self-revelation shine through all anthropomorphic forms of thought and speech in such a way that under the transforming impact of his Word they are not opaque distorting media, but become transparent forms through which his divine Word and Truth are conveyed to us. That is why in the mediation of his self-revelation through the Hebrew Scriptures, which are replete with dramatic imagery, there is a persistent denunciation of all images of God conceived by the human heart, whether conceptual or physical, as forms of idolatry, and why there is built into the self-revelation of God an absolute rejection of all natural-izing of religion such as is found in the worship of *Baalim* and *Astaroth*, with its heathen projection of creaturely gender, male and female, into God.

The proper understanding of 'image' was a crucial issue in the fourth-century church in the debates beween Nicene theologians and heretical Arians about the way in which they were to think of Christ as the image of God, and of themselves as conformed to his image. Stress was laid by the Church Fathers upon the fact that since God is Spirit (Jn 4.24), all the language used of God in biblical revelation and in Christian theology must be interpreted in a wholly spiritual, personal and genderless manner, in accordance with God's intrinsic nature which infinitely transcends all human imaging or imagining. Thus, any images taken from creaturely being such as 'father' and 'son' have to be understood in a diaphanous or 'see-through' way: they are to be used like lenses through which a vision of truth may take place in such a way that the creaturely relations they express in ordinary mundane usage are not projected onto Deity. When used theologically they are forms of thought and speech that refer to truth independent of themselves, and are themselves to be understood in the light of that truth to which, under the thrust of divine revelation, they refer. In short, when used theologically, creaturely images in lan-guage about God have a referential, not a mimetic, relation to the divine realities. It is surely in this way that we are to think of 'father' and 'son': as terms expressing creaturely images which divine revelation uses, and adapts in using, about God, and so as transformed terms which Christian theology is bound to use about God. It is only in and through 'father' and 'son' as they are appropriated and adapted by God for his self-revealing in accordance with who he really is, that we are to know him and think of him and worship him in spiritual ways that are true of him and worthy of him, without reading the creaturely relations and images in them back into his divine nature.

It should be emphasized, then, that the understanding of the words 'father', 'son', 'spirit', 'deity', 'trinity', 'being', 'nature', and so on, when used theologically of God, may not be governed by the gender which by linguistic or cultural convention they have in this or that language, for gender belongs only to creatures and may not be read back into the Being of God as Father. Moreover, since the Son and the Spirit are consubstantial with God the Father, or of one and the same Being with him, they are likewise beyond gender in their Being. This remains true of God the Son, even though as incarnate he is also the Son of Mary, for we cannot speak of his being begotten of the Father before all ages as true God of true God in terms of gender. Moreover, as we have noted, in becoming man it was complete human being and nature that he assumed for our salvation, not just male nature. In all these statements about God, 'father' and 'son' as theological terms and images harnessed to God's self-revelation in Christ are transformed under the impact of his Word and Spirit and are to be understood spiritually in accordance with his transcendent nature. Just as the self-revelation of God as three Persons, the Father, the Son and the Holy Spirit, transcends the category of number, so it transcends the category of gender. Hence, as St Paul has taught us, human fatherhood may not be used as a standard by which to judge divine Fatherhood, for it is only in the light of the divine Fatherhood that all other fatherhood is to be understood (Eph. 3.14-15).

3. A Theological Perspective on the Representation of Christ in the Eucharist

We turn back to our consideration of the place of men and women in the ministry. It should now be clear to us that when we are told that the Lord Jesus Christ is the image of the invisible God, and that we are renewed in Christ after the image of the Creator (Col. 1.15, 3.10), 'image' must be understood in a wholly spiritual and transparent way without the intrusion of material relations and properties such as gender.

What are we to say, then, in view of this theological understanding of image, about the assertion that it is only a male human being who can image or represent Christ at the Eucharist? Fundamentally, that depends wholly on how we are to think of Christ himself as present at the Eucharist, and correspondingly of the way in which he is represented at the Eucharist by the celebrant. At the institution of the blessed sacrament of the Lord's Supper, during the Passover celebration in the upper room on the night in which he was handed over, Jesus ministered himself to his disciples, giving them communion in his own body and blood, which he did in his unique identity as the incarnate Son of God. Thus, it is utterly unthinkable that the body and blood given to us by the Lord Jesus in our communion with him are to be regarded as restricted to male body and blood, for it was the body and blood of *the Son of Man*, the bread which came down from heaven:

> Truly, truly, I say unto you, unless you eat the flesh of the Son of Man and drink his blood you have no life in you; he who eats my flesh and drinks my blood has eternal life, and I will raise him up at the last day. For my flesh is food indeed, and my blood is drink indeed. He who eats my flesh and drinks my blood, abides in me and I in him. As the living Father sent me, and I live because of the Father, so he who eats me will live because of me (Jn 6.53-56).

That explanation of Eucharistic communion was given by Jesus in the synagogue at Capernaum in anticipation of the Last Supper. And so when it actually took place in Jerusalem, as St John tells us, Jesus ministered to the disciples as he who had come from God and went to God, and spoke to them at length of his oneness in being with God in terms of a mutual indwelling of the Father and the Son in one another. The union of the disciples with Jesus through their communion with him was grounded in his own union with the Father. There the image of Jesus as male just did not come into the picture, for in the Supper Jesus was present in the midst of his disciples as the Son of Man clothed with the glory of the Father: in receiving him they received the Father who sent him, that is, the real presence of the Christ, God incarnate, crucified, risen, and ascended, at every Eucharist. Thus, the appointed celebrant on earth acts, not in any representative capacity of his or her own as male or female, but solely in the name of the Lord Jesus Christ who sent them, and only in virtue of his real presence as the unseen Celebrant who in his atoning love communicates himself to us as often as we eat the bread and drink the wine, as he commanded us to do in remembrance of him: 'This is my body, this is my blood given for you'. It is as High Priest and Atoning Sacrifice united indissolubly in his one Person that Jesus Christ comes among us and ministers himself to us in the celebration of the Eucharist, the Lamb of God who takes away the sins of the world and gives us his peace, the Saviour who presents us to the Father in union with himself as those whom he has redeemed and consecrated through his one eternal self-offering.

The general line of our response to the strange idea that it is only a male human being who can image Christ or represent Christ at the altar

which he himself is, should by now be clear. However, three considerations in particular ought to be stressed.

1.   If the notion of image is retained, it must be a diaphanous image
through which the reality to which the image is directed may show itself
unhindered and unobscured. Since the ministerial celebrant acts in
Christ's name he does not and dare not obtrude himself or his gender
into the celebration for, far from imaging Christ in the form of a
transparent medium, that would obscure Christ by coming between
Christ and the communicants. At the Eucharist the minister or priest
does not act in his own name or in respect of his own status as a male
human being, but only in the name of Jesus Christ and in virtue of his
incarnate significance as the one Mediator between God and humanity.
It may help us here to recall what happened at the transfiguration of
Jesus on the mount when a cloud overshadowed the disciples and a
voice came out of the cloud, saying 'This is my beloved Son: hear him'.
When the disciples looked round they saw no man any more, save Jesus
only with themselves. It is surely something similar, *mutatis mutandis*,
that takes place at the Eucharist, when the celebrant is robed with the
garments of office, symbolically blotting his or her own human self and
gender out of the picture so that Christ in his own self-presentation may
be the sole focus of worship, unobscured by the opaque image of the
celebrant, male or female. If the notion of image is used of the celebrant
at all here at the Eucharist, it must be an image not in its picturing or
mimetic sense, but in its referential sense in which the image points
beyond itself altogether and in so doing retreats entirely out of the
picture.

2.   The celebrant officiates at the Eucharist not as a male or female
human being, but as a *person* set apart and sanctified in Christ for this
ministry. Christ himself presides at the Eucharist as he in whom human
nature and divine nature are indissolubly united in his one *Person*. As
we have seen, it was as a human being, not just as male, that the only-
begotten Son of God became incarnate, and it was human nature in its
completeness, and not just male nature, that he assumed and united to
himself in his divine Person. Hence, to claim that it is only a male who
can represent Christ at the altar savours of a heretical Nestorian
separation between human and divine nature in the one person of Christ.
Even St Augustine, in spite of what he had written earlier in the *De
Trinitate* about the image of God, finally insisted that, while the Trinity
himself is three Persons, *'the image of the Trinity is one person'* (*De*

Trin. 15.23.43). That is to say, if reference is to be made to the notion of image, it is strictly not man or woman (or man and woman together) that is to be thought of, but man or woman as *person*. It should be remembered, however, that the concept of person, quite unknown in antiquity in Hebrew or Greek tradition, arose under the creative impact of the doctrines of Christ and the Trinity, and takes its creaturely pattern from the uncreated relations between the three Divine Persons who are the Triune God. This is a concept of person in which the relations between persons are constitutive of personhood, and is not the same as the modern psychological notion of personality in which the person is turned in upon himself or herself. Christ himself is Person in a unique sense, as personalizing Person, whereas we are persons in a dependent and creaturely way, as personalized persons who exist in interpersonal relations, a creation which transcends the distinction between male and female. And it is a person in that contingent, relational sense that is the image of God, which fits in very well with the biblical notion of the creation of human beings for fellowship with God which we noted above, not person as a male or female human being as such. Hence, it should be argued that if Jesus Christ is present to us in the Eucharist as God and Man in one indivisible *Person*, we should think of the celebrant acting in his name or representing him as a human *person*, not as a male or female human being, yet even so, not in virtue of his or her own personal being, but solely in virtue of his or her sacred commission to act in the name of the Lord Jesus Christ alone.

3. Above all, however, we must take into account what the celebration of the Eucharist means, as the sacrament of the atoning self-sacrifice of Christ made in our place, on our behalf, and in our stead, for that governs absolutely the way in which we must think of the celebrant as representing Christ at the altar. We must also remember, as Athanasius expressed it, that the Lord Jesus is both the Dispenser and the Receiver of God's gifts, who ministers the things of God to us and of us to God (*Con Arianos* 3.39-40; 4.6-7). In becoming human for us and our salvation, he became one of us and united us to himself, really becoming what we are in order to be ourselves in our place in his identity as very God and very Man, in such a way that he acts for us and on our behalf in all our responses to God, even in our acts of belief and worship. Thus, we believe in God through sharing in Christ's vicarious faith or faithfulness toward him, and we worship God through sharing in Christ's vicarious prayer, worship and adoration of the Father. In fact, in

a very basic sense Christ Jesus is himself our worship, and it is as such that he is actively present with us and in us at the Eucharist, as through him, with him, and in him, we are brought into such a communion with the Father through the Son and in the Spirit, that we are made to participate in the real presence of God to himself. It is strictly in accordance with this vicarious presence of Christ in the Eucharist that we must think of our part in its celebration, whether as participants or celebrants—'Nothing in my hands I bring, Simply to thy cross I cling'. As participants we hold out empty hands at the altar or the holy table to receive the bread and wine, and by faith to partake of Christ's body and blood, for we bring to it no sacrifice or worship of our own, or if we do we let our worship and sacrifice be displaced and replaced by the sole sufficient sacrifice of Christ, and it is through him, with him, and in him alone, that we worship the Father in the unity of the Holy Spirit.

It is not otherwise with the celebrant. At the Eucharist the celebrant ministers not in his or her own name, but in the name of Christ, acting through him, with him, and in him, and thus in such a way that he or she yields place to Christ, lets Christ take his or her place, never in such a way that he or she takes Christ's place or acts in his stead. That is how the representation of Christ is to be understood, through a personal and liturgical inversion of the celebrant's own role with the role of Christ who is the real Celebrant. The rule of John the Baptist must apply supremely here: 'He must increase, but I must decrease' (Jn 3.30). If we speak of this celebration in terms of Eucharistic sacrifice, as I believe we should, answering sacramentally to the one atoning vicarious sacrifice of Christ himself on the cross, it must be asked how we offer a sacrifice, even sacramentally, which by its essential nature is one offered on our behalf, in our place, and in our stead. The substitutionary as well as the representative nature of the atoning sacrifice must be kept fully in view throughout when, pleading Christ's eternal sacrifice, we set forth the *anamnesis* of it which we are commanded to make. That is a Eucharistic sacrifice in which we may not combine any sacrifice of our own with the atoning sacrifice of Christ, and into which we may not obtrude anything of ourselves or seek to harness it with what we are and do, for that would be to sin against the unique, unrepeatable, and completely sufficient nature of the sacrifice of Christ on the cross.

However, in view of this representative and substitutionary nature of the sacrifice of Christ, to insist that only a male can rightly celebrate the Eucharist on the ground that only a male can represent Christ would be to sin against the blood of Christ, for it would discount the substitutionary aspect of the atonement. At the altar the priest acts faithfully in the name of Christ, the incarnate Saviour, only as he lets himself be displaced by Christ, and so fulfils his proper ministerial representation of Christ at the Eucharist in the form of a relation 'not I but Christ', in which his own self, let alone his male nature, does not come into the reckoning at all. In the very act of celebration his own self is, as it were, withdrawn from the scene. It is surely, partly at least, for that reason, that the celebrant wears vestments (which have no reference to his gender), for he does not act in his own significance, or in his own name, but only in the name of God, the Father, the Son and the Holy Spirit. It is rather in the office of *persona* with which he is clothed to act in Christ's name that the representation of Christ is to be recognized, not in the self of the celebrant, and certainly not in his male nature. It is actually the unseen Christ who in the real presence of his divine-human Person ministers at the Eucharist, not the person of the presbyter or bishop as such except in the name of Christ, and then only in a humble, self-effacing way. Hence the celebrant is not to be regarded as a sacrificing priest who repeats the atoning sacrifice of Christ, even though in an 'unbloody' form, but is only one who serves the Eucharistic proclamation of Christ's full, perfect and sufficient, all-prevailing sacrifice, offered once for all. It is upon Christ, our ascended High Priest, that the Father looks, and only on the celebrating priest on earth as found in him. Thus, however we look at it, to insist that males alone are able to represent Christ would amount to a serious intrusion of male self-consciousness and assumed pre-eminence into one's understanding of the priestly office of Christ, and would be tantamount to some form of psychological sacerdotalism and Eucharistic Pelagianism.

I conclude that, all in all, in spite of long-held ecclesiastical convention, there are no intrinsic thelogical reasons why women should not be ordained to the Holy Ministry of Word and Sacrament, but there are genuine theological reasons why they may be ordained and consecrated in the service of the gospel. The idea that only a male can represent Christ or be an icon of Christ at the Eucharist conflicts with basic elements in the doctrines of the incarnation and the new order of creation, the virgin birth with its setting aside of male sovereignty and its judgment as sinful, the hypostatic union of divine and human nature in the one Person of Jesus Christ who is of the same uncreated genderless Being as God the Father and God the Holy Spirit, the redemptive and healing assumption of complete human nature in Christ, and the atoning sacrifice of Christ, which he has offered once for all on our behalf, in our place, in our stead, and thus also of the essential nature of the Holy Eucharist and the communion in the body and blood of Christ given to us by him. As in Christ there is neither Jew nor Greek, neither slave nor free, so there is no male and female, for all sinful separation and gradations between them resulting from the fall of humankind have been done away, while God-given distinctions have been preserved, renewed and sanctified. Through the incarnation, death and resurrection of the Lord Jesus Christ, humanity has thus been set upon an entirely new basis of divine grace, in which there is no respect of persons, and women share equally with men in all the grace-gifts, or *charismata*, of the Holy Spirit, including gifts for the Holy Ministry.

INDEXES

INDEX OF REFERENCES

OLD TESTAMENT

OTHER ANCIENT REFERENCES

INDEX OF AUTHORS